My Life on Two Continents

My Life on Two Continents

Mathilde Apelt Schmidt

Castro Valley, California

iUniverse, Inc.
New York Lincoln Shanghai

My Life on Two Continents

iUniverse books may be ordered through booksellers or by contacting:

iUniverse
2021 Pine Lake Road, Suite 100
Lincoln, NE 68512
www.iuniverse.com
1-800-Authors (1-800-288-4677)

ISBN-13: 978-0-595-39748-8 (pbk)
ISBN-13: 978-0-595-84155-4 (ebk)
ISBN-10: 0-595-39748-4 (pbk)
ISBN-10: 0-595-84155-4 (ebk)

Printed in the United States of America

Contents

Introduction and Acknowledgements

For years my children and my sisters have been urging me to write the story of my life. Recently, after a wonderful party celebrating our golden wedding anniversary, surrounded by family and friends, I felt like sitting down, getting all my notes together, and pouring out my heart and soul telling about my colorful life, the joy of growing up from a scrawny little girl into a fulfilled woman and the satisfaction of having created together with my husband of now over fifty years a large, still expanding family. Every day brings new growth and there is always a new day. I had started working on my memoirs in 1995 and have been toying with the idea to finish my book and to publish it ever since.

In 1981, when I had reached the age of sixty, my daughter Doris introduced me to Toastmasters, where I chose to give the following speech, *Life Begins at Sixty*. Now, twenty-five years later, I can say that life after sixty has not disappointed me—it still goes on, enfolding, evolving, and expatiating. In many ways life is becoming richer the older one gets, notwithstanding bodily functions may diminish and daily chores harder to fulfill. Every little detail is much more appreciated and life goes at a slower pace. On the other hand, time seems to flow faster; days pass into weeks, months, years so swiftly, photo albums fill more rapidly. It feels like being in a raft on the stream of life. What might the next bend in the river reveal?

My family has its roots in Germany and is now distributed all over the world. Besides having most of our immediate family still living in Germany and European countries, we have descendents of my parents living now in the United States and in New Zealand. One branch has settled in South America. All of our numerous family members are striving to keep up the relationship with their relatives and are making an effort to visit each other in spite of the large distances and growing cost of traveling.

Of great help in writing my memoirs were letters, diaries, recommendation papers, certificates, pictures, and conversations with my sisters, Cornelie Ernst, Dorothee Rohland and Julie Kulenkampff. Never could I have written my life story without the help of my daughters, Barbara Schmidt Cruz, who copied my handwritten pages into the computer and Doris Schmidt Michaels, who helped to edit my memoirs. Thanks for all your help, girls!

I also thank my two readers, Terry Grasso Munistery, the other grandmother of our grandchildren in New Zealand and Phyllis Kreider, my niece living now in California, for their painstaking work to correct my manuscript, so it is now more readable for English speaking people. Above all I like to acknowledge the help of my husband Leo who has been patiently waiting for his dinner whenever I was occupied with my writing and was always there to help when things went wrong with the computer. A great help with computer problems was Bonnie Best, my best computer teacher. Genie Lester, who also writes, is my writing teacher and gave me many good ideas. Last, but not least thanks to my sons, Leo Hermann and Marty for helping with the processing of pictures with help of modern technology. Thanks also to Mary Carey from iUniverse for her patience and her technical assistance.

Mathilde A. Schmidt, Castro Valley, Spring 2006

Life Begins at Sixty

Icebreaker speech for Toastmasters
Mathilde Schmidt
April 1981

Good morning, Mr. Toastmaster, Fellow Toastmasters, Honored Guests!

An old story has God offer a lifespan of thirty years to all his creatures. First He asks the donkey; but *he* begs God to give him less than that—for a donkey's life is hard. So God reduces his lifespan to eighteen years. Then the dog is asked, but he also refuses to take all of the thirty years and only wants twelve. God then turns to the monkey, being sure that this happy little animal would want to live the full offered lifespan. But even the monkey—thinking that this is too much for being silly and laughed at—he only wants ten years to live. At last it is man's turn to be asked if he would like to live thirty years. He not only wants all that God offers; he wants more!

So God offers man in addition to his own thirty years the eighteen years of the donkey, the twelve years of the dog and the ten years of the monkey.

According to this story man's and woman's life is very human and fulfilled for the first thirty years; then it becomes burdensome and laborious for the next eighteen years, then, at forty-eight it turns into the life of a dog, being pushed around and beaten, and finally, at sixty, man turns into a silly monkey.

Is this a good story, true for all mankind? No! I do not agree with it.

I, too, like to take four portions of life from God; but each one shall last the full thirty years and each one shall be a *human* life. Let me share with you the first two portions of my life:

The first thirty years of my life were the hardest. I was born during the inflation in Germany. Hitler started acting up when I was about ten, and when I was eighteen years old, the war began. My goal was to study and become a teacher. It was very hard to get admitted at any German university during the war; so I took a course in seed breeding (since I liked to work with plants) and had a job in Strasbourg when the war ended. Germany lost the war in 1945 and all the Germans in Strasbourg became prisoners of war. The French were very hateful, but the Americans treated us nicely. When we finally returned home again, everything was in ruins and many people dead. I decided to pick up my life where it had been cut off before the war and started to study. Six years later I got my degree at the University in Hamburg and set a new goal: finding a husband. Since there were not many men left in Germany I decided to go to the United States to visit my sister. I was thirty years old at that time.

So the second portion of my life started in America. I found my husband, a German like myself, and we got married in 1953. Now followed thirty very happy and fulfilled years—by no means years of a donkey. We raised a family of four children, I went back to college, received a California credential, and started teaching. Finally, after going back to college once more after thirty years, I received my Masters' degree.

We also had the pleasure to see three of our children getting married. The youngest one joined the Air Force.

Now another portion of my life starts. The life of a dog? A monkey? No, no, no, another wonderful human life; when I finally can do what I really want. I had enough of teaching, the children all left the home, and I am ready to start a new career at sixty. I might go into business. I will enjoy my grandchildren. I will see a long string of presidents, getting better all the time. After all, ought they not to get better, having learned from the mistakes their predecessors made? My husband and I will go traveling all over, I might write books, go to the moon, who knows? I let you know in thirty years from now, so,

Stick around!

See you then. M A.S. Spring 1995

Epilogue written in February of 2006

The third quarter of my life is passing by fast and the years get better and better. Now our six grandchildren are growing up and giving us joy. After fifty years of marriage in 2003 we celebrated a wonderful Golden Anniversary with our family and friends and continue to enjoy life. We do trips together, attend senior classes, see movies and shows, and improve our knowledge of Shakespeare. There is still so much to learn!

Most of all, I like to share with others how fulfilling my life has been. That is why I decided to write this book.

Mathilde Apelt Schmidt

Preamble

All the world's a stage,
And all the men and women merely players.

Shakespeare,
As You Like It

Prologue

<u>Toward the end of April 1945</u>: Weakened from being sick with scarlet fever for six weeks I am crouching in the corner of the high-ceilinged room that is surrounded by tall glass windows. Huddled against me are the other two patients and in the middle of the room stands the Catholic nurse in her black habit, stout, brave and defiant, like a rock, fingering her beads and murmuring prayers. All around the "Isolation House" bombs are falling and every second another window comes crashing down.

Booooom! "That was a big one," Ilse whispers.

"It must have hit the children's hospital next door," says Karla after the noise calms down a little.

Outside it's chaos. Dead and wounded children are carried past our windows. Ambulances are howling; doctors and nurses in white coats are scurrying around.

I am closing my eyes. This must be a dream. What am I doing here? I just came back to the homeland from being a Prisoner of War and we were told that all is well and that Germany is winning the war. Why then are we bombed? Here in Traunstein in the center of Southern Germany? Then I remember. During the six weeks of being isolated and lying in bed with a high fever, I missed what was going on in the world. Of course, the war is not over yet and it does not look like we were winning. A new squadron of planes is approaching; we can hear the rumbling in the distance and the clanging of broken glass tumbling to the floor, already strewn with debris.

The three of us move closer. The first bombs are falling. This time the nurse is trembling slightly, still fingering her beads and silently moving her lips. I feel like praying too.

"Please, my Guardian Angel, if you get me out of this alive, I will never, never feel unhappy again. If I can sit under a blossoming apple tree again, I will forever thank you!" I am not a religious person, but during that moment I know I meant it; I feel my strength coming back, my will to live, to be outside in the fresh air, away from all this. I lift my head and notice that the planes have turned around; no more bombs are falling. After a few more minutes the *Entwarnung* sirens start to blare, a sign that the attack is over. People come out of the bomb shelter across the street from our room. We were not allowed to protect ourselves because we have infectious diseases. They put us here into this building that used to be an art museum before the war because there was no other room available.

Did my prayer help? I believe all of us were praying. It must have helped. The American planes are not coming back and eventually Traunstein, after being severely battered, would be declared a *Lazarett Stadt*. Every house would be signed with a Red Cross so no more bombings and Traunstein would become a safe haven for all military hospitals. We three girls are embracing each other and the nurse is falling on her knees. People start dancing in the street.

Much later, when I was in the land of my dreams, sitting under my own blossoming apple trees, I still remembered how close to dying I came then in 1945. I have kept my promise and do not let small troubles make me unhappy. Not even a nasty car accident or a tree falling onto our cabin and almost killing us could shake me. I am alive and happy for every day I am allowed to live.

PART I
The Old World

1

The 1920s

<u>My First Glimpse of America</u>: My mother had her sitting room next to our living/dining room. In contrast to the gloomy dining room, with heavy dark furniture, Mother's room was light and airy, had rococo-style furniture and was always decorated with flowers in pretty vases. She had a fancy mahogany desk and was often sitting there as she worked on her financial and household papers. My father had nothing to do with all that; he worked and when at home wrote poetry or read his beloved books. There was a secretary too, also of mahogany wood, intricately crafted and with shelves full of memorabilia from her and her father's travels. Her father had been a busy rice merchant and had brought home souvenirs from all over the world. One of the places he visited was San Francisco and he had given my mother prettily carved ivory statues from Chinatown and pictures of the city. I remember standing often in front of those shelves and wanting to go where these beautiful things came from.

In 1928, when I was seven, we heard about plans to build a bridge across the Golden Gate strait in San Francisco and my father, who was very interested in everything that was happening in The United States, got a replica of the Golden Gate Bridge[1] for my mother's collection. This trinket became symbolic to me during my future life.

Bremen

Bremen, my home town, is one of the important seaports in northwest Germany. It is situated on the bank of a small river, the Weser, itself the union of two even

---

1. The Golden Gate Bridge and Highway District was incorporated in 1928 as the official entity to construct and finance the Golden Gate Bridge, "the bridge that couldn't be built". Joseph Strauss, a brilliant bridge builder from San Francisco, was the chief engineer of the project that was completed in 1937. One year later he died in Los Angelos. (Wikipedia)

smaller rivers, the Werra and Fulda, so that there does not exist a source of the Weser. This river tends to become sandy and shallow and has to be dredged constantly to make it possible for ships to get to the port that has been created west of the city.

The fact that there is a port at all can be attributed to the steadfast character of Bremen's citizens, who never gave up the fight against the unfavorable conditions of nature. Only ships of limited depth can make it to Bremen. Over two hundred years ago another port was built downstream to receive the larger ships, and when this port became too shallow for the ever increasing size of the vessels, about 170 years ago, the farseeing Bürgermeister (mayor) of Bremen, Johann Smidt, acquired land at the mouth of the Weser and founded the city of Bremerhaven. He also built the first harbor there in 1825. Now Bremen's future was secured, and she was able to become a formidable rival of Hamburg, Antwerp, and Rotterdam. Bremen was able to capture a great percentage of the trade with North America—tobacco, cotton, and petroleum being the main commodities.

Bremen, an old city whose origins are said to go back to as early as in the twelfth century, is built on a low sand dune that protected the first dwellers, most likely fishermen, from flash floods. Later protection against enemies from the outside had to be constructed, the zigzag shaped *Wall* (dirt ramparts} behind the moat, so typical for old cities in Europe. Gates in the Wall for the citizens to leave and enter the city are still recognizable today by their names: *Ostertor* (East Gate), *Steintor* (Stone Gate), *Schlachttor* (Slaughter Gate) or simply *Vor dem Tor* (in front of the Gate). Now the *Wall* is beautifully landscaped with walking paths and benches to enjoy the garden-like elevation (called *Wallanlagen),* and on the dark, clear water of the original moats white swans and happy ducks live a tranquil life.

The surroundings of Bremen are nearly perfectly flat and, because of frequent rains, mostly green, dotted with black and white Holstein cows. Sun is a rare commodity in this maritime region. From the time I was able to recognize the space around me, I developed a craving for hills, mountains, and sunshine. I dreamed of being in a faraway country where there was a warmer climate and lovely contoured land.

Within the city there are many beautiful historical landmarks, especially in the old part, the *Marktplatz* (market place). Here stands the six hundred year-old *Rathaus* (city hall) with its roof made of pure copper that has oxidized to a brilliant green. The likewise six hundred year-old statue of Roland, nephew of Charles the Great, an ardent fighter for freedom, stands before the Rathaus and is the focal point of the Marktplatz. Roland is holding a shield with Bremen's coat of arms, a double-headed eagle. This statue is the symbol of Bremen's freedom. The marketplace is surrounded by the old and the new side by side, old patrician houses next to ultramodern buildings like the *Baumwollbörse* (Cotton Exchange), all dedicated to commerce and trade. Not far from this old nucleus of the old town are famous narrow old streets with ancient tall buildings, some of these alleys so narrow that only people or bicycles can go through them. Most of the houses are well kept and have window boxes with blooming geraniums. This part of town is called the *Altstadt* (old town), while the part across the Weser is the *Neustadt* (new town).

The people in Bremen love flowers, and in no place is this more evident than the *Blumenmarkt* (flower market) behind the *Liebfrauenkirche* (Church of Our Dear Lady), where one can also view the modern statue of the *Vier Stadtmusikanten* (Four Town Musicians): the donkey, the hound, the cat, and the rooster, all one on top of the other, as they are ready to peek into the window of the robbers' abode deep in the forest that long ago grew around Bremen. It is told that all four of these animals could play an instrument and that they wanted to make music in Bremen to earn their living. However, they were detained by a group of robbers who had to be tricked out of their good food and shelter by our musicians. They liked the robbers' house so much that they never made it to Bremen—and now we can see them, made into a work of art!

There are many beautiful old churches in Bremen, the most outstanding is the *St. Peters Dom* (St. Peter's Dome) with its two Gothic towers, stained-glass windows, and its famous *Krypta* (underground vault) and *Bleikeller* (cellar containing lead) where visitors are allowed to see centuries-old corpses still in good condition, like those found in the tombs in Egypt.

During the 1930s an entire street was dedicated to the exhibition of modern art, the well-known *Böttcherstraße*[2] created by Ludwig Roselius. Here the works of the artists of Worpswede, an artist colony near Bremen, like Paula Moderson-Becker and others can be seen.

Rainer Maria Rilke, the poet, met Clara Westhoff, the sculptress, in Worpswede, and Rudolf Alexander Schröder, a Bremen-born writer, was a good friend of the people in Worpswede. There is also the *Kunsthalle* (art museum), with which my father was affiliated for many years, and there was the *Schauspiel-*

---

2.   The Böttcherstraße one of Bremen's biggest attractions, running from the Marktplatz to the Weser River is a brick-paved reproduction of a medieval alley, complete with shops, restaurants, a museum, and galleries. The street is designed to represent a picture of Bremen's past and present. It was damaged in World War II, but restored after the war.

haus (theater) where I saw my first opera and many famous plays. This building was completely destroyed during the war.

Sometimes we went to the Ottilie Hoffmann house, a restaurant in one of the tiny side streets. When I could read, I would stand in front of that building and read the carved letters above the entrance:

Essen, was gar ist,	Eat what's done,
Trinken, was klar ist,	Drink what's clear,
Reden, was wahr ist.	Speak what's true.

That's what Bremen is about—the people are simple and direct.

We lived in the suburbs that were reached from downtown by streetcar. It took only about twenty minutes to get to the center of town by streetcar, one half hour by bicycle or about one good hour to walk. Bremen is not one of the big cities; it has a population of about one half million, as it did when I was young, while Hamburg is about four times as large.

Not far from us was the *Bürgerpark*, (citizens park), a large area planted with trees and shrubs, landscaped with lakes and lawns and delightful hiking and biking trails. In the center of this park stands the *Parkhaus*, a multipurpose building where conventions are held, balls are given, and even weddings are performed. There is also a popular café, the *Meierei* (the Dairy), where families like to go on Sunday afternoons. Artificial hills in the Bürgerpark allow the children to use their toboggans should there be enough snow in the winter.

Many fond memories come to my mind when I think about my home town!

My Family

I was born in the city of Bremen in 1921, when the pangs and hurts from World War I were still pulsating and when life was hard because of food shortages and inflation. My parents were what you would call in America middle-class people, maybe a little more upper-middle-class. They were neither nobility nor rich—and often I heard my mother complain that it was hard to raise four children on the meager income of a senator's salary.

My father, Hermann Apelt, who was by profession a lawyer, was called to our city during the war to become a senator for our government, Bremen being one of three city-states within the republic of Germany. The other two city-states were Hamburg and Lübeck. Hamburg and Bremen are still city-states. To be a senator in those days meant having a life of full dedication and little reward, the only perk being a car with a chauffeur, since neither of my parents ever learned to drive. The senate in the three city-states consisted of about twelve people from different walks of life: trades people, merchants, blue-collar workers, and professionals, like my father. Two *Bürgermeisters* (mayors) led the senate. During my youth one had been a bricklayer, the other a lawyer. The idea of this type of government was to select a true cross section of the *Bürgerschaft* (citizens) of Bremen, Hamburg and Lübeck. My father had been moved to Bremen from Weimar, his birth place. So he was not a born "Bremer" like most of the other senators. He was recommended for this influential government post by his uncle, Gustav Rassow, who was a well-established merchant in Bremen and also served as a senator, and had influence on the selection of the other senators. Thus, my father was an outsider and had to earn his acceptance into Bremen society.

My mother, on the other hand, was a true "Bremerin". She was descended from a long line of Bremen ancestors. Thus, when we grew up, we "belonged" but not quite as much as the "real Bremers" like the Büsings, the Nebeltaus, or the Kulenkampffs.

I was the youngest of four girls. My oldest sister was born in 1910, almost a year after my parents married in 1909, during the "good" times before the war. Then, my second sister was born also before the war in 1912. But the third sister, closest to me, was born during the war and did not see much of my father when she was very young because he was drafted to fight in the war. As already mentioned, he was called back to Bremen to serve for the government.

Between my older sister and me there was a brother, who was born in 1919, right after the war, but an outbreak of encephalitis took him away in the same year, at the young age of nine months. This sad event took place in December just before Christmas, and an unhappy holiday it must have been for my family. After two years, another girl was born to the family—me. Though everybody tells me it was not so, I am sure that they were hoping for another boy. My mother was nearing forty when I was born and beginning to feel exhausted, so I was the last of the Apelt girls and no heir was carrying on the family name.

We four sisters were as different as the four seasons or better, as the four elements of the Greeks. In fact, when I was about three, my father staged a play for a party given in honor of the birthday of his uncle Gustav Rassow. This play featured the four Greek elements, embodied by us. My oldest sister, Cornelie, represented the air, Dorothee the fire, Julie the earth, and I the water. These were apt choices: Cornelie was a very proper little girl, who was always trying to help my mother, imitating her—her presence was hardly felt but still she was there for us; Dorothee was the fiery one, always on the war path, intent to conquer and the most attractive one of us four; Julie's interests were practical—she liked simple things, sports and nice clothes and liked to work around the kitchen and garden, a born little mother; and I could never sit still and had many interests, like the water that is found flowing everywhere. If I had to represent one of our present elements, it would be quicksilver. There still is that restlessness in me.

Since my older sisters were relatively close age-wise and the gap between them and me rather large, I grew up almost like a single child. My parents were not so young anymore and were less strict when raising me. "She gets away with everything!" How often did I hear that?

Since I was alone so much, inquisitive by nature, and subjected to the literary atmosphere around me, I taught myself to read at an early age. I can see myself sitting in front of the bookshelf of my oldest sister Cornelie and going through the titles of her books. It was a book of Bible stories with illustrations by Ludwig Richter that took my fancy. She allowed me to take it out and I devoured it. I must have been five then, because I was not in school yet. As success breeds success; when my parents noticed that I liked books and could read, they gave me many books and also read to me from books they loved. So I got acquainted with most of the great stories of the classics: Anderson's, Grimm's and Bechstein's fairy tales, *Thousand and One Nights*, the Trojan War, Ulysses' voyages, Aenea's adventures—in short, much of Greek and Roman literature and more. My father enjoyed taking me on long walks and telling me all those stories, then letting me read them in his own collection and giving me suitable editions for myself.

As different as my parents were from one another—as I will describe next—one thing they had in common was their love for good books. We had a whole library in our house; many entire walls were lined with books—probably between 2000 and 3000 of them.

My father, who was listed in the phone book by his title—Apelt, Hermann *Senator Dr. jur*—was usually addressed as Herr Senator Apelt. He came from a family of teachers and scientists. His grandfather, Ernst Friedrich Apelt, a professor of mathematics, had a farm in southeast Germany and wrote books about natural sciences, especially about the solar system according to Kepler. His son, my father's father, Otto Apelt, was a scholar of Greek and Latin. He taught those subjects in school and also translated the works of Plato and other classics into German. He lived most of his life in Weimar, the residence of the great German writers Schiller and Goethe, a small town in the province of Thüringen, and he led a relatively simple and austere life with his family there—his wife Cornelie (Cora) and his three children Else, Hermann (my father) and Mathilde (my Tante Thilde). Some years after the death of Otto's wife, he moved to Dresden, where his younger daughter, Thilde, took care of him. My father's mother died when my father was still a young boy of seventeen. Letters from my father to his father show me that he was sent to visit the Rassows in Bremen several times. Gustav Rassow, my Grandmother Cora's brother, was then married to his second wife, Christiane, and had three young children of about the age of my father. He describes these visits in vivid colors and must have been very interested in the life in a bigger city. I always liked his description of the "Sea of Lights," a week-long affair showing the newest inventions in illumination before the turn of the century. These visits to Bremen instilled in him the desire to move there when he had studied the law for a few years and he eventually settled down in Bremen for good.

My father remembered having to carry books to and from the local library and his father's house. No wonder he was highly motivated to study at the university after having been so successful at school. I remember seeing one of his report cards—every subject graded with a 1 (A), except two subjects graded with a dash (F), sports and music. But he loved music; he just couldn't sing or perform on an instrument, the criteria of getting a good grade in those days. His alma mater was Tübingen, and letters that are in my possession show that he was a normal young man who always needed money and took part in all kinds of roughhousing. We learned much about these memories, as well a good deal of culture, at our dinner table. Never would the four of us forget about Ferdinand and Isabella of Spain, parents of Henry VIII's first wife Catherine, or the lovely Natasha in Tolstoy's *War and Peace*.

Hermann Apelt was around twenty-four years old when he moved to Bremen and first worked for the Court of Justice of that city. Later on he took over the post of *Syndikus der Handelskammer*, (trustee of the Chamber of Commerce) and he subsequently became the senator for harbor and railroads, the general traffic affairs, a position that he filled from 1917 until 1933 and again after the Hitler years from 1945 until a few years before his death in 1960. His uncle, Gustav Rassow, a senator himself, had recommended him for that office. My father was called home from fighting in WWI (1914-1918) and my mother must have been overjoyed to have him with her again.

He was born in the significant year of '76, 1876, that is—exactly one hundred years after the United States of America was founded. Maybe this fact points in a shadowy way to my later life in the States. His death took place when I was already established in America with my own four children, just having given birth to my youngest child, Martin.

A few years after my father came to Bremen, he met my mother and did not hesitate long before he asked for her hand in marriage.

Nobody could have been more different from my father than my mother. He, the scholarly, timid young professional, appropriately raised by strict parents, void of knowledge of right-brain activities, met a circle of four sisters, fatherless and motherless, living at that time independently in an idyllic farmhouse near Bremen. My mother had lost her mother when she was five, when her youngest sister, Luise, was born. There were six children: Carl, a drifter who became a sick, disoriented man and died in an institution; Emma, who was already married when my father met my mother among these four girls—Paula, my mother Julie, Lotte and Luise—all pretty, independent ladies. Their different characters, marriages, and ventures would fill volumes.

When my mother was sixteen, her father, who was a rice merchant in Bremen and partner of the firm Gebrüder Nielsen, passed away and left his four younger daughters under the tutelage of elderly uncles and aunts who were shaking their heads at the adventurous life these sisters were leading. There was enough money for education and traveling for each of the four young ladies—Paula being close to twenty, Julie sixteen, Lotte thirteen, and Luise only eleven. Carl and Emma were out of the picture, the former roaming around in America (though still needing money occasionally) and Emma solidly married and raising her own family. My mother had a strong will and tended to like languages, flowers, and exercise. She studied English and French to become a teacher, loved working in the garden, went swimming without clothes in the river (a thing unheard of in those days) and skated from Bremen to Holland on flooded, frozen meadows in cold winters. To my father, Julie must have seemed like a fairy in one of his books—but she became only too real when she accepted his proposal.

In the beginning of the nineteenth century during the summers the four sisters were—much to the horror of the old guardians—setting up house in Scheeßel, a charming little village where each summer they rented a classic farmhouse, hundreds of years old, complete with thatched roof and stork's nest, a huge *Diele* (vestibule) where the cows used to live the main living area, charming side rooms, a lovely garden, and a river flowing nearby. They also had a guest house where visitors from town were bedded on hay. One of these visitors was my father. At first he could not quite decide who intrigued him more, Julie or Lotte—but Lotte decided to marry the painter, Anton Albers, which left my father no choice.

The story goes that, on the evening of May 2 in 1909, my parents went for a walk in the balmy air of a lovely spring evening. This was the time my father had chosen to propose to my mother. However, when he just started to utter the important words, Julie stumbled and fell into a ditch that ran beside the path, on which the young lovers were strolling. Quickly, Hermann jumped after her, rescued her, and forgot for a moment what he was going to ask. Only when they walked home, a bedraggled Julie on the arm of her beaming rescuer, were they discovered by Paula, who ran out to meet them, holding a big lantern in her hand, with the words:

"Hermann und Julie, ihr seid verlobt!" (You are engaged!). So that settled it, and both lovers were relieved that big sister had taken the initiative.

My parents were married in August of 1909 and rented a room in a rural establishment in the outskirts of Bremen. This building, the *Luisenhof,* still exists and is now an elegant hotel. During this time, they built their own house on *Richard Strauss Platz* in the city, where most of us lived until a bomb destroyed it in the last days of World War II.

This house was situated on a *Platz,* a half-circle or better a "horseshoe", which had a lovely sunken lawn in its center. Since there was hardly any traffic on our Platz, we children had the most wonderful time playing on this green and I still dream about being there in the middle of this grassy field, stretching endlessly toward faraway houses, because I was so little then and our playground was so big. Our house being on the curve of the horseshoe, we had a tiny pie-shaped front yard, just big enough for a few flowering shrubs and our bicycle rack, and a nice backyard, fanning out into almost a field. There was a big lawn in the middle surrounded by flower beds and interspersed with fruit trees. Both my parents made this house a real home, with books and paintings everywhere in the house and flowers and trees in the garden.

A big half-moon-shaped verandah connected house and garden. Here we had our meals in the summer and engaged in many activities. On the front wall of the house, facing north, grew a thick mat of wild grapes in ivy fashion. On the south wall toward the garden we had purple vines of wisteria. My father, who had not known one garden flower from another when he married my mother, studied all the different names under her tutelage and became quite knowledgeable in the field. He had been collecting field flowers as a boy, but it was more a scientific than as an aesthetic hobby. So he had knowledge of plant families and characteristics—but to recognize these lovely things in masses of colors in his own back yard was something he had to learn. He liked learning about flowers so much that he even wrote poems about his newly found friends.

It sounds strange, but over the years of a happy marriage my father absorbed several of my mother's interests: her love for flowers, her love for art (he even was chosen to be the president of the arts council), and her love for living foreign languages rubbed off on him who had mostly studied the dead classical languages. He worked on his English and French, though his pronunciation never pleased my mother, who had studied to be a teacher of these languages. Later, I remember, they took Italian lessons together with an accomplished friend, Meta Sattler, who had been a teacher of the Italian language in her younger years. *He* took the lessons to study Dante in the original language and *she* to go to Florence to enjoy the art there. In fact, all three of us, my parents and I, went to northern Italy when I was sixteen. Very late in life, my father went to Spain, having prepared himself by learning the rudiments of Spanish. My sister Julie accompanied him and took care of him during this trip, since my mother was too frail to go.

My father died at eighty-four in 1960, still partly employed in the senate, as honorable member, after a busy, fulfilled life. My mother hung on for twenty-two more years. She was not well during that time but was the center of her large family of close to one hundred descendants. She died in 1982 at the ripe age of ninety-eight years.

One of our neighboring families on the Platz were the Ulrichs. They were a lovely couple; he a tall, good-looking banker who also loved to travel and hike, a specialist on Italy, and Frau Ulrich, called Mammi by everyone, was petite and graceful, always impeccably dressed, and an expert pianist. Both were very close to my parents, I might almost say, their best friends. They had two children; a daughter, Marie-Luise, who was about Cornelie's age, and a son, Franz-Heinrich, who was a companion of our tomboy Dorothee. Marie-Luise had inherited the musical talent of her mother and became a concert violinist. The son took after his father and became a banker. We were often invited to musical evenings at the Ulrichs, and I loved to be in their spacious living room with the beautiful grand piano, where Mammi Ulrich would play classical music and accompany Marie-Luise who looked lovely in her evening gown playing the violin. My father loved music by Mozart, so we heard many beautiful pieces by this composer who became my favorite also—performed by the Ulrichs. Marie-Luise married at a young age, had a son whom they named Uli after her family name, and passed away when her son was only five years old. Uli Bock still lives in that house on Richard Strauss Platz and is a good friend of my niece Julie Kulenkampff who married Rainer Kohlrausch. Julie and Rainer moved into the house of my parents long after the war, after the house had been destroyed by bombs and built up again and after our father and mother had died. Rainer had suffered a stroke in 1990 when only forty-six, had miraculously stayed alive and had slowly recuperated, and often the two friends, Uli and Rainer were seen walking carefully around the green of the Platz where we had played as children.

My mother was "running" the household. She organized everything from keeping up the house to raising the four girls. My father worked, and in his spare time he sat at his desk and studied.

Our House

When my parents were developing the plans for their new house on Georg Grön-ing Platz, as it was called then (only much later it became Richard Strauss Platz)—with their relative architect, Heiner Rodewald, who was Paula's husband, my mother insisted on a separate study, or den, for my father, so it was carved out of the living/dining room, almost like an afterthought. Heiner warned my mother that it would ruin an otherwise perfect floor plan and create a too small, dark living room and not much space for my father. Since my mother also insisted upon a large, half-moon-shaped verandah, decked completely by an upstairs balcony for the bedrooms, the living room and father's little cubicle were always dark. It gave our living quarters a gloomy ambiance. This was enhanced by very dark, massive oak furniture.

I remember my father sitting in his study, in front of his big desk full of papers, surrounded by three walls of books with illumination from a green-shaded study lamp, which contributed to the eerie feeling. One had to be absolutely quiet and had to tiptoe when father was working. Only Sunday afternoons after his weekly cigar, Father (never Daddy or Papa) opened up and amused us with stories from the classics. He loved to make bon mots and was pleased and amused and loved it when we finally understood how funny those plays on words were—as amusing as those of the jesters in a Shakespeare play. But that was not very often. In short, we didn't see too much of Father.

He also had an unpleasant trait; he had terrible temper tantrums, triggered often by the most insignificant events, like a fork dropping, or even the telephone ringing I was really afraid of him then. I must honestly say that I was much closer to my mother. Since she was not feeling very well anymore after my birth, we had two maids in the house, one in charge of the kitchen and one doing the housework. So much for a "poor" senator's wife. But then, all of our friends had domestics.

Our house had three stories. The ground floor consisted of a large living/dining room, a den for my mother, and the kitchen. Between the dining room and the kitchen there was a *Durchsteck* (pass-through for food and dishes), so the serving maid could receive the hot dishes directly from the kitchen and also send the used dishes back. When my mother wanted help at the table during meals, she stepped on a bell, hidden underneath the rug at her feet. The maids were usually farm girls from outside the city who wanted to learn the intricacies of city households under the tutelage of my mother. These young women spoke *plattdeutsch* (low German), and my mother was able to converse with them, whereas we children were not versed in that language that is in many ways like English. Our maids soon learned to speak High German with a thick Bremen accent.

The second story housed the bedrooms of my parents and my older sisters. Here also was the one bathroom, which had two convenient wash basins, a bathtub on four feet, a large *Wickelkommode* (chest of drawers for changing the babies), a console specially designed for brushing teeth, and four chairs for the children to neatly stack their folded clothes when they went to bed. Toilets were separate in small cubicles called *Klosett*. Germans in America have to be careful when asking to find a toilet; "*Wo ist das Klosett, bitte?*" they are led to a closet.

There was one more bedroom on the top floor, where my sister Dorothee had her room. Also the spacious attic was there with huge armoires for the laundry. Above the attic was the *Hahnebalken* (part of the roof construction), from which my swing was hanging. I loved to use this during rainy days. A tiny room facing north was occupied by the maids.

Where did I sleep? I shared a room with each one of my sisters over the years. While my sisters had their definite rooms—Cornelie and Julie on the second floor and Dorothee on the top—I never had *my* own room until they started to move out. I was finally given my own room and I loved to furnish it the way I wanted. The other emptied rooms then became guest rooms.

The basement served as a work area. Here the washing and ironing took place and the potatoes and apples were stored; a small pantry held the perishable foods. The wine cellar, a real treasure, was also in the basement. The heating system also deserves mentioning. It was called *Zentralheizung* (central heating). A huge oven was installed in the basement and next to it the *Kohlenkeller* (coal cellar). Every morning during the cold season this monstrous oven had to be started by building a fire with kindling and coaxing coals onto it, and then the fire had to be fed by shoveling more coal onto it several times a day. The heat created by the fire was led to the *Boiler* (hot-water heater), which in turn heated water that was sent to big *Heizungskörper* (radiators) in every room of the house. These radiators were usually installed on inside walls and were often used to dry hand-washed items quickly. In more modern times these radiators were placed under the window sills to create a more even heat in the room. Between the garden and the basement was an entrance where our garden tools were kept. One part of this entrance was used as a shelter for a goat during World War I, when the children needed more milk than they were allotted with food stamps. Much later, during World War II, this part of the basement became a temporary bomb shelter.

Washday was a big affair with two washer women coming in and taking over the tubs and washboards in the basement with two washer women and all of us helping. This took place once a month, so we had to have enough laundry and garments to last for four weeks. After everything was boiled, scrubbed, rinsed, and inspected by my mother for spots, long wash lines were strung all through the backyard (heaven forbid it would rain!), and all the laundry hung and air-dried.

Then came taking the laundry off the lines, folding it, and preparing for the next day, ironing day. Only one woman came in for that, since we only had one ironing table. On a stove specially fashioned for this purpose, two or three irons were constantly heated, and when one cooled down (even I knew how to lick my finger and test if a hissing sound could be evoked from the iron), the next was ready. The final stacking of the laundry was supervised by my mother. There had to be a full dozen of everything, and every blemish or defect of a particular piece was noted in a little black book, the *Wäschebuch*. Armed with *Wäschebuch* and stacks of clean, ironed laundry, my mother went up to the third floor of the house, where, in the large attic, the two huge armoires were waiting to be replenished. I had my swing set and other physical equipment close to those armoires, or *Wäscheschränke*, and loved to observe my mother carefully stacking the linen with no one piece sticking out while I was leisurely rocking back and forth on my swing.

Another big day in our house was sewing day. For years Frau Zweibrück was our seamstress. She was a tiny humpbacked creature who always seemed to be at the verge of collapsing. My mother had a stack of clothes ready for her to be altered. For me there were usually garments whose hem needed to be let down because I was growing so fast. Also the dresses from my older sisters were carefully inspected to see if they still had some wear in them left for me. New dresses were seldom made, at least not for me. Later when I was a little older and needed something new, Frau Zweibrück came armed with a fat pattern book and she and my mother pondered over it as to what style to chose. Though our seamstresses (others followed Frau Zweibrück) were usually quiet persons, the entire household was affected by their presence. They were always cold from sitting so long, though the house was overheated and stuffy just to please them. From the sewing room, one of my sisters' bedrooms, came the clacking noise of the foot-operated

Nähmaschine (sewing machine), only interrupted when meals were brought up to our slaving employees.

We had to be at my mother's beck and call all day for fittings of our new or hand-me-down garments. I still remember standing half-dressed in front of a high pile of clothes to be altered, itching to go outside to play with my friends. To buy ready-made clothes at the store—heaven forbid the thought—I often wondered if seamstresses had a life of their own. They were in such high demand that they had enough work to fill their lives.

So my mother was fully occupied supervising all her helpers in house and garden, and still she always managed to have time with me. Consequently, I was very close to her and very jealous of everything and everybody that took her away from me. This went so far that I sometimes faked sickness by complaining about some aches and pains, and when my mother, who was a born nurse, had put me to bed, I rubbed the thermometer that stuck in my armpit to fake a high temperature. Now *that* got her attention and she only found me out by checking my forehead and finding it surprisingly cool.

I loved my mother deeply, though she never cuddled or kissed me. That kind of endearment just wasn't done in our family. The pinnacle of affection was expressed when she sat down by my bed during her busy day and read me a story. Unfortunately she was often sick and had to rest regularly. *Mittagsruhe* (nap) right after *Mittagsessen*, the main meal in the middle of the day, was a time of absolute silence in the house. My father also took a brief rest after *Mittagsessen*, before he went back to his office.

Earliest Memories

My earliest memories go back to a scene close to our house when my mother had taken me with her downtown to do some shopping. We were both tired, and when we got off the tramway and started walking home, I decided that I had had it and had a temper tantrum fashioned after my father's. I threw myself on the ground in the middle of the street, kicked both legs furiously and screamed at the top of my lungs. My poor mother was wringing her hands when a policeman came by, gripped me firmly by the hand and dragged me home, handed me over to my mother and probably thought, "You take over from here, Lady. Good luck!"

Another event also arises in my earlier memories. I must have been close to three years old when all of us children were invited for afternoon tea and games to the house of a close friend of ours, whom we fondly called Großmutter Becker

(Grandmother). Her first name was Mathilde, so I felt especially drawn to her. She lived in a little house in the suburbs of Bremen that reminded one of the candy house in *Hänsel und Gretel* and had an enchanted garden behind it. We children grew up with her grandchildren and we loved to go there to a party. At dinner on this particular Sunday (the main meal was always held at noon), my father had just finished carving the Sunday roast, my mother and the maid were distributing the food onto our plates, and I felt on top of the world. My father had a preoccupied look on his face and I could not help teasing him.

"He looks mad," I piped up and aroused Father's anger. It only meant that he looked a little crest-fallen, but it hit a nerve.

"If you say *one* more word, you are *not* going to the party," he growled.

Now *that* was a challenge to me. I had to test him, so sure was I of my right to go to that party. "He looks bedraggled" or something like that, I said boldly.

That did it. My father exploded, threw down his knife and fork, took me by the hand and whisked me to the sitting room next door while the others watched in horror. "She is *not* going to the party," he told my mother in no uncertain words.

After having slammed the door, he sat down and they continued the meal without anyone eating much, I assume. I spent a very dreary afternoon in the room I was having my bed at that time and only cheered up when my sisters came home and brought me all kinds of leftover cookies and shared their toys with me.

My mother must have hated these scenes—nobody but me had ever dared to stand up to my father. After such a scene my father became soft as butter and was extra friendly with me. Maybe he admired my revolutionary spirit somehow.

Otherwise, I was not much to brag about. When I was four years old, I remember standing in front of the floor-length mirror hanging in the entrance hall of our house and looking at that scrawny long-legged creature with mousy hair and runny nose.

"That is me," I thought. "Why don't I look beautiful like my sisters or my parents?"

I also sucked my thumb and bit my nails, much to the chagrin of my mother and the ridicule of my sisters.

When I was five, I started to play with other children. One of our neighbors was an English family with a son named Johnny who was my age or maybe a little older. In the morning after breakfast, my father left for work, my sisters for school, my mother was busy running the household, and I was left to my own devices. There was no compulsory kindergarten. School started when a child was six years old. So when Johnny came over, we played, sometimes in the basement, and were forgotten by the adults. Johnny had plans for me.

"Pull your pants down. We'll play grown-ups," he demanded.

Obediently, I did so, wondering what kind of game this was. After he had carefully looked at and fingered my private parts, he asked me politely if I wanted to do the same thing with him. I was getting bored by this and told him, "I'd rather play marbles." I didn't know that the difference between boys and girls went beyond different clothing and length of hair—I had never seen a naked man. My modest mother fiercely protected us from seeing my father in the nude, though we only had one bathroom. So I only knew one kind of physique, that of my mother and sisters. Why more of the same? Grudgingly, Johnny told me to pull up my pants again and took out his marbles. So much for my first encounter with sexual harassment. Soon after this, Johnny and his parents moved away and an elderly couple with no children lived in the house.

I now turned to the neighbors on the other side for company. Those were the Kottmeiers. Their family seemed tailor-made for us. There were three girls at first, almost exactly of the ages of my sisters and promptly all these girls became best friends.

During the years 1920/21, both my mother and Frau Kottmeier became pregnant with what they hoped was their last offspring. Now Herr Kottmeier, whose occupation I forget, was one of those people who must have everything bigger and better than everyone else. He had the biggest house on our Platz, the best furniture, the prettiest and smartest daughters, and so forth. His wife tried to play up to his ambitions. She took singing lessons to become the best singer in Bremen; hard on us, because there was only *one* wall between our houses and their bathroom as well as their piano were located close to this mutual wall. So we were bombarded by alternating sounds of scales and flushing toilets.

So in the spring of 1921, when my mother gave birth to yet another girl and the Kottmeiers produced not one but *two* strapping boys, the joyous father could not contain himself with pride and my mother had to concede. She was beaten. My father did not care—he was beyond this race with the neighbors.

I then became the playmate of the twins, Hermann and Markus. Both strove for my attention, both tortured me and alternately made up for it just so that I would come back to play with them, after I had run away from them to the arms of my mother. They were horrible, constantly fighting, and sometimes hatching dangerous plans, like building a fire under their parents' bed. They were as competitive as their father and never could I do anything to gain their respect. In spite of loving the game, I hated to play marbles with them. They always took my prize pieces and then had to go home, leaving me with an empty feeling.

Since my father tended to throw temper tantrums and got away with it, so did I. My mother had a unique way of dealing with these outbursts. When I was asked to do something I did not like doing and showed signs of throwing a tantrum, she quickly took me by my hand, dragged me up to the third floor where we had a storage room, locked me into it, let me rave there for a while, and when I had quieted down, knocked softly on the door, asking in a friendly voice, "Is the *Bock* still there, Tita?" We all envisioned a temper tantrum simulating a male goat with big horns. *Tita* was my baby name and people in Germany still call me that, though I hate it.

"It's almost gone," I would answer hesitantly, or, if she asked too early, "No!"

"Then I'll come later," Mother would say, and give me the chance to sit still and wait for the Bock to disappear.

To this day I do not know if my mother made this thing up or if it was a well-known tactic of educators in those days. With my own children I hesitated to use this method; should signs of a looming tantrum arise, I just ignored it.

On Sunday afternoons we sometimes went for a walk in the Bürgerpark and had coffee and cake at the Meierei. At other times we visited the Rassows at their elegant residence not far from our house. Onkel Gustav had remarried and his new wife was much younger than he. Tante Ilse, or *Ilschen* (little Ilse, pronounced "Ilsken") as he lovingly called her, was a wonderful housewife in addition to her other womanly graces. Others in the family had thought it almost "scandalous" for an older gentleman to marry such a young woman and even found her rather coarse, but my parents received her graciously and admired Gustav for his virility. He must have been over seventy when he married Ilse, who was barely over thirty.

Their house was always spotless and filled with laughter and happiness. Onkel Gustav used to come down the wide steps from the living area to welcome us at the entrance, and Tante Ilse came smiling from the kitchen, took off her apron, and embraced us. She loved her Gustelchen, white hair and all, and his friends were hers. A scrumptious repast was served in the sunny *Wintergarten* (sun room), and she took special care that Titalein—that was me—had enough to eat. That silly name was a diminutive of a diminutive of my name Mathilde. She was the model hostess and knew how to make her guests feel at home. She was still a good friend of ours after her husband passed away in 1944 and came often to visit. She had to sell the big house and lived in a tiny rented room in the outskirts of Bremen. Even after she had suffered a terrible operation—due to mishandling of a tiny wound on her foot—that left her limping for the rest of her life, she always managed to look neat and fashionable and had an aura of radiance about her.

Fond memories also are connected with our summer vacations at the seaside close to Bremen and at a castle on the Upper Weser, called Fahrenholtz. My parents always insisted on taking at least one trip a year with the family to "get away from it all."

Elementary School

I was happy when school started. In Germany at that time the school year started in April, so I was exactly six years old, since my birthday is on April 21. In some ways I was more than ready for school. I could read, but I did not know much about numbers, and I certainly did not know how to react with other people. So far, my experience with people outside the family had not been much more than the brush with Johnny, Hermann and Markus and some other children on our Platz.

On a beautiful spring morning, satchel on my back, and armed with a bouquet of flowers picked by me for my teacher, my mother and I set off for my first day of school. The flowers for the teacher had been wrapped around the stems with a piece of paper, over which my mother had slipped a rubber band, and while we were walking and talking, I swung my arm around so that the flowers fell out. When we arrived at my classroom, I proudly stuck out my hand with what I thought were flowers and saw to my horror that the paper roll was empty. That was my teacher's first impression of me. She was one of those maiden teachers close to retirement with ample experience of recognizing signs of future problems.

Elementary school was obligatory and paid for by the government. Everybody had to finish the first four years of *Volksschule* (public school). This school was tuition-free. Then there was a choice of either staying for four more years at the *Volksschule* (at the expense of the taxpayer) or go on to a private *Oberschule* or *Gymnasium,* depending on the purse size of the parents and the future goal for the child. The classes at the *Volksschule* were numbered from one to eight going down, so that a child started with grade eight and left school either at grade five to go on to a private school or at grade one, which would be the last year of school.

I proved to be a dreamy, inattentive, always preoccupied pupil who had to be told everything at least three times and was hesitant to follow rules. I did not learn to play the school game easily. Since I knew how to read I was bored during German class and made slow progress with writing.

During my first year of school, called *achte Klasse* (class 8), we had to learn the old German script. Manuscript writing was briefly touched upon in order to aid our reading and right away we had to indulge in the ragged, pointed, nonfluent construction of Gothic script with pens on penholders dripping with black ink from an inkwell. After most of us had mastered at least the rudiments of this ordeal, the school board of the city decided that Gothic script was becoming out-moded and that we all had to learn to write using the easier, rounder, flowing Latin system. So, in 1928, we who had begun writing with Gothic, had to change to Latin and all new children started with Latin writing. The printed materials changed too, but this took much longer. I was able to use both styles and changed from one to the other occasionally.

As I mentioned before, elementary schools in Germany were composed of four grades, which everybody had to attend, so that a healthy mixture of children met each other during the ages from six to ten years.

In my particular school there was one track for boys only (8A to 5A), one track for girls only (8B to 5B), and one mixed-gender classroom (8AB to 5AB). It was decided by the parents which track the child was attending. I was in 8B and wished to be in 8AB. But this secret disappointment turned into a feeling of relief after a few boys from 8A and 8AB had beaten me up for asking them silly ques-tions. Unlike Miranda in Shakespeare's *Tempest*, I had found out that not all boys are wonderful creatures. I should have known better from the treatment I had received from Hermann and Markus.

I also found out that not all girls are like little mothers as my sisters were, so I had a lot to learn in the social arena. Since my teacher, Fräulein Hellmann, who only wore dark brown or gray high-buttoned blouses, did not turn me on very much—she seemed to dislike my absent-minded attitude—I turned to my stud-ies. I was fascinated by arithmetic and did all those boxes of addition, subtraction, multiplication, and later, division problems faster than most of the other chil-dren. I made lots of careless mistakes, too! My grades in arithmetic were therefore mediocre—as my report card showed.

Reading was satisfactory, but I had never read aloud before, and since the grade was given only for expressive fluent oral reading, no one cared how many books I had already read. I was an average reader who stumbled a lot and got very frustrated over my own shortcomings. This frustration over oral reading did not leave me until I had my own children to read to. I liked art, but it was also taught by Fräulein Hellmann, who had little imagination.

Sports were really grotesque. For this purpose an old spinster, even older than Fräulein Hellmann, was always busily checking out our royal blue sports outfits with baggy pants cut in one piece for spots and missing buttons, then told us what not to do, what we would get if we did it, and then let us run several times around the school building. I was on the warpath with her for often having missing buttons and the rest and having recited a poem about her without noticing that she stood directly behind me.

Fräulein Sand,	Miss Sand,
liegt am Strand,	is lying at the beach,
mit dem Bauche auf dem Sand	with her tummy in the sand.

The other children wanted to warn me, but it was too late and I was sent to the principal.

I had a hard time buckling down to do my homework. Since my mother was used to having her older children do their homework without much prodding, she never *made* me do it. Father, of course was completely out of the picture. So, one day, when I again came to school without completed homework, the teacher asked me: "And why didn't you do your homework, Mathilde?"

I answered truthfully, "I didn't feel like it," and Fräulein Hellmann almost swooned. This was serious and I had to take a letter home to my mother stating what I had said and expecting her to let me feel the consequences. My mother took the situation very lightly and even laughed when she told Father about it. But she asked from then on that I do my homework, so the incident was forgotten. The teacher had time to zero in on other system offenders.

Schooldays were always half days. They started at eight o'clock in the morning and ended at one o'clock in the afternoon. There were only brief five-minute recesses between classes, so the teacher and the children could have a breather, and at nine o'clock we had a break of fifteen minutes to eat the sandwich we had brought from home. Only the very young children were sent home at noon. Most families had their main meal right after the children came from school. After this meal, the *Mittagessen,* my mother usually took her nap, while the children did their homework.

Other Pastimes

There was life beyond school, though. I just loved our big, beautiful garden. I helped my mother pick out flowers at the Blumenmarkt in town or I went with her to the nearby nursery, then coming home loaded with flowers and plants of all kinds that we planted together. I picked fruits and nuts and I dug and tended my own garden while I let my imagination go wild.

We had a large sandbox where I spent hours. The big lawn was great for playing croquet with my friend from two houses away who was one year younger than I, Lotte Kruse. There was also Margret Siebert, another girl my age living on the Platz, who was a little sex kitten and taught me some secrets about how to deal with boys.

My mother, who never could get enough garden space, had rented a plot of land outside the city to raise vegetables and more fruit. She had sublet the front part of this land to a retired man who also took care of her land by doing all the digging and hard work as payment for his part of the parcel. We called this plot *unser Land* (our land) or *die Parzelle*, and here we spent many happy constructive, as well as relaxing, hours. Each one of us children was allowed to plant a fruit tree of her choice and tend to it. I chose a Golden Delicious apple tree, which proved to be very prolific and gave me much joy every fall. There were all kinds of vegetables, potatoes, beans, peas, spinach, lettuce and many more, also different berries, bushes with red and black currants, and a large variety of fruit trees. We also had flowers on our land. I remember a large field with daffodils. Huge dahlias that were too big for our backyard at home had to be stored in our basement during the winter, since it froze frequently and the frost would have destroyed the fleshy rhizomes. All the heavy work was done by Herr Pestrup, our helper and we children also did our share of work. I remember pulling our little hand-cart full of plums, potatoes, or dahlia clumps and storing everything away at home. Herr Pestrup was of such importance to my mother that I was quoted as having said: "When Father dies, Mother will marry Herr Pestrup!"

There was also swimming, outside in lakes or swimming holes or inside in pools. All four of us were encouraged to exercise and we had to walk and run every day. Of course, we had bicycles and I even took my bike to school. I had a scooter, roller skates, and ice skates and would have gone skiing if there had been snow or mountains in Bremen. My parents did not have the money to send us to southern Germany or Switzerland where more affluent citizens of Bremen would go in the winter. When I was older, I played tennis. The children on the Platz liked to play a game called *Völkerball*, something like dodgeball. I don't quite remember the rules but recall clearly how captivating the game was. One had to avoid being hit by the ball and I, being so thin and quick, was good at that.

My mother and I liked to go on trips in the surrounding countryside of Bremen, either by train, by foot, or by bicycle. Walks in the city opened my eyes for the beauty of the historical buildings like the six hundred-year-old city hall, the churches, and the quaint narrow streets in the old center of town. We would spend hours ambling through the luscious parks that are found throughout the city. On Sundays our whole family would go to nearby Lilienthal or Oberneuland (meaning the "Upper New Land", though there was no Lower New Land or Upper High Land around) for a nice hike and subsequently end up in a lovely café for coffee and cake. Or we would go for longer trips to the only "mountain" close to Bremen, the 150-foot-high Weyerberg, visit the nearby artist colony in Worpswede, and again end up in some inviting restaurant. Unforgettable are the trips to one of the rare primeval forests of northern Germany, the Hasbruch, (a copse where the bunnies roam), where there still stands an ancient oak of more than one thousand years of age. (Of course, that is nothing compared to the much older Redwood giants!)

Winter was full of activities too. Most winters were cold enough to freeze the shallow waters that were covering the endless meadows around Bremen. The meadows were flooded purposely to ensure better growth of the grass for the many cows that were an important part of our agriculture and depended on fodder from these meadows. As soon as the ice would hold us, we went out to the Blockland, our favorite skating ground and donned our speed skates to do hourlong tours. As on our summer hikes, we often refreshed ourselves in picturesque inns with hot soup, mountains of *Butterbrote* (sandwiches), and pitchers full of beverages. The flatness of our countryside lent naturally to this sport of speed skating, as no obstacles of hills or valleys obstructed our path. My mother had even skated thus to Holland in her youth.

When I started class 6B, the third school year, I learned to knit and sew. These were new crafts for me and after the first awkward attempts, I actually finished my first sock—not very well proportioned and with a few mistakes, but knitted by me! Very proudly I took it home and my work was greatly admired by everyone. Also the sewing went well, and soon I was busy making wardrobes for my ever-growing doll family. Since I was alone so much, I played very often with dolls. They all had names and personalities, had to learn to read and write, had swimsuits and hiking outfits and their own toys, and had to brush their teeth before they went to sleep.

For Christmas I received books and things for my dolls, and sometimes a game that I soon learned to play by myself. I had such a vivid imagination. It really didn't matter if my opponent was a real person or someone I made up. My feelings even changed when this other imaginary playmate was losing or winning. One of my games could be played with up to six people. It was a board game called *Mensch ärgere dich nicht* ("Man, don't be angry" or maybe "aggravation"). It could be compared to Parcheesi that comes from India, a dice game that sends little colored pawns across the board following a path. Each person had four pawns of the same color. In order to get out onto the board, a certain number has to be thrown with the dice—a Six in our game, a Five necessary in Parcheesi. Whenever the throw of the dice hits a pawn of a different color than his own, this one has to go off the board, back to "start". The object of the game is, of course, to bring all four pawns into a goal which is a safe place, and the person who has brought all four pawns exactly into their goal positions first, wins.

I could spend hours with this game, sitting either on the floor with my legs bent outwards, a position that resembles an awkward Yoga stance, or half-lying on my bed with a wooden board over my lap on which the game board was propped up, giving me enough room to throw my dice. I even constructed a small game board for my dolls. Knitting and sewing was done in the same Yoga position and reading could be done anytime and anywhere.

My parents, and in this case especially my father, were concerned and did not want me to read at night after I went to bed—at least not past a certain hour, nine o'clock or so. But when I was at a particularly interesting point in my story and just could not turn off the light and resolve to sleep, I had a flashlight and continued to read under my bedcover, so the parents, whose bedroom was the next to mine, could not see the light on my nightstand, which, of course, I had turned off. I remember the horror that struck me when one time my father tip-toed into my room, then shared with Julie, saw some light coming from the bed, ripped back the cover, and discovered me in fetal position with a fat book beside me. It must have been close to midnight and Father was absolutely furious. My parents were concerned about my eyes and lack of sleep. I understand that now, but then, as a child, I wanted them to understand me and my drive to devour the printed pages.

Of course, I was selective in my choice of books. My favorites were books like all the children's novels written by Johanna Spyri (author of *Heidi*) and Selma Lagerlöf (author of *Niels Holgerson*), Grimms' Fairy Tales, Teutonic hero stories, Greek and Roman sagas, and so forth. These were read over and over by me. Other classics, like for instance *Tom Sawyer* highly recommended by my father, were not touched—partly maybe because he recommended it so highly. To read it in English was not feasible (English classes started in the new school when I was ten) and the German translations were flat and hard to get into.

Trashy books did not exist in our house. So when I once stumbled on *Wahre Geschichten* (True Stories) at a friend's house, I was appalled by the style and contents of this kind of writing and soon tired of it. We have a word for trash in the German language that means something like "artificial art" or "non-art" or even "trash". This word is *Kitsch*. I was not sure what *Kitsch* was; it is hard to define. We did not have any in our house supposedly. It was something to avoid yet still many people seemed to like it.

From reading numerous letters to my mother, I realize now, how often she was away from home, mostly to spas or quiet places in the country to recuperate from frequent illnesses. In one of my earlier letters it says: "I still remember you. You have curly hair." Sometimes both of my parents went together to places where they enjoyed art or just wanted to get away from the children. These time spans ranged from a few weeks to months or even half a year.

No wonder I clung to my mother when she was with us. Until I was about ten, someone was hired or invited to keep house and take care of us children, mostly Tante Marie, the wife of Uncle Fritz who was the oldest son of Uncle Gustav Rassow. I did not like her because I found that she was very strict with me. My sister Julie told me, "You got that all wrong. Tante Marie was strict with all of us, but she preferred *you*. You got away with everything. She used to tell us *"Passt auf, Tita steckt euch noch alle in den Sack* (Watch it, Tita will outdo all of you)." I did not realize my exalted position then. Now, I think that she was not a good judge of character and did me no favor.

Later, when my older sisters were gone and my father went with my mother, I had to go to someone's house. I remember two elderly sisters who both watched me carefully and wrote to my parents almost every day. I felt cramped and longed for my parents to come back. Another time friends of our family took me for several weeks. The Abbegs had three daughters, Clara, who was already a young lady, Gretel, who was my age, and little Christiane, who was a baby. This time I almost forgot about my parents; it was wonderful to be together with other young people. Tante Margarete and Onkel Fritz were very nice to me; they treated me exactly as one of their own.

I got a lot of culture in this household. For one thing, I was encouraged to practice piano, more than at home, where it often interfered with *Mittagsruhe* and Father's work. Then they took me to several operas and shows, more than my "poor" parents could afford.

My sister Cornelie was sent to England to polish up her English when I was about eight. She had just finished her *Abitur* (Maturity diploma) and needed to decide what to do with her life. Since she was definitely talented for languages and also motivated by our mother, she thought of becoming a teacher in this field. When she came back from London, her English was excellent, but now she almost had to translate back into German in order to talk to us. For example, the German preposition *"nach"* could mean "behind" or "for". So she asked me, while telling us all about her wonderful experiences, "Tita, sieh doch bitte hinter den Kaffee". Now that means: "Please look *behind* the coffee." What she meant was: "Sieh doch bitte nach dem Kaffee" because she wanted some more of that beverage. So I mocked her and looked behind the coffee can and all of us laughed. It did not take Cornelie long to get back into our mother tongue.

Little by little my sisters left us and when I became a teenager, I was the only one left with my parents, *das Nesthäckchen* (the little nest hook). And I became a teenager.

2

The 1930s

Widening My Horizon

Trip to Bremerhaven: My father was senator for Bremen's port and railroads. In this capacity, he had to travel often to our seaport Bremerhaven and also abroad. The big ocean-going vessels—like the steamers *Bremen, Europa,* and *Columbus*—could not come up to Bremen; our river, the Weser, was not big enough. Even for smaller ships that brought goods like rice and cotton, the river had to be dredged constantly.

When I was still less than ten years old, I was allowed to go with my parents to Bremerhaven to see the christening of a new ship, and on the way down, we observed a huge dredger at work. This impressed me so much that I had to make a painting of this big machine when I came home, a colossal black monster with many shovel-like containers, scooping up mud from the river and dumping it on the shore. This trip also impressed me with the importance of my father's work—he gave a speech when he christened the new ship—and gave me a glimpse of what was lying ahead for me on the other side of the big ocean that would be crossed by the new ship.

About twenty years later I would go down this stretch of our river on a much smaller ship, waving goodbye to my father forever and starting a new life for myself in the United States. But now I was only a little girl with dreams about California and the Golden West. I had a lot of growing up to do!

Trip to Dresden: When I was nine years old, my mother took me to Dresden to see my only living grandparent, my father's father, Otto Apelt. He had lost his wife, Cornelie or Cora as she was called, in 1896 and was living with his younger daughter, Mathilde, another Mathilde Apelt. The family had moved from Weimar to Dresden. Mathilde, called Tante Thilde by us, was highly educated and had achieved her doctor's degree in Latin and Greek philosophy, but had never married. She was a soft spoken, sweet person, very much liked by me, and she had treated me very nicely on a previous visit to our house, when she taught me how to play dominoes. I think that the attraction between us two namesakes was mutual, so it could have been that she had invited us to their home in Dresden to see Großvater Apelt one more time before he passed away. He was close to ninety years old then in 1930. I had met him once before in Bremen, when he celebrated his eighty-fifth birthday with us. I was four years old and my father had fashioned a poem for me to recite to him as a birthday present. I remember this poem clearly:

Eins, zwei, drei, vier,	One, two, three, four,
Ich gratulier'	I congratulate
Fünf, sechs, sieben,	Five, six, seven,
dem Großpapa dem lieben,	dear Grandpa,
Acht, neun, zehn,	Eight, nine, ten'
zum Geburtstag schön.	to your birthday.
Elf, zwölf,	Eleven, twelve,
Daß Gott helf'.	With God's help.

I remember turning and twisting before the words came out, and only a strict look from Father made me say my little poem so fast that Grandfather could hardly understand it. Now it was five years later and my mother and I set off on our big trip to Dresden. Grandfather's birthday was on December 27, so if we wanted to be there for his ninetiest birthday, we would have to leave right after Christmas, My mother had prepared food and games for the long train trip, and I enjoyed having her all to myself. My aunt, Tante Thilde, picked us up and brought us to their house where Grandfather was working in his study by the light of a green lampshade, just like my father. The house was very dark and uncomfortable and I had to sleep on a black leather sofa that stood in the hallway. Food was also very simple, but both my grandfather and my aunt were so happy to see us that I quickly got acquainted with the new surroundings. I don't remember a party—if there was one, it must not have impressed me.

What I do remember clearly is a visit to the Zwinger in Dresden, a famous art museum, where besides many immortal classics I met the *Sistine Madonna* by Raphael, alone in a room; like the goddess Athena in her own temple, filling almost one entire wall of the sacrarium. A dedicated scholar of the arts sat in one corner trying to capture the brilliant colors and angelic smile of the Virgin Mary, and the two little Roman-looking angels at the bottom—gazing so admiringly and lovingly at Mother and Child that I felt chills all over me. My aunt had to take me by the hand and lead me out of the room. I would have stayed all day. That picture had to do some traveling: during the war it was brought to Russia and was exhibited in the Hermitage in St. Petersburg. Now it is back in its old home in Dresden.

I think I stayed until New Year's Day and the following year Grandfather died. Tante Thilde visited us several times after Grandfather's death, and each time I saw her, she seemed to have shrunk some more. She sold the house in town and moved to the outskirts of Dresden, where she lived together with two Jewish lady friends in a charming little house among flowering peach trees. I visited her there a few times when I was older, and my sister Julie became especially attached to her during the hard times during and after World War II.

The new school: The age of ten brought many changes. I graduated from elementary school and started *Oberschule*. The word "high school" would be translated *Hochschule* or *hohe Schule,* but neither one means the same as "high school" in America. This term is reserved for universities in Germany. I will call high school "upper school."

When a child had finished four grades in elementary school, grades eight to five, which was public and paid for by the state, the parents had to decide among several options. They could leave the child for four more years in elementary school, grades four to one, and then let him or her learn a trade or go on with a private upper school, or gymnasium, to prepare for university. Colleges like we have in America didn't exist in my time. There were special schools that offered complete preparations for certain careers—like photography or physical therapy—usually taking up only a few years to complete. The first three years of upper school could be compared to our junior high schools, though the children were younger. They would compare to our grades five, six and seven. My two older sisters had been put into an upper school with a more classical curriculum, modeled after the gymnasium for boys, and had done well. They both had finished the *Abitur,* a difficult exam that is needed for university entrance, when they were nineteen. My sister Julie was not a prize student and my parents were advised to let her finish the upper four years in elementary school. But my parents did not agree to that and selected an upper school for girls with a slant toward natural science where Julie took the entrance exam. She passed with flying colors and was enrolled. She sailed through the first six grades of that school, which were called *Sexta, Quinta, Quarta, Untertertia, Obertertia* and *Untersekunda.* But in the sixth year, Julie had second thoughts about doing the *Abitur* and wanted to quit school. My parents talked her into taking one more year, *Obersekunda*; then she could study to be a *Krankengymnastin* (physical therapist), a new field in medical therapy, which only took two years to complete, a study which Julie wanted to pursue. So while my sister was in her last year of upper school, I was enrolled in this school also, *Deutsche Oberschule für Mädchen* (German Upper School for Girls), and had the privilege of having my older sister in the same school. She was thrilled, too, and we spent happy times together in the courtyard of the school during lunchtime.

In those days, teachers had the same homeroom for three consecutive years. We called it *Klassenlehrer.* My homeroom teacher was an old exhausted man, ready for retirement. His name was Herr Schnelle (Mr. Quick). We called him *Papa Langsam* (Daddy slowpoke) behind his back. He taught German and some other boring subjects.

Besides him, we had about eight other teachers who had to come to our room. Only for sports, music and art did we go out to the appropriate facilities. Later, for physics and chemistry we left our homeroom also, because these subjects were taught in labs. I loved almost everything about my new school. So much to learn! So many new faces! Some of the daughters of my parents' friends were in my class, so not every face was new.

Now I started learning English. My mother had taught all of us some phrases—like "How are you?" and "Thank you very much!"—and I was motivated to learn more. I remember sharing my first lesson in English with our maid while drying the dishes: "I am, you are, he/she/it is," and so forth. She was quite impressed. Later, when I was a teenager, I started reading English books that our teacher ordered for us and even tried some of the classics like *The Secret Garden* by Frances Hodgson Burnett is fairly easy to read. My father wanted me to read *Little Lord Fauntleroy,* but I found it too difficult. Also *Tom Sawyer* was too hard for me in the original—I read the German translation.

Since I showed interest in reading Shakespeare, my parents sent me to their knowledgeable friend Meta Sattler, who had helped them to learn Italian, to study *Julius Caesar,* in German, of course. Fräulein Sattler, who had never had the time to get married, was well versed in Shakespeare besides knowing about everything there was to know about anything. Though I was rather young for reading this particular play, I still remember most of the drama, especially the two impressive speeches by Brutus and Anthony.

Soon all the excitement calmed down, and I settled down to my usual routine of daydreaming and getting away with as little as possible in the way of homework. Because of these poor traits, I never became a star pupil; my grades were middling, hardly ever above a C average (that would be 2-3 on a scale of 1/2/3/4/5, corresponding to the American A to F). But every year I was promoted and started the new class with high expectations, which soon fizzled out.

Music: Simultaneously with upper school, I started piano lessons. This was my own decision, since my parents were not very anxious to add to the already high costs for high school during the depression. The year was 1931, bad times all over, four children to be educated, and "only a poor senator's salary." So I was sent to Frau Marschall, a patient widow who made her living by teaching the children of many families in Bremen. I loved my first piano books with notes as fat as blueberries and quickly got into the world of classical music. We had a piano, a black upright; since my oldest sister had taken lessons. Dorothee had started learning to play the piano, and then dropped it. Julie had wanted no part of it. So, I decided to give it a try and held out for four years, well into the Clementi and Kuhlau sonatinas and the easiest Bach, Mozart, and Beethoven compositions.

I think Frau Marschall passed away or moved and I did not have enough drive to look for another teacher. Later our black upright was found shattered among the rubble of our bombed-out house and I did not have a piano to practice on. But the love of music has followed me all my life and I am now picking up where I had left with a new "Frau Marschall."

When I was about twelve, I saw my first opera. Operas were presented in the Schauspielhaus in Bremen, where plays were also performed. In this cultural aspect we were behind Hamburg and Berlin, where the opera houses were world famous, so our performances were secondary—but adequate. My parents' choice was *Der Freischütz* (Free Shooter) by Carl Maria von Weber. It was a very good selection, because it is a dramatic opera with an exciting plot and beautiful, impressive music. I loved it and even wanted to see it again. It was a great initiation into the wonderful world of opera. When I told my piano teacher about it, she gave me sheet music with arias from *Der Freischütz: O wenn die Wolke sie verhülle,* and *Wir bringen Dir den Jungfrauenkranz;* along with other pieces by Weber in easy arrangements, very easy, because I was still a beginner on the piano. I also discovered the recorder and taught myself how to play it. Someone must have given me my first recorder for my birthday or for Christmas.

Holidays

This brings me to the wonderful tradition of German holidays that are so dear to our family that even though I raised my own children in this country, the spirit of German holidays still shines through. Let me begin with birthdays.

Geburtstage: My birthday was on April 21—around Easter, *Ostern*. Sometimes it even coincided with Easter. My parents, not regularly church-going, but belonging to and subsidizing our local church and being good Christians, instilled in all of us the true meaning of all church holidays, especially the whole Easter week, Ascension Day, Pentecost, Luther's birthday (our Veterans Day), Advent and Christmas, followed by New Years and Heilige Drei Könige (Epiphany). Lent was not observed in Bremen, because we were Lutherans, not Catholics. Lent and *Fasching* (Mardi Gras) are observed in the west and south of Germany, for example in Cologne and Munich—not in the north.

So, as Jesus rose from the grave, I rose to a new year of life in the spring of every year and the twenty-first of April was my "Special Day" in many ways. In the morning I found a wreath of flowers around my breakfast plate, a custom that my family here still observes. Then I was allowed to do as I pleased. I didn't even have to go to school if I so chose; my mother thoughtfully wrote excuses to my teacher. I chose what Lina, our cook, had to prepare for dinner. I could invite some friends over to help me eat the huge *Schichttorte* consisting of layers and layers of fine biscuit alternately filled with chocolate and whipped cream and topped with the sweetest, best-looking frosting. It depended upon how good a mood Cook was in, so I was extra nice to her during the week before my birthday. At night I could stay up as long as I wanted and even read through the whole night if I so pleased. But next day all was over; it was back to reality.

Needless to say, *every* member of the family was treated this way on his or her birthday; it was a regular "Spoil Day"! Since our birthdays were thus celebrated, we had no need for elaborate parties and gifts, nor did my parents want to observe Mother's and Father's Days.

Other Spring Holidays: There were other special days in the month of May. On Ascension Day, *Himmelfahrt*, we had an official holiday from school. My mother told me the story of Jesus going to heaven and Father also mentioned it at dinnertime. *Pfingsten* (Pentecost) was celebrated almost as much as Easter. Thus we children lived through the most meaningful period of Christ's life, death, and resurrection year after year, just by observing these holidays, without even going to church. Every one of the three big holidays—Christmas, Easter, and Pentecost—was celebrated by everyone with two free days, Sunday and Monday. Schools and businesses were closed on Mondays following Easter and Pentecost and on the second Christmas Day following Christmas Day. As far as I know, this custom was observed all through Europe in countries that are mainly Christian. But I don't know if that is still true. The holiday customs that are so very important in the United States, such as the fineries on Easter Sunday, the big egg hunt, the parties and merriment around Christmas, the fat and jolly St. Nick, and so forth, did not exist in Germany, certainly not in our house.

On Easter Sunday there was a small egg hunt usually between church services (if we went) and dinner. My father had the honor of hiding the eggs, put into little baskets that held the eggs, either in the garden when the weather was good, or in the house when it rained. These little baskets were used over and over and when after a while of searching I asked if this was all, Father would say: "That little yellow basket is still missing," and I knew exactly what to look for.

My hygienically inclined mother did not want to put the eggs in direct contact with the soil, hence the baskets. Some of the eggs (never more than ten or so) were boiled, colored eggs, eaten by us at supper or next day's breakfast. For Easter Sunday's dinner, there was usually roast lamb with young vegetables from the *Parzelle*.

I remember a nice custom my mother's sister, our Aunt Luise, observed and once shared with me: she prepared one big basket, or nest, containing seven little bags filled with candies and marked with weekday names. This was a supply for the week following Easter and I was not supposed to eat any more than the bag contents for that certain day. I carefully observed this rule, though I could have eaten the entire nest in one setting. I could eat constantly and never became fat.

Pentecost was similar to Easter, but without goodies. In fact, I remember now, schools were off for not only two days, but for two entire weeks around these holidays and Christmas was embedded in three weeks of free days or "Ferien". For that reason, summer vacation only lasted for six weeks

After Pentecost came the long summer, cherished especially in northern Germany and the Scandinavian countries, because these countries have longer days with a relatively low apex of the sun during summer. Bremen is located on the 52nd degree latitude as is, for example, Calgary in Canada or Ketchikan in southern Alaska.

Fall and Winter Holidays: An old tradition in Bremen was *Freimarkt* (fair celebrating the freedom of Bremen citizens). This tumultuous affair is always celebrated during October and has grown over the years from a small country-fair-like event in the center of the old town to a huge event covering a vast field behind the Bremen train station. It was part of every Bremen-born person's childhood. Like everyone else, I received special *Freimarktsgeld* (allowance to spend at the Freimarkt) and spent many happy hours indulging in all the special foods, purchases, rides, and sideshows the Freimarkt had to offer. Even adults seemed to loosen up and were diverted from their usual sedate life styles to follow the motto "Ischa Freimaaakt" in Bremen accent. (It's Freimarkt, so anything goes!) In Bremen accent the internal "r" is omitted, so "garden" would sound like "gaaaden."

There was not much going on in terms of holidays until the beginning of December, when Advent started. *Erntedankfest*, our Thanksgiving, was only celebrated locally and obviously in villages where the harvest was brought in. Of course, we had our very own harvest to bring in from our "Land," but no special holiday. Luther's birthday on November 11 was a mere calendar holiday. We stayed home from school and enjoyed the free day.

Advent was the time before Christmas. It started on a Sunday exactly four weeks prior to Christmas Eve, the 24th of December. If Easter was celebrated as Christ's resurrection, *Advent* was the coming of Christ and Christmas Eve, the birth of Baby Jesus, whose first and second days of life were celebrated on the first and second days of Christmas. The first of *Advent* frequently fell at the end of November, when those gloomy days of dark afternoons and long sunless mornings approached. In addition, the weather was rainy and dismal, so we children could not play outside. We sat indoors and worked on our Christmas presents and listened to stories my mother read to us. We had an Advent wreath made of fragrant twigs of fir or pine with four red candles, and each week before Christmas, one more candle was lighted until, during the fourth week of Advent, all four candles were burning and Christmas was around the corner.

December 6 was the official church day of St. Nikolaus who was a saint in Asia Minor. We pictured him as a haggard old man, clad in burlap and carrying a sack with gifts of different kinds: sweets and toys for the good children, switches and black coals for the bad ones. On the night before *Nikolaustag*, the children went from house to house in a costume, carrying a small bag, and asking for gifts, much like our tradition of Halloween which comes from England. The difference is that the costumes were always modeled after St. Nikolaus and each city had certain songs for the children to sing. Our song in Bremen was:

> *Nikolaus, de grode Mann,*
> *Kloppt an alle Dören an*
> *Grode Kinner gift he wat,*

Kleene Kinner steckt in'n Sack.
Halli halli hallo,
So geit in Bremen to!

This is *Plattdeutsch* (Low German), an old language spoken by the people from outside Bremen. My mother could speak it fluently and often conversed with our helpers who usually came from the country side to learn about house-keeping in the city. The little song above means roughly:

Nicklas, the great man,
knocks on all the doors.
He gives something to the big children,
Small children he puts into his sack.
Halli halli hallo,
This is what we do in Bremen!

Weihnachten: As Christmas Day drew nearer, the holy mood in the house became more intense, and finally we could hardly stand it anymore. My mother and our maids talked secretly to each other, packages were observed being wrapped and hidden, we were not supposed to anticipate anything this year, because of the poor senator's salary, and so forth. We played the game, and also acted very secretly with our little handmade presents. We covered them up, and when Mother came in we faked absolute innocence. On the morning of December 24, *Heilig Abend,* or earlier, the tree was put up. We children were held at bay, either sent off to relatives or to our rooms so that we were not underfoot on such a busy day. Our dinner that day usually consisted of a thin soup, in order to let us look forward even more to the evening. When the, for us, seemingly end-less, gloomy afternoon was over, we were told to dress and we went to church at our *Dom* (cathedral) in the center of town, where the most beautiful requiem or other great church music was performed. Live candles illuminated the old spa-cious cathedral, and we all felt the birth of Christ really happening.

I could not refrain from picturing the lighted tree—with real wax candles—at home with all our presents around it. And there it was, after we came home from church, and after we had waited in line outside the living room door, while the parents put the last touches on the Christmas room: Father lighting the candles and placing a bucket with water next to it (because of fire danger), Mother arranging and rearranging all the presents on little tables for everyone. And now, a little bell rang, the door opened, and there was the tree in all its glory, hung with glistening ornaments and freshly baked *Kringel* (cookies strung on threads), the well-known nativity scene in front of it, the beaming parents and the whole room lit by candle light. This was the moment we were living for all year, the pinnacle!

Shyly, I glanced toward my table, but a stern look from my mother restrained me. First, we had to perform! My oldest sister Cornelie played the piano and we sang Christmas songs, the last of which was *Stille Nacht* (Silent Night). Then Dorothee and Julie had something to perform and I played a little piece on the piano or recorder. After that we recited the Christmas story according to the second chapter of Luke together, and I always had the last part when the shepherds returned to Bethlehem to bring *Good Tidings to All Men on Earth*. Then my father led us to the piano where he had placed us four girls in paper miniatures with little poems describing our personalities and special happenings of the past year.

Then, and only then, we were led to our tables. First, my table, because I was the youngest and most impatient one. Everyone stood around and watched me unwrapping new books, toys, additions to my doll house, and a plate with sweets, and then settling down happily to absorb it all. Then the family turned to Julie's table and so on until Father and Mother received their frugal gifts on a table together: our knitted and stitched presents, a new pen to Father from Mother, a book to Mother from Father. Finally, our two maids got their own little tree and presents to take to the kitchen.

Now it was time to eat the Christmas dinner. For this special time of the year, all the furniture had been rearranged. The big oak table and chairs were now placed in the small living area next to Father's study cubicle, and the former dining room was filled with the tree, the little tables for presents, the sofa, and easy chairs. We all squeezed into our chairs around the dining table and were served by Lina und Minna (cook and maid) with the traditional Christmas Eve dinner: chicken ragout on a bed of rice served with freshly baked crescent rolls and a huge bowl of fruit salad for dessert. We all were hungry after eating only thin soup at noontime. After dinner we enjoyed each others company, our presents, nibbling off the tree, and happily relaxing. We were allowed to stay up as long as we wanted, and I was sometimes found sleeping under the tree the next morning.

First Christmas Day as well as New Year's Day was visiting day. Friends dropped in, handing their calling card to the maid, who put it on a silver tray for just this purpose and brought it to my parents. They evidently had expected this and happily invited the guests into the living room. When all expected guests had appeared and disappeared, my parents made their rounds, sometimes with, sometimes without, us children. Usually we were too occupied with our presents or my older sisters had their own friends to see.

On the second Christmas Day things began to look a bit seedy—new candles had to be put onto the tree, a general cleaning took place, all my books were read, and I was ready to go outside and try my new scooter, bike, or sled. It sometimes snowed for Christmas and I could use my sled on the slope of our sunken green on the Platz. We had up to one foot of snow at times; unfortunately, it usually melted fast and turned into a messy looking slush. A fine misty rain fell on this slush and this was typical *Bremen Schlotterwetter*. But the uglier the weather outside, the warmer and cozier it was in the house with every room fragrant with the scent of fir.

When New Year's Eve came around (we called it *Sylvester*, according to the name of that day's saint), everything was almost back to order. Nothing could match Christmas, so even the tempting offering of "staying up until midnight" wasn't too exciting. Only the old tradition of *Bleigießen* (throwing melted lead into cold water and reading meaning into the strange shape that formed after the hissing bubbles had subsided) made the waiting for the New Year bearable. The big moment finally arrived and big and little fireworks were thundering and screeching all over. We children had a certain noisemaker called "frogs" that my oldest sister hated, and she sat there, holding her ears tight, so none of the frogs would shatter her delicate nerves. I was usually fast asleep by midnight and had to be awakened. When the fireworks abated, the church bells could be heard, ringing in the New Year for at least fifteen minutes.

Ties to America thicken

Sister Cornelie Marries. When I was twelve years old, several things happened. My oldest sister Cornelie married Walter Ernst, who lived in America and came to Germany with his mind set to marry a German girl. He knew our family well because his father, who was a writer, had married my father's sister Else after Walter's mother had divorced him. Paul and Else Ernst were living idyllically in a castle in Austria and it so occurred that Walter and Cornelie had met there once.

If Walter had specifically come back for my sister or just any German girl, I do not know, but what I do know is that one year around Christmas, just before their engagement, a huge box with chocolate candies arrived from America, big enough to feed an army. If this swayed my sister to accept his proposal or if she would have done it even without the candy, I'll never know, but it did impress me. In order to completely convince me of his qualifications to take my sister to America, he invited me to Bleekers, our best café, to select whatever I wanted in any desired quantity. He succeeded; I trusted him with my sister.

This was the first wedding in our family. Walter, who was used to living very "American," meaning that he dressed casually and rather informally, had not even thought of bringing a black suit for the wedding. He was married in a brown suit, a fact that our mother considered *unmöglich* (impossible), though he thought nothing of it. He had brought an escort from America, a good friend of his named Russell, who was different from Walter in regard to apparel. Russell always appeared impeccably dressed, mostly in white seersucker.

It must have been hard for my parents to see their first child leave home to go so far away—but every parent has to go through this in one way or another. There were occasional visits from and to the United States until the war broke out in 1939.

The Ernsts Visit Us. One of these visits took place when I was about sixteen and in my last year of school. Cornelie came by herself with her then two year-old Walter Jr. who took us all by storm. He was the first of his generation and the first baby I had encountered. Walter Jr. was just learning to talk and pronounced his name as "Wutz". Consequently, he became *Wützchen* for us, and I was amazed at the speed at which Wützchen learned new words all the time. I was learning Latin in school and practiced my vocabulary every day. One day the word *avus* (grandfather) came up and I decided that this was a good word for Wützchen to start on his Latin. I pointed to my father and said "This is *Avus*", and from that day Grandfather was addressed thus. Soon followed *Avia* for grandmother, and for a long time these names stayed with my parents.

Of course, all the neighbors were introduced to our visitors too. Mammi Ulrich thought that little Walter was the most promising creature on earth with his prominent lineage, and she dubbed him *Erbmasse*, meaning a "conglomeration" of genes of brilliant ancestors. Later Cornelie's husband came from America and took her on a second honeymoon trip to England. Wützchen stayed with us and we took good care of him. After the parents returned refreshed and happy, the little family left for their home again. We all were sad and missed them, especially our little boy. I then vowed to myself that someday in the future I would go and visit them!

Silberhochzeit In 1934 my parents celebrated their silver anniversary. For this occasion we all were invited to the summer cabin of our uncle, Gustav Rassow. This little house was situated in the Alps, near Obersdorf, perched below a tall mountain, where Tante Ilse was able to spot deer with her powerful eyes and hiked with us on difficult mountain trails that her *Gustelchen* could not muster anymore. They had a housekeeper living in this cozy little abode, called *Burgstall* (castle stable) who had the place ready at any time the Rassows wanted to leave and take a little vacation. We all met at this beautiful place, all except Cornelie, who was married by then and had left us for America, and celebrated the wedding day amongst mountains and summer flowers in the lovely scenery of the Alps. My mother wore a wreath of silvery *Parnassia,* a mountain flower, on her head and looked as young and as pretty as on the day of her wedding twenty-five years ago.

Introspection: And so the years came and went and I grew up. I became a teenager very gradually. I did not want to grow and clung to my beloved childhood. Girls and boys around me of the same age were already approaching adulthood while I was still an immature *Backfisch*, the German word for female teenagers. When I look back at that time objectively, I see that I had other undesirable traits: forgetfulness, carelessness, disorganization, and an inability to look people straight into the eye. I suffered from that for a long time. I also chewed my nails and was tormented by this self-mutilating drive, since I hated the feeling of short fingernails. My thumb-sucking had stopped when I was six, but the nail biting lasted until I was married and had too much to do to continue this nasty habit. But it reveals that I was high-strung and nervous by nature.

I also overate (without ever becoming overweight), maybe as a way to get attention. Other teenagers, who had to be careful with their intake, saw me gorging my food and wondered where I put it all. They envied me but did not become my friends. People also accused me of being very self-centered and queer, so much more reason for withdrawing into my room and biting my nails. Other girls went out with boys. I was not popular with them, to say the least. Even Markus, who later on confessed to having been in love with me all his life, shunned me in those days. In fact, I was so filled with *Minderwertigkeitsgefühle* (low self-esteem) that I felt like a mouse wanting to crawl into its hole.

I was even unhappy with my name. I was named after three old ladies: Großmutter Becker; Tante Thilde, my father's sister; and Tante Thilda, the daughter of Onkel Gustav Rassow. Though I loved these three people dearly, it was such an old-fashioned name. I wished that my parents had given me a name like that of my friends, Susie or Lotte. Since I did not like any of the abbreviations of Mathilde, I was called by my baby name, Tita, and I am still called that by my family.

Then there was the fate of the wrong gender. Boys seemed to be able to do anything they wanted, or so I thought.

Neither was I happy with my surroundings. I loathed the never changing flat landscape and the monotonous weather and wished to be in a country with hills and mountains and everlasting sunshine. I wished that I could have gone with my sister to America!

Rise of Hitler

Change of Power. A big political event in 1933 was the rise of power by the Nazis under Hitler. This was done in a sneaky, but legal way. already in 1920 Hitler had hatched the plan to worm his way into the *Reichstag* (constitutional government) and to persuade the members to give him the majority of votes. Thirteen years later, on January 30, 1933, he had reached his goal—without firing one shot. The frail, old, and weak President Hindenburg was ousted, and Hitler, who declared himself *Führer, Präsident,* und *Reichskanzler* (Leader, President, and Chancellor) all in one, took over. I was never much interested in politics but could not help noticing what was happening. All of a sudden our handsome *Reichsfahnen* (flags of the Empire), black, white and red stripes, had to be replaced by red flags with a big *Hakenkreutz* (swastika). For a short time, both flags were allowed in equal size; however, my father decided to show his true colors by hanging our huge *Reichsfahne* with a tiny bicycle swastika flag. Promptly, a policeman appeared at the front door and told us, in no uncertain terms, that this was inappropriate and asked if we would kindly buy a larger swastika—Heil Hitler!

On January 30, 1933 the whole nation voted for Hitler, a mere farce, since there was just one ballot entry to vote for! So now we were a nation of Nazis and had to be careful what we discussed at the dinner table, because there might be wire taps in the walls! We did not know then what was still to come. So, for the next twelve years, we were oppressed by the *Partei*. My father had to leave his post and office in the senate instantly; the old senate left the *Rathaus* by the back door; the newly elected senators walked proudly in by the front. Fortunately for my father and Bremen, the new senator for port and railroads was an able, understanding man who had great respect for my father and often asked for his advice.

In fact, our lives during these first years of the *Machtübernahme* (change of power) were not too different from the ways we had lived before. In some aspects, they were even better, because Hitler was ambitious to get Germany out of its chaotic stage of the years following World War I. These were the years when the

Autobahn was created, the Volkswagen (the car that everyone could afford) was constructed, unemployment was combated by starting big projects all over the country, young people had to work before they started college, sports and recreation facilities were enhanced and the nation really looked up to a brighter future. *Kraft durch Freude* (strength through happiness) was an organization touching all ages, all wakes of life.

I became a *Jungmädel* (young maid) in the preliminary stage of *Bund deutscher Mädel*, (League of German Girls); in short BDM, and had to conform to all kinds of new ideas that did not seem to thrill my parents when I poured it all out at the dinner table, the only time we all were together, by this time *without* Cornelie.

The BDM as well as their male counterpart, the *Hitlerjugend* (Hitler's youth), had as principle of their belief young people as leaders. *Jugend führt Jugend* (young leading the young) seemed to guarantee that none of the old fashioned, dangerous ideas were being taught and rubbed off on the precious young ones. Since they could not get rid of parents, we were told to ignore what parents told us; to do what we thought was right and only listen to them, the young leaders. In a way I liked being a *Mädel*. It fulfilled a need for healthy activities with other girls. We sang, hiked, did crafts and projects, and really had good times. There was also a uniform to be worn at the meetings, copies of which were promptly sewn by me for all my dolls. There was a fresh breeze blowing, and I came out of my closet and started to be happy.

But not for long. The stress of being pulled in one direction by the Nazi Party and another by the home was starting to irritate me and gnaw at my, until now, so seemingly solid picture of the world. Who was right? The Nazis, who were everywhere, or my parents, who seemed to be isolated, though not outspoken against Hitler and certainly not delighted with the course of events. Father had more tantrums; Mother looked tired and worn out. Even at school, the tension was felt. Old accomplished and beloved teachers had to hide their true feelings or they would be removed. They were dismissed if they could not conform and replaced with young, enthusiastic Nazi teachers. Especially in history and geography, as well as German classes, teachers were scrutinized carefully as not to "contaminate" us.

No Jewish people were allowed to teach. Hitler had gradually built up his loathsome theory of seeing Jews as undesirable people, partly because he was ousted from an art academy by its Jewish director. There was a Jewish girl from Poland in my class, Josephine Posnanztky, a sort of outcast like me, so we were drawn to each other. I was invited to her birthday party in March of 1937 and a few days before the birthday, Josephine was absent. I never saw her again. The whole family disappeared and on November 10 of the following year, *Die Kristallnacht* (Crystal Night) was happening. Nothing about it was mentioned in the papers, but we all could see the evidence. Downtown stores that had belonged to Jewish merchants, were broken in and looted. There was broken glass all over.

These events were so hushed over and so taboo that no one really knew they were happening. But the concerns about Crystal Night could not be completely silenced. We all could see that our beloved jewelry store, run by an old Jewish Bremer family, was shattered and destroyed, and the owners deported. What was going on was sad and terribly wrong, but we could not do anything about it.

Last Three Years of Upper School. After three years in the Upper School, we got a new homeroom teacher. Up to now, I had not really met a good teacher, with the exception of Miss Shilling, our young English teacher. She was a native Brit, not at all a Nazi and she gave us an excellent foundation in her mother tongue. Now we were home students of Fräulein Dr.Hermine Ruschmann, a tall, bony, strong woman who was an excellent teacher. Her personality did not quite match her teaching ability—she could be rather unfair—but I did not care; for the first time I was motivated and challenged to do my very best. I learned things that still are part of my knowledge today.

I can still remember those excellent lessons. She even inspired me to want to become a teacher myself. She taught all the natural science subjects—physics, chemistry, biology and math, and left little room for other teachers. The whole class was under her spell. We would have gone through fire for her! She looked through all my frailties and lame excuses for being lazy and induced me to produce A's instead of C's. I would sit up all night to work at a project she assigned. Once, when I was sick for several weeks, she sent me a detailed outline of the lessons I had missed and I learned the entire theory of magnetism in my bed. My mother also was enthused and bought me a box with tools at a science store to do experiments about magnetism on my wooden tray that had formerly carried the *Mensch ärgere Dich nicht* game board. I became a good student in just a few weeks and was obsessed with doing my homework.

Unfortunately, this deluge of enthusiasm for studying did not rub off onto the other subjects: German, history, geography, religion, etc. Once, in German class, when studying Schiller's *Wilhelm Tell*, we were assigned to learn an entire monologue by heart, in which Tell debates with himself how to best kill his opponent, the *Landvogt,* in order to save Switzerland. It starts:

Auf diese Bank von Stein muss ich mich setzen,
Dem Wanderer zur kurzen Ruh bereitet….

I shall sit down on this stone bench,
prepared for the wanderer to rest briefly….

Only about four girls were called when reciting time came. I knew this, had considered the odds and not studied. Well, I was among the four that were called, started boldly and stopped after the second line. "Go on, go on," probed the teacher and I couldn't go on. I received a 5 (F). On the next day, I thought for sure that she would not call on me, but she did, ditto the next day, so I had three 5's under my belt. That afternoon I sat down and learned the entire monologue by heart, forward and backward. The whole house was tired of it. Proudly I went to school, my head high up—the teacher did not call me. I still know this monologue by heart.

Our class at that time consisted of a variety of girls from all walks of life. There was Susi Milarch, our top student. Susi made A's in everything, she was a natural perfectionist. The wonderful thing about her was that she never bragged about her accomplishments and she was a nice companion. From my vantage point now I could compare her to my daughter Barbara, quiet, efficient, and just excellent by nature and hard work. The real action wheels in class were Irmgard Sander and Paula Spitta, both in some ways connected to our family, Irmgard being the daughter of a born Becker and Paula the daughter of our friend Bürgermeister Spitta. My parents might have thought that I would keep company with these two girls, but they were too overwhelming for me.

On the other side of the spectrum there was Mareili whose mother was a poor widow—so the rumor went, because little Mareili only wore impossible badly fitting clothes that were either hand-me-downs or homemade by the mother. That was really cruel; I had to wear homemade clothes also, but was not snubbed as badly as Mareili. Maybe my clothes fit better or whatever the reason was. She was very good in languages, but had no sense for math and sciences which made her an outcast in our class that excelled in these subjects thanks to Dr. Ruschmann. I associated with some of the mediocre girls who were nice, but not outstanding and did not overpower me. Of course, there was Josephine Posnantzki, the Jewish girl who disappeared so mysteriously in 1937.

Fräulein Dr. Ruschmann was not married and could pour all her energy into her students. Every year she arranged a trip to some attractive place in Germany and invited members from her class to come with her. Every year she had a tight little group of participants, Paula and Irmgard being the leaders of this inner circle. My parents could not afford these extra-curricular activities—at least they said so and did not let me participate. Neither did I really want to go; I felt that I did not belong. But somehow I developed a craving to belong to Dr. Ruschmann's disciples and in *Untersekunda* I almost decided to go to the Bavaria with the group. My parents, though, were adamant. They took me with them to Italy instead and had a sulking daughter to content with.

This trip that should have been a treat for me was all but that. Here I was, a girl of not quite sixteen, traveling with my rather ancient parents—at least from my perspective—in a land I was not interested at the time, having to look at art objects day by day and missing my life in Bremen. I half-heartedly agreed to go with them because I was involved in playing tennis and would miss important matches. But staying home by myself was out of the question. So I trotted along, to famous places like Ravenna, Milano, Florence and Rome. My father loved the Italian arts and my mother and I were dragged around until we were tired out.

"Just one more museum, palace, church," my never tiring father would plead, after having studied his *Bädicker* tour guide, the bible for all travelers. We lodged at a *palazzo* in a damp, musty smelling room and took our meals between visiting every sight to see. I silently yearned for my tennis matches and also for being with my class in Bavaria.

There was a certain danger about Dr. Ruschmann's power over her students that almost triggered obsession. My parents felt this, and when, after three years of being our homeroom teacher, she was chosen again to take our class for the last three years, *Obersekunda*, *Unterprima* and *Oberprima*, to lead us to the *Abitur*, my parents revolted and took me out of school. I was heart-broken and could not understand why my parents did this to me. The reasons they gave were unsatisfactory to me:

"You are not cut out to go to the university."

"We are too old to go through another eight years of paying for education."

"Your sister Julie didn't finish school and is doing fine, she even supports herself."

All these reasons did not help me to see why I had to give up school now, when everything was going so well and I was finally a good student.

Burtenbach: My parents decided to send me away from home for one year to a boarding school in southern Germany to learn household management, cooking, gardening, and other womanly graces. I had to submit and went to Burtenbach near Augsburg, still rebelling inside. This school, called Schertlinhaus, was situated in the picturesque little town of Burtenbach which otherwise consisted of farms and rural dwellings and was recommended to my parents by Emma Ernst, the sister of my brother-in-law in America. She had been a student in the Schertlinhaus herself and had liked it. For me it meant that I had to leave home when I was barely sixteen years old. I was homesick and still aching from the abrupt severance from my school. But gradually I got used to the new surroundings, made friends, and tried to see positive angles of my situation.

As consolation for all the boring lessons in household-related subjects plus a course in German history from the Nazi view, I found an outlet in the nearby swimming pool, where I soon excelled in swimming and diving and was even selected to perform in Munich at a big party event. Sports were always on the front burner in the party. Another outlet to survive the year at Burtenbach was to send for the school books my class was using this year and to try to keep up with Dr. Ruschmann's lessons, so I could join my class again the following year.

But when I asked for an appointment with Dr. Ruschmann during the next spring vacation and poured my frustrations and wishes out to her, her first question was:

"Do your parents know about this?" and when I denied this timidly, she said,

"I know you really want to do this, Mathilde (Fräulein Apelt, it was really, I believe), but you missed too much and I cannot do anything against the wishes of your parents."

So she did not support me and I felt very unhappy.

I had a few friends during this time. One of them was Sybille Wagner, an older girl who had decided to do her *Abitur* first and *then* learn the graces of housekeeping. She tried to make me into a more responsible person and pointed out my shortcomings.

"Äpfelchen, you have to think before you leap," she used to say when I did anything impulsively; as it was the case quite often. Äpfelchen or "Little Apple," derived from my surname, was her endearment for me. She was well liked by the others and it could be that they resented the fact that she took *me* under her wing and not any of the others. She was well-built and had a classical profile—a good model to follow. I still don't know what she saw in me. Another person I felt drawn to was Gaby von Herrenburg, a sixteen year-old unpretentious girl from an old Adelsfamilie (nobility), with whom I could kid around.

One more event connected to the *Partei* that took place during my stay in Burtenbach is worth mentioning. All of the girls at the Schertlinhaus had to belong to the BDM. In September of 1937 it was decided that we had to go to Munich in our uniforms to receive Mussolini and Hitler at the train station. This is described by me in a letter to my mother, which I translated and am inserting here, translated, of course.

Schertlinhaus, Sept.27, 1937

Dear Mother,

I must write to you about Munich with the BDM in order to greet Mussolini. So, we left here on Friday at 6:o'clock in the morning and had a very bad connection with the trains so that we only got to Munich at 1:30. Usually it takes only two hours to get to Munich. After this tedious journey we had to stand for two hours and then we got "refreshments" consisting of an inedible sausage and a roll as hard as a brick. After that we had to stand again and to practice marching. In the evening all BDM girls who came from outside Munich were led into schools. Our group was brought to a school far away from the center of town. We slept in classrooms with fifty girls on very thin mattresses, almost directly on the floor.

On Saturday morning we had again to stand and march and got another meal of sausage and roll. Then they selected from all the columns of BDM girls the blondest, tallest and most Nordic looking girls (I was too dark!). These girls were clothed in bright red gowns and had to stand in front of the Haus der deutschen Kunst (House of German Art). The less desirable non-blond girls were led into the train station where they were lined up in columns on the left and right side of the gate. The blondest and tallest of this group were placed into the first row and to my great joy I was selected too. We had to stand like soldiers for three hours. At ten o'clock the Führer came through in order to greet the Duce at the train. Shortly after this the Duce, the Führer, and all the Großen des Reichs (Big Wheels) came back. I could see everything incredibly well; it was fantastic! In the evening the same performance took place once more; this time the Führer and the Duce went together to the train to go to Mecklenburg.

On Sunday we had to get up at 5 o'clock in the morning and went back to Burtenbach, just as laboriously as before. The weather was absolutely perfect all the time. You must have read about the details in the paper.

Love, Tita

Doesn't this sound like fun!

Undecided: After I had finished my year in Burtenbach, we had to decide what to do with me. My parents offered several options, all brief courses, none exceeding two years. Nothing seemed to please me. There was photography—because I liked taking pictures, chicken raising—because I liked animals, Saatzucht (seed breeding)[1]—because I liked plants or Krankengymnastic like my sister Julie, even Metallurgie (research of metals). Nothing short of university appealed to me and that was out of the question. I was seventeen and should have been motivated to earn my own living.

Finally, after being back in Bremen, my parents enrolled me into a preparatory class for secretarial work in a local business school with the secret hope that I might be fit for work one-half year later. That did not work, even though I graduated somehow from business school with passing grades. I refused to work as a secretary, so it was back to the drawing board.

Into this time of indecision falls the courtship of Christoph Kulenkampff to my sister Julie. He was a real Bremer, deriving from a distinguished family of merchants and had my parents' whole-hearted support. But what he wanted was Julie's support. She, too, had a period of indecision and, being a very popular girl, had a hard time whom to choose from all the beaux around her. I distinctly remember Eric von Forell, a stocky, older man, very rich and very determined to marry my sister. She was intrigued by his nobility and his flashy life style and tended to give in to his pleading. When he invited her for a trip—I forgot where—I was asked to come along as chaperone, not an easy task, but you could not go by yourself on a trip with any man unless he was your husband, in those days. Christoph, who had waited too long to pursue Julie, must have endured tortures during this time. When we came back from the trip and nothing had happened, Christoph did not risk waiting any longer and asked for Julie's hand right away. Julie, who had become increasingly irritable with Eric during our trip, now was cured from her fling with Herrn von Forell and gladly accepted Christoph. The wedding took place at the family church of the Kulenkampffs, the Liebfrauenkirche, and the reception was held at the *Glocke*, a special hall for family celebrations. My mother even had a new dress made for me for this occasion.

Of all my parents' options, I liked the seed breeding best, especially when I learned that at the end of two years of work on experimental fields there would be an accredited state exam that entitled me to do genealogical work at universities.

---

1.   The word "breeding" is mostly used for creating new strains of animals, but it can also be used for plants.

For instance: Most of the seeds sold all over the world are produced by seed companies, which are using methods like cross pollination and careful selection. One of these companies is *PanAmerican Seed Co.* They describe themselves as "an internationally renowned seed breeding & producing company." From a seed catalog.

So, my mother set all her wheels in motion and by spring of 1939 I was supposed to start working as a seed breeding assistant under Herr Dr. Lembke on the small island of Poel near Wismar in Mecklenburg.

Pflichtjahr: But then came the blow; all young people who had left school, no matter in what class, had to spend one whole year of working in a household other than at home. This was called *Pflichtjahr* (year of duty). There was no way around this. I had to do it; it was the law. How I wished to have stayed in school. Those lucky classmates of mine were left alone to finish their *Abitur* in peace. Then, before they entered universities, they would serve their *Pflichtjahr*. Anyway, who knew what the law would be then?

Part of the condition for *Pflichtjahr* was that we had to find our own jobs. So I scanned the papers for want ads for *Hausgehilfin* (assistant for housework) and picked out a household close to our home that could be reached in three minutes flat. I was inspected and found satisfactory, especially when the lady of the house heard that *Pflichtjahr* girls only had to be paid twenty-five marks (four marks then were equal to about one American dollar) a week, whereas the usual wage for help was at least a hundred marks. I think she got her money's worth, but not a penny more! I started to work on December 15, 1938, an important date, since my *Pflichtjahr* would end on exactly that day one year later.

As soon as I had done my chores, dusted and vacuumed the flat, helped with the cooking, cleaned up the kitchen after dinner, polished the floor, washed and dried the dishes, I was off and gone to do some living for the rest of the day. My boss put up with me for about four months, then both of us had had enough and I quit.

This time, my father, who must have had a bad conscience when he saw me so unhappy, ventured to help and got me a position in the farm household of one of his friends, André Bölken, to finish up my *Pflichtjahr*. This period gave me a completely new outlook on life and I'd like to go into it in a little more detail.

The Bölkens: André Bölken was the son of a Bremen family and had rejected the wish of his parents that he go to college. Instead he rented some land and raised vegetables and fruits, which he sold all over town in a little hand-pulled wagon. In time, he had made enough money to acquire a farm outside of Bremen and had a dream to turn this rather run-down property into a model dairy farm. Little by little, dreamy-eyed André fulfilled this wish. Every year he brought more farm animals into the stables, had fancy equipment for milking installed, and the surrounding land cultivated to raise fodder for his cows. Also, the farmhouse was renovated. It became one of the most beautiful thatched-roof buildings in the area. André had great taste. Everything he did had to be right, stylish and functional. He was a never-resting inventor and as soon as one plan was put into action, the next one was hatched. He married a simple country girl who became his closest companion in all his ventures. Everything her André did was wonderful, and it was her task to realize and fine tune his ideas and make them run smoothly day after day. In time, she also became inventive and triggered many new ideas in her husband's head to improve the farm.

In earlier times, about 1925, André Bölken had a fleet of about five light blue and white one-horse carriages that proudly displayed the name *Bölkenmilch* to distribute his dairy products. One of these he drove himself and I remember him knocking on our door: "How many quarts shall it be today, Frau Senator?" He was such a proud and simple man; one had to like him. After World War II, when my father was back in the senate, he recommended André Bölken for the post of agricultural senator.

He had many workers on his farm: *Schweizers* (milkers) who tended the cows, farm hands who took care of the horses and farmland, and a manager who was his overseer in all the operational tasks that are necessary to run a large farm. The word "Schweizer" derives from the fact that dairy farms in Germany were modeled after Swiss dairies, but the milkers were not necessarily from Switzerland, ("Schweiz" in German).

Frau Bölken, affectionately called *Annie* by her husband, called all of those helpers with the same title, *Jungens* (boys), and took good care of them. They were fed, clothed, housed, and even morally supervised by her. From the simple little farm girl that André had married, she became a strong-willed, very capable organizer of their mutual empire, but never forgot her simple upbringing. While the dairy farm grew into a respected *Sanitätsmeierei*, a new concept developed by Herr Bölken to produce entirely germfree healthy milk and milk products, Annie was content with a tiny, tidy and comfortable room next to the big *Diele*, the large central room in the typical German farmhouse. In the old days the whole family used to live here and all the animals were housed in stables around it. Frau Bölken's room was a former stable for cows. She had put checkered curtains in front of the tall windows, arranged comfortable chairs surrounding a round table with a checkered tablecloth and fresh flowers in the center, and a sewing machine with projects in progress in a big basket next to it. On the floor lay a clean thick carpet, matching the homey atmosphere of the room.

Here Frau Bölken received us, my mother and me, when we came to the Bölkenhof to start my employment. Both Mother and I were very favorably impressed with the whole situation. Frau Bölken explained to us what time she expected me to arrive in the morning and when I would be done with my work. She and her husband, who later joined us, expressed their joy about our decision to have me complete my Pflichtjahr on their premises. After a brief tour through the farmhouse, kitchen, dairy facilities, stables, and garden, we were dismissed and went home happily. I liked the Bölkens and really hoped to please them. The farm was much farther away from our home than any of the sites of my earlier activities. I either had to use the tramway or, if using the bike, had to leave home by 6 o'clock in the morning, because I had to start work at 7 o'clock. This was a new experience for me; school had never started before eight o'clock, and the way to school had never taken more than twenty minutes. Now it meant setting the alarm clock the night before, getting up by the crack of dawn and pedaling through the empty streets of our suburbs.

Frau Bölken had two other helpers in the house and kitchen: one adopted girl, Martha—the Bölkens never had children of their own, much to their sorrow—and another *Pflichtjahr* girl like me, Rose.

For some strange reason, Frau Bölken and I were instantly drawn to each other, although she soon discovered my many shortcomings. I had a deep respect for her and tried hard to please her. Rose, on the other hand, acted like a prima donna doing the Bölkens a favor and aroused a smoldering anger in her boss. We were treated exactly alike, had to do the same chores, but reacted very differently. It obviously hurt Frau Bölken to seem favorably inclined toward me, but Rose showed such obvious resentment to her work, that it could not be overlooked. Martha was a little older than Rose and me (she must have been about twenty, while I was eighteen, and Rose seventeen). Martha, who came from the country and was raised by the Bölkens since she was a little girl, hovered over both of us like a wise little mother hen, knowing about all our chores almost as well as Frau Bölken, and trying to smooth out rough edges that were bound to develop. Our chores included keeping all the rooms of the farmhouse clean, including the *Jungens* quarters, premises in a separate building that used to be the barn. In the kitchen, we had to prepare the meals for over twenty people, do all preserving and pickling of the garden produce, prepare meats and sausages on slaughtering days, do all the necessary baking, *and* make the yogurt for the Bölken's dairy business. Otherwise, we had nothing to do with the dairy; that part of the farm was run by the manager.

It was exciting to be part of such a large enterprise, and for the first time in my life I felt proud to work and contribute to the flow of life. Frau Bölken unlocked in me latent domestic talents, and my yearning for going to college was superseded by the sheer joy of physical work. After peeling two buckets full of potatoes that had been harvested the day before in the vast garden and having prepared masses of green beans, all of which were simmering slowly on the huge iron stove, I felt a great sense of accomplishment. Also, the fact that I was no longer on the lowest part of the totem pole in this household, but one notch above Rose, was good for my ego. Rose, by the way, did not last her whole year. Things became so heated that her contract was terminated by mutual consent. We all breathed more easily. Frau Bölken never replaced Rose and we all willingly worked harder to make up for the loss of one hand.

When my *Pflichtjahr* ended just before Christmas in 1939, I was eighteen years old and hoped to start a life chosen by me at the beginning of the following year. But things did not work out that way.

3

The 1940s

The War Starts

Arbeitsdienst: While we were busily working at the Bölken farm, the first of September, 1939 came upon us like a thunderbolt. Hitler had declared war and boldly entered Poland to seize that nation. The years before had been filled with annexation of several neighbors—Czechoslovakia, Austria, Schleswig Holstein, and southern Tyrol—without even entering into war, and now it was Poland's turn. She proved to be more problematic, and Hitler could not avoid declaring war. Everyone, even the most nonpolitical-minded persons, became shocked by this event, and all else seemed to fade into insignificance.

The fact that our nation was now officially at war triggered new laws and regulations, especially for young people. Now, not only men had to complete the *Arbeitsdienst* (work service) after schooling and before doing anything else, as had been the law since the first years of Nazi regime, but also girls were drafted to serve for one half year in the *Arbeitsdienst*, and this new ruling went into effect right away. On December 15, 1939 I finished my *Pflichtjahr*, and already on January 2, 1940 I had to report to my headquarters in Bremen to be sent to the *Lager* (work camp) by Wildeshausen, southwest of Bremen.

I arrived at the *Lager* in the middle of the term, which had started in September and would end in April.

Neither my parents nor anybody else, least of all me, could believe the bad luck I had. The fact that I had just completed my *Pflichtjahr* did not count a bit. I had fallen between the cracks of Nazi bureaucracy and was deprived of nine more months of my freedom. None of my sisters had to serve the *Reich* (meaning "empire."—this word was used for the ever-expanding Germany during the Hitler years). Cornelie was far away in a better country, Dorothee had been married to Wulf Rohland since 1937 and had graduated shortly after that from the university in Graz, where she had studied medicine. Julie was working as a physical therapist and engaged to be married to Christoph Kulenkampff.

So, in the middle of winter, I was ensconced in one of the big barracks in our *Lager* and had to adjust once more to something not of my choice. But the rewarding experiences at the Bölkens had given me a positive feeling about myself and I tried to make the best of the current circumstances.

The Nazi principle of "Youth leading Youth" was fully implemented in the *Arbeitsdienst* system, and thus our *Lagerführerin* (work-camp leader) was not much older than I, about two years my senior. She was barely twenty-one, while I was almost nineteen. Most of the other girls were between sixteen and eighteen, depending on how far they had gotten in their schooling. Our leader was a difficult person to work under, and she was a very poor teacher. Most of us hated her.

We were militarily addressed and had a strict daily schedule. Our work consisted of aiding farmers with their chores. It happened to be one of the coldest winters in decades. All of northern Europe was frozen over, and I remember stomping over the solidly frozen ground with my heavy boots, wearing several layers of winter clothes and gazing at the crystal-clear starry sky above me on the way to my farmer.

We had to get up at 5 o'clock in the morning when it was still dark for several hours and make the fire in the big stove in the mess hall. Girls who had fire duty had to get kindling and coal from a shed nearby. Since it was a newly erected work camp and ill equipped with supplies, and since the majority of the girls had never learned how to build a fire, most of the kindling wood as well as the coal—from a heap of something that resembled dust more than pieces of coal—was soon exhausted, and fire makers had to use their own devices for starting and maintaining the fire. We slept in bunk beds with sacks of straw for mattresses that were held in place by slats of wood. If one or two of those slats were missing, the straw mattresses were still held up, but when, after the long, cold weeks in January and February, most beds were left with only three slats, the others having been smuggled out by the inventive fire makers, a general collapse of beds took place and higher authorities had to be addressed to check our management. It was a no-win situation: if you slept in the upper bunk you were apt to crash down; if you slept in the lower bunk you were crashed from above.

This and other signs of mismanagement finally led to the closure of this *Lager* and the girls that had been serving from September of the previous year, were dismissed. The others, who had started later, like me, were relocated to a camp near Oldenburg, close to the Dutch border. The cold weather was over now, and I remember a beautiful spring followed by a lovely summer. Now our work consisted mostly of out-of-door chores. We had to turn manure piles, pack them onto wagons, and distribute them with *Mistgabeln* (pitch forks for dung) onto the fields. We donned long rubber boots for this work and became muscular and tanned from the spring sun. Also not so sweet-smelling. There also were garden plots to be dug and fences to be erected and painted. We even learned to hitch horses onto wagons and drive to and from the fields.

At the end of summer an epidemic of some infectious disease broke out in the camp, and all the afflicted girls, including me, were sent to nearby Oldenburg and put into a hospital there. Patient nurses cared for us and we almost felt like being on vacation. My mother came to Oldenburg to visit me and received permission to take me home to gain my strength back. Thus ended my "career" in the *Arbeitsdienst*.

Office Work: Since everything ended so abruptly and the administration must not have felt very proud of their medical care of us, nobody insisted that we had to report back to the *Lager*. They were glad to let our parents take us home.

I was free once more and had to choose what to do with my life. But again my parents chose for me. I was put into an office of my father's business friend, who hired me as a filing clerk. That was all I could accomplish with my scant knowledge from business school two years ago. It was such a boring and unsatisfactory job that I gladly got out of it with "mutual consent" after only two months. So much for a secretarial career, my parents thought, and again I was presented with a list of two-year courses to choose from. What I really wanted was to go to a university—but that I could not do because I did not have my *Abitur*.

Seed Breeding, Mecklenburg: So I consented to go back to the seed breeding training offered by Dr. Lembke in Mecklenburg that I was willing to embark upon before my *Pflichtjahr*. The offer still stood and Dr. Lembke expected me on his large farm at the beginning of 1941. This farm was beautifully located amidst fields of white, yellow, red, and blue crops on the small island of Poel in the Baltic Sea near Wismar. In order to get to Wismar from Poel, one had to ride by bike to the center village of the island, Kirchdorf, board a ferry there, and then pedal on the mainland fourteen kilometers to town, which sported shops, offices, and movie theaters, and sometimes dances. The island itself did not offer much excitement for a young girl of twenty. But I enjoyed the beauty of the island with the large yellow fields of *Raps* and *Rübsen* (rape, a plant used for producing cooking oil; Rübsen, very similar), blue fields of flax (used for making linen), and white and red fields of poppy (used for making poppy seeds for baking and heroin for medicinal purposes). Also large potato fields that bloomed in a variety of colors, had different shades of green, and were fragrant and aesthetic.

All these fields belonged to the Saatzuchtgut (seed breeding farm) of Dr. Lembke, and the resulting seeds and potato spuds were sold all over Europe. We did the initial cross-pollination and creation of new strains of plants in our special gardens. We had two divisions of seed breeding on Poel: Herr Keller managed the potatoes together with an assistant, while Fräulein Dettweiler worked the remaining plants such as clover and grasses for fodder and raps and flax for industrial purposes. The ground on the island was very productive; black, fertile loam, and easy to cultivate. I was assigned to help Fräulein Dettweiler and tried very hard to please her, which was not always easy. She was a robust, commanding woman, very dedicated to her work and had a talent for selecting the best specimens among hundreds of plants that had resulted from cross-pollination.

It was a tedious procedure to finally breed a new brand of seed, and took many years of painstaking selection and bookkeeping. I had to stand for hours in the fields writing down characteristics of plants that seemingly all looked alike, mark plants, collect seeds from the best plants into little plastic sacks that were carefully marked, store these in appropriate places, and record everything into fat record books. There was much repetitive work, the pinnacle of which was copying the thick record books so we had doubles (no Xerox machines or computers in those days), and more of the same forever. I also had to supervise the workers who did the hard manual labor, like all the digging, sowing, and harvesting of the crops. We, the seed breeding people, were not supposed to do menial work; this was hard for me, having been used to working out, and I was aching for exercise.

But I found my own opportunities for letting out excess energy. The island was surrounded by beautiful beaches; so frequent bike trips to these beaches and swimming in the Baltic Sea was a great relief for me. Also, there were other young people, apprentices like me in the big farmhouse, who learned cooking and household management and general husbandry. All of us went together on Sundays (Saturday was a regular workday) to the beaches or with the ferry from Kirchdorf to the mainland and made excursions there.

Only when we went to Wismar to the movies did we notice that there was a war going on, since bombs never fell on our peaceful island. There was not much bombing going on in 1941, but increasingly more enemy attacks happened after Pearl Harbor, and when I came home during holidays and vacations, I had to spend more and more time sitting in underground bunkers when the howling sirens warned us that war planes were coming. I was almost glad to go back after such holidays to our peaceful island.

We always had plenty to eat. Herr Dr. and Frau Lembke offered us simple nourishing meals in their spacious dining room, sitting with him at the head of the table, and presiding over the distribution of the food. We all could eat as much as we wanted of the tasty dishes and felt well cared for. I was happy on Poel, but also lonely.

My Love Life: At this point I would like to go back to the year 1935 when I was fourteen, was still in school, and had my first dancing lessons. This was a great event for me, since, for the first time, I was confronted with a whole class of boys. My experiences so far had only been those with Johnny, Hermann, Markus, Margret Siebert's explanations, and the reading of "True Stories." Here in dance class, the boys were supposed to choose the girls and since our teacher, a bony lady with the pompous name of Fräulein von Hofmeyer and regal deportment, had seen to it carefully that every maiden had a man, no one had to be a wallflower. But somehow, the most desirable young men dashed to the most popular girls and the rest had to be satisfied with what was left over. Many times I prayed silently that one of the slick-looking great dancers would choose me, but mostly it was the sweaty-palmed, short young men who were not fast enough to grab the attractive girls and tripped over my feet. Also not helping was the fact that my mother was not inclined to buy brand-new dresses for me but had our seamstress alter some of my sisters' dresses to look more modern.

One evening in dancing class, I was praying again secretly that some "real" boy would ask me, and a very nice young man actually hurried to invite me to dance. I was so happy that *I* tripped over *his* feet, but not for long. He even brought me to our doorstep after class, something I never even had dared praying for. Later I heard that his mother was a good friend of my mother and that those two mother hens had hatched the plan to get us together. We really liked each other and one pretty Sunday afternoon in spring, August asked me to go for a walk with him in the beautiful area of the Blockland (where we used to skate in the winter). Both mothers consented and we took the bus out to the Blockland and had coffee and cake in the café garden by the little river Wümme. After one cup of coffee, August became bolder and ordered one whole bottle of *Liebfrauenmilch*, a heavy white wine. Well, we consumed the entire bottle before commencing our planned walk through the pretty meadows of the Blockland. I do not remember much about this walk, only that I got home somehow, and that our mothers did not encourage us to do Sunday walks thereafter.

In fact, August's mother had warned my mother, "You know, Julie, I would not put too much stock into this relationship. August has *many* girlfriends and he is quite a social butterfly. Don't encourage your daughter. I am afraid she might get hurt if she thinks that August really loves her." Maybe she had hoped that I could tame her son a little? So my mother tried to talk me out of socializing too much with August and with that killed my first love in the bud.

When dancing lessons were over and we were able to move gracefully on the dance floors, we were invited to balls and parties and a little social life started. Unfortunately, as soon as the war started, a curfew was initiated and the parties had to end before 11 o'clock or last all through the night. This sounds romantic, but proved to be rather tiresome. I had a girlfriend when I was in upper school, Elisabeth Noltenius, the daughter of one of Bremen's leading families, who was unfortunately rather overweight but knew how to arrange parties. Those festivities were always all through the night and we had to play games and charge ourselves up with food and drinks just in order to prevent going to sleep in some quiet corner.

During these parties, I made friends with two tall lanky youths, who actually fought over me and settled their dispute by picking me up and bringing me home together. Since I had a hard time deciding whom of the two to favor, they lost interest in me and their ardor fizzled out. Later I heard that both of them had been killed in the war.

While attending a party given by a very rich and influential Bremer family, I must have looked rather nice in a frock of the latest fashion that I had pressed my mother to buy, because the best looking tall, dark, and handsome dreamboat danced with me all evening, brought me home before 11 o'clock (it was a "before curfew" party), and invited me to a *Katerbummel* (hang-over party) for the next day. I was thrilled and counted the minutes before his arrival. He came and took me to a shabby little room where some of his friends sat on beds with their girlfriends, all of them smoking cigarettes. He offered me one and I tried to smoke but couldn't do it. His countenance obviously fell and I felt like sinking into the floor. After that, I did not hear from him again, but I saw him a few days later on my way home from school, wooing a popular girl from my class and carrying her satchel for her. My heart broke, but not for long.

During *Pflichtjahr* and *Arbeitsdienst,* there was no room for boys and now, being tucked away on my island, I began to dream about real men.

Herr Keller, the potato breeder, was a very handsome man with black hair and white teeth. He always wore elegant green riding breeches. He was married and had three adorable children. His wife was plain and uninteresting and always had a pained look on her face. I fell in love with Herr Keller the minute I saw him. Both of us were held in check; he by his wife and I by Fräulein Dettweiler. What was happening must not have been new to the people around us. In fact, Fräulein Dettweiler had warned me that Herr Keller was a wolf. Nevertheless, we managed to meet on balmy summer nights on fragrant meadows or at the nearby beach and I got my first lesson in a loving encounter from an experienced man. He was gentle and careful and I was feeling wonderful. Even winter evenings were romantic when we picked fir branches together and made Advent wreaths.

This affair went on for two summers, after which time I became restless and asked Dr. Lembke to dismiss me, since I really wanted to prepare myself for doing the *Abitur* to be ready for the university. He advised me to finish my second year, take the exam in Kraftborn and then, if I still felt like it, enroll in courses to prepare for the *Abitur* and after passing it, go to a university. He was right and I agreed to finish my apprenticeship at the estate of his son-in-law in Pommern (Pomerania), which had lighter soil and would serve as a good complement to my experiences with heavy soils on his farm. Those four months in Neu Buslar went by fast and were uneventful and then I was ready for the big exam in Kraftborn that was held on April 16, 1943.

Success Story. Kraftborn is a small town close to Breslau in the southeast of Germany, not far from Bunzlau, where the Rohlands lived. Now all of that area belongs to Poland. At that time Wulf was director of the wool treatment plant in Bunzlau; and with his well-paid job came a comfortable house close to the factory. I stayed for a few weeks with my sister who was busy raising three children and was pregnant with her fourth. I had ample time to prepare for the upcoming exam in Kraftborn. When the big day came I was looking forward to it and very confident.

At the institute where the exams were held, I met a variety of young people who, like me, had spent their practical years on farms or at institutes, but unlike me, were eager to end their learning period and to start working. (For me, learning came always first and work secondary.) We were called in front of a panel of seed breeding experts and asked pertinent questions about various subjects. I had been well prepared by my employers and also had studied industriously.

I passed with flying colors, received three *sehr gut* (very good) grades out of five and was given the general grade of "excellent". It was a great feeling to having done so well.

The Abitur at Last

Strassburg, Elsaß: I wanted to go to a preparatory school for my missing *Abitur*, but again my parents interfered and insisted that I look for work in the field of seed breeding and genealogy. The political situation had gone from bad to worse; American, British, and French bombers came every night, and food and clothing shortages became more and more noticeable.

I wrote to several universities, but only Strassburg (now Strasbourg) in the province of the Elsaß answered positively. Strassburg and the entire Elsaß (now Alsace) had been annexed to the German *Reich* in 1940 and every post at the large university had been filled by a Nazi in good standing within the party.

Strassburg is situated in the fertile Rheintal (Rhine Valley) and was then a German city close to the border of France. It has a special, warm and humid climate and has all the conditions to produce an abundance of fruits and vegetables in its surrounding fields. Strassburg is famous for its enormous *Münster* (Cathedral), which towers majestically over the red tile roofs of the city.

Herr Professor Knapp: The Strassburg University was at that time supervised and equipped by the University of Tübingen in the *Reich*. Natural sciences, especially genealogy, were favored subjects, so someone like me was needed. I was hired to work under Herr Professor Knapp (notice, no "Dr.") who was sent to Strassburg from Tübingen. Hitler was very interested in all facets of gene inheritance because he wanted to breed a new German race, so it was not so much the goal to create new strains of plants and animals, as research about mutations and other chromosome variations. Mendel's laws were the bible of our science that hovered between biology, chemistry, and physics. Most of the plants raised on our fields outside Strassburg were the snapdragon and the *Mirabilis* (four o'clock), both already discovered by Mendel as having only one difference in one chromosome. Also, peas and soybeans (the source of Tofu) were investigated. My special care would be directed to rows and rows of peas with one, two, and three chromosomal differences, such as the color of the seed (green and yellow), the shape of the seed (smoothed and wrinkled), and one more, which I cannot recall clearly. I think it was round and square. Thousands of plants created by cross-pollination had to be raised and documented to find new chromosome constellations or mutations besides the distributions to be expected according to Mendel's laws. Powerful microscopes, with which chromosomes could actually be seen, were then just being developed and DNA was discovered later in the 1950's by two scientists called James Watson and Francis Crick. There was much tediousness connected with this job, but it was also interesting, especially when new discoveries were made.

In the lab at the institute were thousands of Petri dishes and flasks dedicated to the studies of *drisophila melanogaster* (fruit fly), a creature with huge chromosomes in its saliva, already used by one of Mendel's followers, Thomas Hunt Morgan. The chromosomes of this creature could be seen through our microscopes. Two assistants were working in the lab, Fräulein Bähr and Fräulein Hofstätter, both having worked under Herr Professor Knapp in Tübingen.

He was an ardent Nazi and thus well equipped to head the genealogy department in Strassburg. I always had the suspicion that genealogy was the only thing he really knew and that his realm of knowledge was rather limited to this narrow field. I don't even remember that he had the doctor's title (the prerequisite to becoming a professor).He was short, stocky, and had a raspy voice. According to him, it was more important to be a good follower of the Führer than to be a good scientist and anything that resembled independent thinking was suspected of being "sabotage."

I had started my work in Strassburg in May of 1943. It is interesting that among my very complete papers of reference the one of Professor Knapp is absent. The reason for this is that I never left him; *he* left before me. But that happened later.

For the first two weeks I was invited to lodge in the building where the institute was housed, an old patrician mansion with super-high ceilings in every room. Professor Knapp also resided there. I have tried to block this period of my life out of my memory, so I don't even remember if he was married or not. Should we meet at any time in the hallways or even at night on the way to the common bathroom, it had to be *Heil Hitler* (Hail to the Führer), with the right arm stretched out in front of you. After two weeks of this, I moved out into a three bedroom apartment with a living room, kitchen, and one bath on the fifth floor of an old house on Kirsteinstraße, about ten minutes by bike from the university. I lived there with two roommates; a young girl also working for Professor Knapp and the other one a thirty-six-year old lady who sang in the choir of the Strassburg opera. Her name was Sabine and she gave me a precious gift. Because of her I was able to see the entire repertoire of the winter season of 1943-1944 at the opera house of Strassburg. She always had tickets for me at reduced prices, or, should she not be able to give me tickets, I purchased one for standing on the uppermost gallery of the opera for two marks and enjoyed this just as much as if it was the best seat in the house. I had brought my own bicycle from home and went everywhere on this beloved vehicle.

Abitur: Another thing I did while I worked for Professor Knapp was to enroll in an evening course at the *Abendschule* that was held twice a week in the evening to prepare people like me for the *Abitur* (very much like our adult school prepares for the GED).

Finally, I was working on the fulfillment of my secret dream, to go to the university! I was told at the Office for Adult Education that my night school class was a three year course, but I was in a hurry and tried to enter the second year of the course that was already in progress. Somehow I managed to further consolidate my studies so that I was ready to take the big exam already in March of 1944—it had taken me less than a year to cram everything into my head. I tried and passed the exam with fair grades and the gates of the university were open for me! I must have sensed that something was going to happen, hence the hurry to get my precious *Abitur* document.

Professor Knapp had observed my outside interest with mixed feelings. He thought that I was too much distracted from doing my job satisfactorily; and I must confess that he was right. One morning, when I was busily sorting out results of sampling specimens of our research material, I was barely able to hide my math problems—homework for that night at school—under my large blotter when he came in suddenly and wanted to see some of my figures. He must have been suspicious, for he went right away to my desk, picked up the blotter, and saw the clear evidence. I had been working on *my* math on *his* time.

"Sabotage," he screamed. "Do you know, Fräulein Apelt, that I can report you to the authorities for this?" Why didn't I leave then and there?

In those days before the tragic end of the war (heaven forbid to mention this possibility to a Nazi!), everyone had to be working. By law, even mothers of small children had to work in factories. There was a special department just to enforce all the new rules about working, the *Arbeitsamt* (office regulating work). Whoever had a job was clinging to it; otherwise, they had to make warheads and other munitions; a kind of work that was highly undesirable. So when Professor Knapp threatened me with reporting about my "sabotage," I was afraid. I thought long and hard about what to do to not offend him anymore. On the other hand, I needed time to study for my exam. Something told me it is now or never that I take this exam.

I wrote to my parents asking them to send me a small amount of money every month and went to Herr Professor declaring boldly that I had decided that I work only half a day for him from now on, for half of my salary. He agreed to this, since his budget had become tight lately, and he made me promise never to do outside work during my job again. I happily agreed to everything and was very relieved. At noon, when everyone else had to slog back to work after lunch, I was free as a bird and hurried home to my studies.

On weekends the other young people and I went on trips to the lovely surroundings of Strassburg. The Elsaß is a beautiful country, situated in the Rhine Valley, between the *Schwarzwald* (Black Forest) and the Vogesen, interspersed with many lovely cities. Strassburg itself is a picturesque city with its majestic cathedral, the *Münster,* interesting pile buildings on a small river, old narrow winding alleys and lovely suburbs. Even my daily bike rides between my apartment and our fields were never boring.

Shortly after my *Abitur* exam, which went well for me, the faculty of the night school at the Friederiken Schule, which managed the adult courses, gave a big party for all the teachers and students with their parents. This must have been sometime in June, when spring was still in full swing. I invited my parents, and to my great joy they came. They had planned to visit me anyway, so this was a wonderful occasion. The party was held at Sesenheim, which was very dear to my father, the Goethe scholar. In Sesenheim, Goethe had met his great love, Friederike Brion, (maybe the school was named after her) while he was studying in Strassburg in 1771, only twenty-two years old. On the way, Father was talking about this encounter, which is described so beautifully in *Dichtung und Wahrheit* (Poetry and Truth), which I had read and now experienced. My parents got acquainted with all my teachers. Especially the math teacher, who had taught us about the cone sections and the beginning of calculus, impressed my father very much. They soon were deeply involved in a discourse about infinity. My mother found common ground by talking to the English teacher, so we all were happy. The weather was great, the birds were singing, and the first flowers of spring were blooming. We sat at long picnic tables and had plenty to eat and drink. War was far from all of our minds.

It is strange that nobody knew yet about the famous invasion on June 6, which happened in 1944, just around the time we were having such a good time; when American air-born troops landed on the coast of Normandy. Since we never mentioned political events in order to avoid being accused of sabotage and since we had neither radio nor television and seldom bought a newspaper, we were fairly uninformed about the world-changing events that were going on not far from us.

My parents also visited my apartment, where they met Sabine. They were a little shocked at the free lifestyle she obviously led—she smoked, drank, and had many boyfriends. But Sabine knew how to mollify their doubtful feelings by praising me to heaven and sitting down at the piano and expertly playing my parents' favorite classical music.

One reason that I did not leave my job at the institute right away in March of 1944, when I had the *Abitur* in my hands, was dictated by the politics of the time. As I mentioned before, anyone without a job was put to work in a factory. Also, I would have had difficulties being accepted at the University of Strassburg with my sketchy records and having only the *Fremdenreifeprüfung* (something like the GED in this country). The places at the university were coveted, there was overcrowding and other applicants with full *Abiturs* and better records would have been preferred. Moreover, I would not have had the money to pay for tuition and living costs, so I decided to stay on at the institute and postpone my college education until after the war.

Sabine: Let me describe Sabine some more. She was a middle-aged, sensual, overweight woman and took me under her wing like a mother hen.

"Look at her, how beautifully slender she is, only twenty-two years old and reading all those books," she used to introduce me to her friends.

She was a great musician (at least I thought so) and had studied the piano since she was a little girl in her hometown, Graz, in Austria. She could play anything either from memory or by sight from printed music. Since I always loved classical music, she often played for me and also explained the music to me in her fashion. When she played the *Liebestraum* (Dream of Love) by Liszt, for example, she would say, "Listen to the build-up and then the beautiful orgasm. *Wunderbar*," as the music flowed from her apt fingers. "*Und die wundervolle Apassionata!*" she raved about the beautiful piano sonata by Beethoven.

Yes, Sabine was opening a whole world of music and sensuality for me that I had not experienced until now.

During the last month of the war the opera house as well as all other institutions related to the fine arts was closed down and all the performers sent to the munitions factories to work. This was very hard for the poor artists who were not used to menial labor. Poor Sabine complained and suffered and finally managed to get away with her boyfriend. I missed her terribly and almost felt orphaned.

Much later, when the war was over, I visited her once in Braunschweig, where she and her boyfriend had moved, and to my great sadness, I found a completely dispirited, unhappy Sabine, a mere shell of her old self, living in the poorest of conditions, being brutalized and abused by the man she was then married to. Her former boyfriend had left her soon after their move to Braunschweig. She had been in contact with me by first writing to my parents (whose address I had given her), who then in turn wrote her address to me. I was studying in Hamburg at that time. After this sad encounter, I lost track of Sabine. Meanwhile the war was dragging on.

Bombings: The bombings started to become more frequent during the year 1944. The Germans had been bombed ever since the Japanese had attacked Pearl Harbor in December of 1941, and the Americans had joined the Allies by declaring war. People were advised to keep all windows tightly masked at night so that the enemy fighters would not make out the cities easily from the lights. When Elsaß-Lothringen (Alsace-Lorraine) was captured during the first years of the war, those countries, too, were attacked with bombs. These attacks escalated during the years and became a way of life for the Germans.

I was tucked away on my island in Mecklenburg and later in Pomerania, where there was little reason for the enemy to throw bombs, but whenever I was at home, I had to march to the nearby bunker when the ugly sound of the sirens started. These loud wailings going up and down were given in advance, if possible, and sometimes it took hours of waiting before we heard the droning of air fleets approaching and then infallibly, the thumping sound of falling bombs, followed by explosions.

"That was a big one," we would whisper to each other in terror,

"Hope it wasn't our street!"

When finally, the level sound of *Entwarnung*, the signal that the attack was over, came, we could leave the bunkers and inspect what was left of our homes. Our house in Bremen was miraculously spared until the last days of the war; almost the last bomb hit our house on May 4, 1945, when Hitler was already dead and gone. He had taken his life on April 29, or rather, had ordered his chauffeur to roll him into a blanket, pour kerosene over it and light it. At least this is what we heard.

Anyway, when I came to Strassburg in April of 1943, I had to learn to live with bombings all the time. Many a night we spent in the cellar of our house at Kirsteinstraße because there were no bunkers nearby. We had to climb down five flights of stairs each time the alarm started and up again when the Entwarnung came. In 1944, the frequency of alarms was stepped up and many people got used to it. It was just a way of life then. While I was studying for my exam, I got tired of going to the cellar in the middle of the night. I just stayed upstairs in my bed since most alarms came after midnight and I was out almost every evening to go to the opera, theater, or night school. I had just captured my first good sleep and was not willing to interrupt this for any dumb alarm in the world.

There was also the *Verdunklung* (darkening all sources of light at night). In the beginning of the war it had been a suggestion, now it became law. At the onset of dusk, which varied according to seasons, everyone all over the *Reich* had to go through the painstaking procedure of darkening the windows *completely*, so that not a speck of light could be detected from the outside.

On September 29, 1944 there was a real big attack on Strassburg. The sirens had started early and kept on wailing until even diehards like me climbed down the stairs to the cellar. It was a strange-looking group of people, mostly clad in sweat suits or robes, some clutching photo albums, others with suitcases always ready in case the house was bombed and not all of us buried under the rubble. All night the bombers flew over the city, throwing carpets of bombs onto the frightened citizens. Their real targets were the munitions factories, but those were cleverly camouflaged, therefore many bombs hit civilian areas. Next morning, when it was finally quiet, all we saw was mass destruction in town. Whole districts and streets were wiped out. The university was still intact. So was our street, and I was happy when I heard that neither Münster nor the opera house nor the adult school had been hit. All the rest of September through October and into the second half of November, we had air raids, day and night.

When I think back to the winter 1943/44, I marvel at how I juggled my life. I went to adult school, had learned many new things, saw a variety of operas, plays, and movies, worked everyday, had to cook or go out in order to eat (for the first time in my life nobody was cooking for me), enjoyed music with Sabine—all that in-between air raids. But I was young and healthy and life was great.

The Last Months in Strassburg: On June 6, D-Day, when the invasion of the allies took place, and the Americans had landed in Normandy, we were almost untouched by this historical event. Our lives went on as if nothing was happening. Of course, I am speaking for myself mostly—others knew and worried but didn't talk about it. Our professor knew; he had orders from Tübingen to plan on relocating the institute back into the Reich. All this time he gave lectures at the university and I, his assistant, had to help him.

In Germany at that time, the study year was divided into two semesters: the summer semester from April to the middle of August and the winter semester from September to the middle of March. During the summer semester of 1944, I had to assist my boss during his lectures on genealogy by running the slide projector and carrying his illustrative material to and from the lecture hall. The hall was packed with students of both sexes, who were fiercely envied by me. They might have envied me for having a job. They seemed to be leading such carefree lives, sitting there and taking notes of wisdom from many different professors about a variety of interesting subjects, while I had to stay with just one professor, one subject, and hearing the same stuff over and over again. My work in the fields was continued; so altogether I led an interesting life. Meanwhile, Sabine got entangled with a fellow from the male choir and decided to move back to the *Reich* with him.

Without Sabine, a part of my life in Strassburg was gone and then when our third renter, the gardener from the institute, left, I was alone in the apartment. Sadly I sat in our living room and looked at the piano that belonged to the flat, and recalled how Sabine had played Beethoven and Mozart sonatas for me, and how she and her girlfriend, the leading soprano that year, had practiced together the wonderful arias that I would hear later on the stage. The air was full of the fragrant scent of the geraniums and petunias that our gardener had raised in planters on our little balcony overlooking the city. I felt change coming and I hoped it would come soon. And soon many things happened

The Fall of Strassburg: The week before Strassburg fell, first into the hands of the French on November 23, 1944 and then of the Americans on November 25, there had been rumors about such an attack. Of course, my boss, Herr Professor Knapp, forbade us to speak about this or to send our belongings home into the *Reich*. As I learned later, *he* had secretly sent most of *his* belongings and part of the institute's assets to Tübingen "just in case" something should happen. And it did.

On November 21, we heard shooting from the west. On that day I had sent my last letter to my parents, not mentioning any suspicions, because I was afraid someone might open my letter and accuse me of sabotage. My parents received this letter on November 22 when the siege of Strassburg was inevitable. On that day, November 22, all able-bodied persons in the city, except small children, had to dig a ditch around Strassburg. We had the crudest tools to do so: shovels, picks, even wooden boards. Old men hardly able to walk worked beside teenagers and women of all ages. While we were working, we heard the awesome shooting coming closer and closer from the west, where French troops were assembled with their tanks.

Prisoner of War

Strasbourg, Alsace: On November 23 these tanks rolled over our ditches with ease and took over the city. All the Nazis, including my boss, had vanished like cockroaches, so had smart Germans who had been reading the handwriting on the wall. All of these people had crossed the bridge going across the Rhein leading to the city of Kehl in the *Reich*. (During the time when the Elsaß was German territory Strassburg and Kehl were practically one city, just separated by the Rhine, but as soon as Strassburg fell the bridge separated two countries, France and Germany.)

On November 22, Herr Professor had given me some letters and packages to bring to Kehl the next morning with the strict order to return to the institute *after* I had delivered everything. On the morning of November 23 I packed all the mail and packages into the basket of my bicycle and headed for the Rhine Bridge. It was raining buckets as I made my way across the Rhine. At 10 o'clock I had delivered my mail at the post office in Kehl and obediently and stupidly started on my way back into Strassburg. I had to fight the stream of refugees and hardly could get through. When I finally arrived at the institute, my boss and both assistants were gone! I decided to look for a handcart, go back to my apartment to fetch my belongings and go again across the Rhine to get home.

But, when I had loaded my things onto the little cart (I left my bike at the house in Kirsteinstrasse) and wanted to get onto the bridge, it was already too late. French and American tanks had occupied all the streets. I observed people jumping from the bridge into the river just to escape being imprisoned. Allied soldiers were shooting at them. I had to turn around. A little later a loud explosion was heard. A German suicide squad had been successful in placing dynamite and blowing up the bridge. I had failed to get out in time and was trapped in Strassburg.

Since my apartment was empty, I decided to go to a work colleague who was an *Elsässerin* (a native of the Elsaß) who used to work with me at the institute and had stayed in the city. She and her sister were German-friendly and they took me in. I lived about ten days in their house, with one interruption that I will go into shortly.

The besieged city soon looked quite different; instead of swastikas, there were tricolors, and French street names were substituted for German names, Hitler Platz became Place de Gaulle, and Strassburg turned into Strasbourg. The city was occupied by French soldiers for the first two days after the siege. The Americans came a day later, on November 25.

On the first day of French occupation, November 24, French tanks came down our street to look for Germans from the *Reich*. Since I did not want to cause trouble for my hosts, I gave myself up and was added to a long column of Germans, many of them people who had helped build the ditch around the city two days before. Elsässers, who had quickly turned around and became French again, lined the streets and pelted us with rocks and French slogans. We saw our German soldiers lying dead or wounded on both sides of the street. We had no idea where we were headed until they marched us into the city prison and dumped us into big cemented halls without any beds, blankets, or anything to lie down on. Was this where I would spend the rest of my life? In the evening our guards put a bucket full of raw potatoes in each hall; that was our dinner! People of all ages and all kinds of health conditions were thus spending the night without knowing what would happen next. There was much weeping and wailing going on, and babies were crying pitifully, because there was no milk for them.

Next morning, on November 25, we were set free again—obviously the Americans had come and given the order. We walked back to our homes, among the hand grenades thrown by German diehards who were too fanatical to give up the fight for the city. When I came back to my friends, they were happy and assured me that I could stay as long as I wanted. During the next days, the Germans were allowed to walk in the streets, but only until five o'clock in the afternoon. Food was available at the stores. The Nazis had put big supplies into warehouses, so we could eat, and I went back a few more times into my old apartment to get more of my belongings (including my bicycle).

Even before the Americans had captured the city, I had taken a course in Red Cross First Aid and had also applied for a permit to donate blood to our wounded soldiers. On December 3, when everything had quieted down on the streets, I rode on my bike to the hospital to pick up the permit. The same gentleman to whom I had applied was still there and asked me how I was doing. He advised me to go to the head of the hospital and try to get onto the list of DKS Schwestern (German Red Cross nurses), because the Americans might want to exchange these nurses for allied prisoners in the *Reich* and would probably transport them out of Strasbourg. I followed his advice immediately—but it was difficult. The list was already full and had been given to the Americans. But I should try anyway, the leading doctor and the head nurse indicated to me, and I should move into the hospital with my things. Maybe I could slip in when the nurses were transported. So I rode to my friends' home, packed a few things, said goodbye to my friends and set off (without my bicycle) to the hospital. On the way I almost got caught by a French policeman who was going to put me into prison again; only by flashing my permit for blood-donation was I able to evade him. Following the advice to join the hospital staff most likely saved my life. But I did not realize that then.

In the hospital I was put in a group of *Krankengymnastinnen* (physical therapists) who were studying under Professor Kohlrausch who, as was revealed later, was also a fierce Nazi and not much better than my Professor Knapp. I stayed with these girls, called *Kohlräuschlinge*, the entire time of my stay as a prisoner. We waited for three more days in the hospital. By now the hospital administration had been taken over by a German-American doctor from Mannheim. He and his staff were very civil to the German nurses, doctors, patients, and us. We had the feeling that the Americans tried to save us from the hatred of the French.

We were looking forward to being transported away from Strasbourg. The first transport consisted of wounded Germans and other patients. We did not know what happened to them. Then, on December 6, the rest followed, about two hundred persons, doctors, nurses, assistants, helpers, kitchen personnel, and *Kohlräuschlinge*. We were loaded onto LKWs or *Lastkraftwagen* (big trucks). After an eight hour drive, we came to Epinal, a town on the border of Alsace (the former Elsaß) and France. It had rained all night and we were all, in spite of the canvas covers, drenched and frozen stiff to the bones.

Epinal: Here American soldiers received us and brought us into a large stone building. It was in the middle of the night. In a short while a large kettle full of coffee appeared, along with sugar and cream, and then we were led to cots with three blankets for each of us. Next morning we had a wonderful breakfast consisting of hot oatmeal with brown sugar and raisins, scrambled eggs with bacon, and as much French-bread toast as we wanted. Things were looking up. Such breakfast was not possible in Germany anymore! We hoped to stay at least for a few days in Epinal, but right after breakfast we were told: "Pack everything. In two hours we are leaving!" LKWs brought us to a train station and we were distributed onto the train.

Marseilles: The trip from Epinal to Marseilles took four days. We were guarded by the same Americans who took care of us in Epinal and were told never to stand by a window, so the French, who hated us, could not see us and throw rocks at us. We had more than enough to eat: cans with heavy food like pork and beans (which had to be eaten cold; I still can't stand pork and beans from cans) and light cans with cookies, cacao, candies, and so forth. Water was limited during the whole trip. On December 11 we arrived in Marseilles. We stayed the entire day in the station and had to remain on the train. Our guards played catch to kill time. The sun was brilliant. French girls were wearing summer dresses and socks. In the evening we continued our journey toward the west. We stopped at a small town, Septenes. Again, we had to stay on the train.

After a bitter cold and starry night, we had to get off the train, were put into trucks, and away we went though the beautiful hills of southern France. Our goal was a huge prison camp near *Aix* off the Mediterranean coast. About 30,000 German soldiers were held here behind barbed wire. For the first time, men and women were separated in this camp. We received a good dinner and then had to line up to hand in our watches, pocketknives, pencils, and all the money we had. For all of this we were handed a receipt—but doubted if we would ever see our things again. Afterwards, we were inoculated against typhus.

In the evening we were led to our tents, big enough to hold thirty people—but we were twice as many. Each woman received two blankets, which were not nearly enough for us—we had to sleep on the floor and it was bitter cold. Later we were told that our soldiers had only one blanket. For washing ourselves, we had to use big tubs that stood outside the tents. So we washed off the dirt from our long trip under the stars and had an unforgettable view of the huge camp with thousands of lights. It was December 12, 1944.

In the middle of the night we had to get up, walk to the office in a long line, and turn in our personal data with fingerprints. After this procedure we, still all weak from the inoculation, were led back to our tents. We started to think that all of this bureaucracy was done to torture us.

The next morning we had to get up early, were given a good continental breakfast consisting of French bread, butter, marmalade, and coffee, and then had to line up with our baggage. We were really wondering why they bothered to let us keep the baggage. In fact, German soldiers had to bring our suitcases and bags and it seemed important that we got everything we had taken with us (except those items they took from us during the night). Our guards divided us into groups and we were loaded into the trucks again. Black drivers took us in the direction of Marseilles. The leading truck driver evidently did not have clear directions, because we drove randomly about the city for quite a while. At one time we saw the harbor, so I already hoped to get to America and see my sister! Through the inner city, through many tiny alleys, we finally reached our destination: the rail station.

Chartres: This time we traveled north. Different American soldiers were guarding us. We had no idea where we were going—home maybe? We passed through Lyon, Dijon, Paris, and finally came to Chartres. The beautiful cathedral at Chartres we could not see because it was nighttime. In Chartres we were again loaded into trucks—by this time we felt like cattle—and transported to a prison camp for women only. Our men had been left in Marseilles. Our group now consisted of the nurses, cooks, *Kohlrausch* girls, and also fifty *Nachrichtenhelferinnen* (news transmitters) who had later joined us. Our women's camp was situated between two men's camps, one for German soldiers and one for deserters.

Between those camps were barb wired fences. Our camp was still under construction when we arrived.

The weather was very bad. It was cold and rainy. Our tents were erected by German soldiers. We were told not to "fraternize" and were closely observed by the American MP guards (Military Police) who were posted in guard towers on the four corners of our camp. Ten women were put into each tent. It was not easy to place ten cots into the small tents that measured six meters by six meters (about three hundred square feet). Cooking was done by German women who had been captured in the west and were supervised by our cooks from the hospital. The kitchen was a primitive building made of corrugated iron. During the first ten days, we suffered greatly from the cold weather. On December 22 it started to freeze—we had no stoves in the tents and had to eat outside.

Christmas was a sad affair. I remember sitting on my cot, next to my friend Hanni Korthals, both of us crying and thinking of our parents who had no idea where we were.

Especially humiliating were the bathroom facilities, one barn like building with rows of latrines, with no privacy possible. There was another girl in camp, Helga Singer, who was my friend. She used to clown around and make fun of everything. "Let's go and lay eggs," she said when we went to the latrines. In fact, it looked very much like a chicken coop with busy hens, when we were all sitting there.

We got used to these things in no time at all. How we cleaned ourselves, I don't remember—we probably didn't wash at all.

In January things began looking up. We all received warm clothing, German navy outfits that had been taken by the Americans, complete with long johns. Then a mess hall was erected that had a stove, and we were even given stoves for each tent. Now we started to fight for wood! In time our captors provided us with enough wood and coals. I was the official fire maker, having had good training in the *Arbeitsdienst*. Food was plentiful and nutritious. We also started classes in the New Year to use all the free time we had. We selected teachers from those with special talents among us and soon developed English, singing, poetry, math, and science classes, even a course in religion. Every Sunday afternoon we were invited to one of the neighboring prison camps for a *Varieté* performed by our fellow Germans. I remember us putting on our overalls marked with POW (Prisoner of War) and being led by the MPs to the neighboring camp. We were not allowed to "fraternize" and, of course, did it anyway. Usually on the day following the show, a lively exchange of little notes, written on bits of paper and crumbled up, took place over, through or under the barbwire. The leader of all the camps, whom we had to address as "Colonel," had a mean streak. Usually he ordered regular contributions of candy to the women and tobacco to the men. Once, when it absolutely rained with messages via fences, he ordered distributions of tobacco for the women and candy for the men. When this became an incentive for the frequent exchange of goods, he curtailed the meals on both sides. Otherwise, we lived comfortably for about five weeks at Chartres.

Cherbourg: In the morning of January 23, 1945, we were told abruptly: "Get everything ready. We are leaving in two hours." Nobody told us where we were going. Two weeks before, some of our nurses had been transported away on trucks and we had heard nothing about them. At noon we were loaded up and we said goodbye to Chartres. After twelve hours of driving, with only two stops for stretching our legs and warming ourselves, we arrived at a hospital in Lison near Cherbourg. It was in the middle of the night. We were brought to our lodging, tents for thirty women as in Marseilles, but this time with cots and enough blankets. Next morning we had a chance to look at what we thought was our new home. This camp was much larger than our small camp in Chartres. The hospital was part of the camp and was for German prisoners. We supposed that we had to care for these soldiers. To our surprise, we met all those nurses who had left us two weeks ago! They had already started to work and seemed very pleased with all the conditions. One of the nurses had even met her wounded husband.

There was only one drawback. The leading American doctors and policewomen were often rather unfriendly. The American nurses, under whom the German nurses were working, were bossy and demanding. During the afternoon, after our arrival, we had to line up at the office to record our personal data. However, after only half of us were processed (these procedures always took a long time because we were around two hundred persons), it was announced that that was enough for today. And on the same evening we were told to pack up again, that we would leave the next morning. We could hardly explain this seeming contradiction of orders. But only a week later we would know the reason for this chaotic state of events.

Back to Chartres: Again we sat in a train. This time we went to the east. This train was very dirty, as if it had been used several times and never had been cleaned. The floor was full of empty bottles, leftover food, paper, and so forth. We received French bread and canned meat as meals. At one station I had an animated conversation with one of the American guards (my school English came in handy) and he told me that he was a singer and had plans to study voice in Vienna after the war.

After a day of travel, much to our surprise, we arrived in Chartres again around midnight and were picked up by our colonel himself. The trucks stood ready for us in front of the station and took us back to our camp after a three-day trip. We were heartily welcomed by the crew of women who had cared for us before. The tents were clean and there was fire in the stoves.

We stayed for one more week in Chartres. During this time we had more shots and were given back all our things that had been taken in Marseilles, even the money. The personnel in charge of this procedure even had us present our receipts to check if everything was given back to us. But we were also carefully checked for any suspicious papers by having to undress completely in front of an MP woman. My only important document was the *Abitur* and I clung to it like a tigress. On January 29 our camp leader, Captain Cliff, a stern lady, announced that we would start on one more journey tomorrow—the way home!

Later we learned that there had been a successful attack by Hitler in the Ardennes, the Battle of the Bulge on December 16, 1944, during which two hundred American nurses had been captured and imprisoned. For these nurses, we were now exchanged. It had taken five weeks of red tape and contradictory orders to achieve this exchange. We were hysterical with joy, packed our belongings and slept for the last time on our cots. Our baggage had expanded considerably, because the Americans allowed us to keep the navy clothes and the three army blankets they had given to us. This time we bade farewell for good from the camp, to the Americans, and some German civilians who wanted to stay.

Back to the Reich

Traunstein, Bavaria: Trucks brought us and our baggage to the train station. A long train stood in readiness. Every one of us had her own seat (on the previous train rides, we often had to share seats). There was enough food for all of us. It took two days to get through Lyon to Geneva. Here we were cordially received by Swiss agents, given a full dinner, and then brought to an express train headed for Germany. On this clean train we felt much better than we did in the run-down French wagons. Now followed the journey through beautiful Switzerland; though it was nighttime, the moon was shining and we could make out the contours of mountains and shimmering lakes. Nobody could sleep; we were free again!

Toward morning, we arrived in Konstanz and were received by the members of the Nazi Party with a thundering "Heil Hitler!" We were back in Germany! However, to our dismay, we were told that we could not go home right away as we had hoped, but that we had to report first to the *Heimkehrlager* in Traunstein (collecting camp for homecoming soldiers and prisoners) in Upper Bavaria. Since the rail system in Germany toward the end of the war (the date was February 2, 1945) was already in bad shape, it took us two full days to get to Traunstein. My two friends, Helga and Hanni, and I managed to get a place in the front of the train with the leaders of the transport, Germans this time, and we had a very good time. In Traunstein, it was again "Heil Hitler" and "Sieg Heil" (the victory slogan) and we were put into cars and escorted to the collection camp.

Here in the *Heimkehrlager* everything was prepared for us. We had beautiful airy rooms with eight beds and were offered spacious hot showers to wash off the grime of imprisonment. Then followed a lavish meal in the huge canteen. In the course of one week, all the homecoming men and women, six hundred altogether, were asked for personal data for filing purposes. Every evening we had performances of a political or entertaining nature. On Friday, February 9, a big party was arranged. Actors and other artists from Munich gave a variety show in our honor. Every one of the home comers received a bottle of wine. The only thing that baffled us was the joyous mood all our guests were in. Didn't they know that the end of the war was near? However, the confidence in the *Endsieg* (final victory) and the Führer's ability to tackle his enemies rubbed off on some of us and we had a good time.

On February 13, we were sent on our way home. From our files the management knew where our homes were and provided us with the appropriate train tickets. All people with the same or similar destination went together. I had to say good-bye to my friends Hanni and Helga, since Hanni's parents lived in a different part of Germany and Helga, who didn't have a family, decided to stay in Traunstein. Let me talk a little more about Helga Singer.

I met her first when I joined the staff of nurses and *Kohlrausch* girls in Strasbourg at the beginning of my imprisonment. She struck me from the start as an unusual person. She was an orphan and had a variety of experiences in her life. Among other occupations, she had been an actress. She was older than most of us girls, I think about twenty-seven or so. At the time I met her, she was a helper at the nurses' station in the hospital and we were both in the same situation. I enjoyed her wit and her intelligence and most of all her beauty. She carried herself very well and always looked pretty, even in our men's navy outfits at camp. When we came to Traunstein, the camp there was headed by a young lieutenant, Fritz Simon, dashing and vigorous, whom everyone fell in love with. Helga just said, "I would like to marry this man!" She was noticed by him soon and he obviously courted her. The two of them made a beautiful couple. When we all left for our homes, Helga stayed with Fritz Simon. I liked both of them so much that I decided to return to Traunstein after two months at home and even asked at the war hospital in town if I could get a job as a nurses' aide there. I still had my certificate stating that I had completed a course in First Aid. The hospital management was glad about my decision, as all hands were needed. They would have a workplace for me in April of 1945.

So I left for Bremen, and since mail service was practically out-of-order in those days, I arrived at our home on Richard Strauss Platz before my letter from Traunstein. After seven weeks of prison, where we were not allowed to write at all, we finally could send mail to our families. However, because of the failing mail nobody knew I was coming. I did not know that then, though.

The train trip went without major difficulties. Only before Fulda, we had a long wait because of air raid warnings. We stopped at a little village and had a chance to buy milk and bread without food stamps. Stamps had been necessary for everything from food to clothing since the beginning of 1944 and had to be used in Strassburg too, so I was familiar with them.

Last Days of the War

Again in Bremen: On Thursday, February 15, 1945, I arrived in Bremen. The train station had been bombed and was hard to recognize. But the tramway was still functioning and I was home quickly. I had seen many signs of destruction on the way and was relieved when I saw our house still standing. I rang the bell. Never will I forget my mother's surprise when she opened the door! "Tita, is that you (I was still called by my baby name at home)? Is that possible?" I saw then that none of my letters had arrived. My father was at work but both of my sisters were there with their children. My mother had not seen me since the visit in Strassburg, and she could not believe that she had her missing daughter back again.

Dorothee had been living in Bunzlau in Lower Silesia with her family—her husband Wulf Rohland and her four children, Julie, Regula, Jane, and Dorette—for many years until the Russians captured that area in January of 1944. During the later years of war her husband had been drafted to fight in Greece. Julie's husband, Christoph Kulenkampff, had come from Riga, where he had been wounded and had been sent to the *Reich* to recuperate. He had come to Bunzlau and was staying with Dorothee when the Russians came. The Russians came from the East and the Americans from the west and the border between the two occupied territories was just a small distance away from Traunstein. Julie, who had been living in Bremen with her first child, Hedwig, had been bombed out and had just come to Bunzlau to care for her husband. When the Soviet attack came, my sisters packed up the children in two cars, each of the children wearing a small backpack. One car was driven by Dorothee, the other one by the recently wounded Christoph, with his one functioning hand. On Christoph's car a chicken was dangling in the back. Someone had given it to him when they left. So they had driven slowly through the bombed and burning Germany and had arrived in Bremen just a few weeks before me. When my father came home from work that night, he found a full house. We were all very happy to be together again.

Later on, from 1946 to 1955, my two sisters would have more children, Dorothee had Wulf Jr. and Constanze, and Julie had Cornelie, Julie, Bettina, Christine, and Charlotte. So six more family members joined the Apelt clan after the war. I would start with producing my own clan much later: from 1953 to 1960. But that is looking into the future.

Our house on Richard Strauss Platz sheltered twelve people now: my parents, my two sisters with their husbands (Wulf Rohland joined us soon after I had arrived), five children, and myself. It was crowded, and I don't remember how my mother bedded and fed us all. But then everything was topsy-turvy in those days before the war ended. Most likely she had hired help, but I don't remember clearly.

Next morning I looked around and found many signs of destruction. The entire inner city had been bombed repeatedly, and it was a miracle that some businesses were still open and tramways were functioning. My father told me that the port area was almost completely destroyed. I remember that on a Sunday morning my father and I had to go to his office on the Schüsselkorb, a street downtown close to the Weser River. There had been an air attack and the attic of the building was in flames. The lower stories were drenched with water from combating the fire. We tried to retrieve his most valuable papers.

That same Sunday afternoon my father gave a speech at the Goethe Institute. Air raids happened now day and night, and whenever the alarm started wailing, Dorothee and Julie dutifully went to the nearby bunker with their families.

After a while, both husbands found jobs in Blumenthal outside Bremen and took their families with them. Now I was alone with my parents. I was amazed how nonchalant they both acted. They took everything in stride, as long as everyone was still alive. My parents told me how worried they had been about me since November 22, 1944, when they received my last letter. They had heard rumors about the siege of Strassburg and did not know if I had escaped or not; if I was dead or alive. They had even written to Professor Knapp in Tübingen, but he did not know anything either. (Neither did he care, evidently, according to his letter.)

It was quite a shock for them when I told them that I had intended to return to southern Germany to work at the hospital in Traunstein, but they understood my restlessness and desire to be useful. Of course, I should have stayed with them and could have easily found work in a war hospital in Bremen. It was another very unwise decision of mine but I felt obliged to go.

The political situation was still critical. The Russians had occupied most of Silesia. The Americans gained territory in the west.

Back to Traunstein: On March 12 I started out on what would become a long, adventurous journey. Just when my father and I left our home—he had insisted on bringing me to the station—there was a terrible air attack that wiped out most of the electrical tramway system and the rail system around the Bremen station. We had to walk for an hour and a half to Sebaldsbrück where I was able to catch a train to Hanover.

My father and I talked about many personal things on this walk. I will never forget how close I felt to him then and how thankful I was that he and my mother understood that I would not stay with them because I was driven to venture out into the world again after all my hardships. In short, they too felt that I was not ready to settle down.

The train to Hanover was supposed to connect to an express to Munich, but it went so slow that it missed the connection by five minutes. So I decided to take a train to Frankfurt instead. At first the journey went well, until the train stopped just before Treysa. We waited, but nothing happened, and all the passengers got off the train to walk to the station. I had found nice companions who offered to help me with my baggage. My good mother had helped me pack and given me some bulky foodstuff, and my father had allowed me to take some of his books. There was even a bottle of wine in my bag.

In Treysa, we had to wait for two hours and then got on a train to Marburg. In Cölbe, one station before Marburg, the train stopped and we were told that Marburg had suffered a severe air raid the same afternoon (it was night by now) and that we had to leave the train. So we had to walk again. Marburg was on fire; it was a horrible sight. We had to walk twelve kilometers to the southern rail station that was still intact. When we finally arrived there, completely drained, we heard that the next train would leave in nine hours, at 6 o'clock in the morning. Then we had to look for a place to sleep and found nice people who took us in for the night. Germans were used to these happenings now and rolled with the punches. To show my gratitude to our hosts, I shared with them my bottle of wine and the food my mother had packed.

Next morning at 6 o'clock we continued our journey in an overfilled train on which people even sat on the roof. We got as far as Friedberg, where everything looked almost the same as in Marburg. Friedberg had just had a terrible attack. Again we had to walk seven kilometers until we reached a cattle wagon standing on the tracks that brought us to Hanau. In Hanau, more of the same, nothing but smoke and rubble.

At a center for the army, my soldier friends, my traveling companions, and I warmed ourselves, got something to eat and drink, and decided to spend a little time in the beautiful Odenwald. A little train carried us to Eberbach, which was untouched by the war and situated in a lovely wooded valley. We went on a beautiful hike through the forest and felt as if we were on vacation.

From now on it was smoother sailing. We had to change trains only in Neckarels and Heilbronn, then we caught the Express to Rosenheim and finally arrived in Traunstein at 6 o'clock in the evening. It was March 15 and the journey from Bremen, about eight hundred kilometers (five hundred miles), had taken three full days!

Scarlet Fever: I needed a few days to straighten out all my personal affairs and find a place to sleep. I could not stay at the hospital since this was already overcrowded. I found a small room in a basement, with only half a window sticking out from the ground. My reunion with Helga Singer and Fritz Simon was disappointing. I could sense that they had never believed that I would actually come back. I could hardly believe it myself! They were too occupied with themselves to be very interested in me. So I tried to forget about them and reported to work at the war hospital. There was so much need for help that I was soon completely wrapped up in work. I was put into a room with severely wounded soldiers, most of whom had been shot in the lungs and had breathing tubes sticking out of their mouths. Some were shot in the face and had to be fed. I was mostly in charge of emptying bedpans. I also had to assist in changing sheets whenever necessary. One very severely wounded man died while I was tending him.

In spite of all this misery, the spirit of the wounded soldiers was rather high. They laughed and made jokes; some read, some played cards or chess. I remember two soldiers lying on opposite sides of the room playing chess with each other, and I had to go back and forth between them and report their moves: "White Rook from G7 to G4 or Black Queen back two spaces," and so forth.

This activity went on for three days when, on the morning of March 21, I felt feverish and could hardly stand on my feet. I remember holding a full bedpan and handing it to a nurse in the hallway because everything was swimming before my eyes and I was ready to collapse. She took me to the nearest doctor's office and there it was determined that I had scarlet fever, already fully developed. In all the excitement of the previous days, I had not had the time to feel the disease coming on.

Now, work was out of the question! I was put into an isolation station at the hospital, which was above earth and had tall glass windows and doors. It had been an art museum before the war. Stout Catholic nurses took care of me and others afflicted with infectious diseases. I was put together with two other young nurses, Ilse, a young, lively girl who talked incessantly and the much quieter Karla, always composed and quiet. In order not to contaminate others, we were not allowed to go to the bunkers when the bombers came. We had to stay in the tall glass building, and the dedicated nurses stayed with us.

I remember clearly to this day one horrible moment of attacks when first the nearby children's hospital was bombed and corpses of children were carried by our isolation house. Then followed another attack, and this time a bomb fell so close that most of the tall windows were shattered and fell all over us. We all had left our beds and sat huddled together in one corner of the building close to the entrance. On that day I was afraid for my life for the first time and prayed to my Guardian Angel to let me get out of this alive, and once more sit under a bloom-ing apple tree. The wish came true and today I own not only one but several apple trees that remind me of our perils in spring of 1945. These heavy attacks took place on April 18 and on April 24 as I find mentioned in my diary. Traun-stein had received heavy damages; the entire region around the train station was completely destroyed.

The political situation became more critical everyday. We were betting with each other about who would first arrive in Traunstein, the Russians or the Amer-icans. On April 25, one day after the second heavy air attack, the Russians entered Berlin and stood in the annexed protectorate of Austria-Czechoslovakia before Brünn. The Americans were positioned outside before Bremen in the north, thirty kilometers west of Berlin in the middle part, and at Augsburg and near Nuremberg and Regensburg in the south. There were rumors that Traun-stein was going to be declared *Lazarettstadt* (a safe haven for military hospitals) and thus it would not be bombarded anymore.

During all these weeks in the isolation house, I devoured all the books my father had allowed me to take along. They were mostly paperbacks. I read almost all of Ibsen's plays and some Russian books by Tolstoy and Dostoevsky, Gogol, and Turgenev. I still have most of these *Reclam* books, inexpensive paper editions that were easily accessible in the years of the war.

During the beginning of May of 1945 the situation became really critical. On May 4, on the day my six weeks of isolation were over, we were told that the Americans would take the city this evening. Around 1 o'clock in the morning, the first American tanks drove into town. Traunstein had surrendered without struggle. Our German soldiers—those who could walk—had been continually discharged during the last week. The ones who had not been discharged yet left on the morning after the siege.

I was discharged that day. When I walked through the city, still weak from my bout with scarlet fever, I was reminded of occupied Strassburg—already Strasbourg then—every street was taken over by heavily armored tanks and there were Americans all over, chewing gum and joking with each other.

Bergen and the Schröders: On May 5 I ran into Helga Singer, who quickly talked me into leaving Traunstein and going to northern Germany with her and her boyfriend, Fritz Simon. I packed my remaining things (some of which had been stolen during the last hectic days), got permission to leave work, and set off on the morning of May 6 toward Bergen where Helga and Fritz had some friends and were waiting for me to start their journey northwards.

I got to Bergen with a few hitches. First I found an abandoned bike on the road, put my baggage on it happily and pedaled away, then a group of American soldiers stopped me, took the bike and also my wristwatch, but mercifully let me keep my bag with the precious books. I observed one of the soldiers putting my wristwatch on his arm where it joined many other watches. They were not supposed to do this! I now had to walk again. Helga and Fritz were waiting for me and we set off together.

Actually, I was so drained and tired that I almost decided not to go, but the determination of Helga and her friend gave me back some courage. Moreover, I had nothing left to keep me in southern Germany. And so we commenced our journey, each one of us with a pack on our backs.

But after only two hours of marching on the Autobahn, we were stopped by MPs, asked to show our identification papers, and told that we girls were allowed to go on, while Fritz had to stay with them and would probably be transported into a prison camp in Munich. These soldiers even offered us stolen bicycles for our trip.

This was a heavy blow for us and caused a sudden end to our endeavor. Helga decided to stay with her friend and I took one of the bikes and turned around.

Before parting, we went through our belongings and Helga gave me one of her army blankets while I let her use my heavy boots. Since I had a bike now, I didn't have to walk anymore. Much later I heard from them once more; they had weathered the stay in prison camp (Helga having been a real professional at being a former POW), had married, and my boots would be sent to me shortly. That was the last time I heard from them, and I never got my boots. I kept the blanket and had a winter coat made out of it later.

Now what to do? I remembered that my parents had good friends somewhere in Bergen, the writer and famous "Son of Bremen", Rudolf Alexander Schröder, (mentioned in Chapter 1) and his sister Dora. Since Bergen was a small town, I had no difficulty finding the Schröders and on May 7, 1945, I arrived with my new bike and my backpack on their doorstep, where I collapsed. I had hoped to stay with the Schröders just one night, but that night turned into months!

The Schröders were delighted to take me in once they understood who I was. They were good friends of my parents and were glad to help their daughter. My first task was now to fully recuperate. I was delirious for many days and had forgotten where I was. Then slowly, my health came back and I could get up and think about what to do next. Hitler had been dead since April 29. The war was officially over on May 7, and only a few pockets of resistance remained. I had to make plans for the future. The Schröders graciously invited me to stay as long as I wanted and shared their precious food stamps with me. This was difficult because as soon as I started feeling better, I had a great appetite and was constantly hungry. As soon as I could ride my bike again, I pedaled to the nearest center for distribution of food stamps to register and to receive my own ration of stamps. I also went berry picking to supplement our scant supplies. There were other people from Bremen in Bergen, and I soon made many friends. There were also the American soldiers, the *Ammies* as we called them, who were friendly and supplied us with excess cans of food and chocolate. I even had a little love affair with one of them. Again, I tried to let my sister in America know of my whereabouts, and asked an American to send my letter to her—but to no avail. It was even hard to write to my parents since all mail connections were severed. Somehow they got the news that I was alive and at the Schröders, but I never knew that they knew.

Through the months of June and July of 1945, I stayed in Bergen, helping the dear old people with their chores and really having a peaceful, pleasant time. But in August I was gripped by wanderlust again and became anxious to go home to Bremen. The Schröders pleaded with me to wait until the rail system was functioning again—but I could not wait. I packed up and boarded a northbound truck whose driver was willing to take me half through Germany for a little money, which the Schröders helped me out with. I think they must have been relieved to see me go—it was not easy for two elderly persons, used to a peaceful existence, to have a young fireball living with them and upsetting their routines.

Back to Bremen: I was on my way home again, this time to stay. After a slow, uneventful trip on various trucks, cattle trains, and other vehicles, I finally made it back to Bremen, even with my bike that had become my best friend. On the way home, I had seen the most beautiful part of Germany, the Romantische Straße, and had been carried under apple trees lining the road, loaded with ripe apples. It was an unforgettable ride and how I managed to get through all these adventures on open trucks and other transport unharmed makes me still wonder. I must have had my Angel watching over me! Much later I learned that my husband, after having miraculously survived the war, had been on the very same road at that time, searching for his sister.

When I came to Bremen this time, there was no longer a tramway to take me. I had to ride my bike to get home. When I entered the Richard Strauss Platz, I saw that on the place where our house had stood, there was nothing but a heap of rubble. The very last bomb of the enemy had destroyed the house, where I was born, down to the ground. My parents, who were tired of going to the bunker whenever the alarm sounded, had had some fortification built in the old goat shed in the basement of the house and had been huddling in one corner of this makeshift bunker when the destructive bomb fell. By a true miracle, the house collapsed on the opposite side of the bunker and neither killed my parents nor buried them alive. They crawled like Phoenix out of the ashes (fortunately not their own) and continued with their lives.

They were immediately invited by a colleague of my father, Dr. Degner-Grischow, to move into his spacious house on Parkstraße, at least for the time being, an offer which my parents gratefully accepted. It was a spacious patrician dwelling with three stories. He, a widower, lived on the ground floor and he offered them the second floor, but his daughter, homeless at that time also, did not let this happen—*she* would move into that story. My parents had to climb all the narrow stairs up and down to live in their quarters on the third floor, under the roof. My parents, of course, did not object and were happy to at least have a roof over their head.

Postwar Time

End of the War: Shortly after that last terrible air raid that destroyed our house, the war was officially over. On May 7, 1945, Admiral Dönitz, the man who succeeded Hitler in taking over the lead in Germany temporarily, declared unconditional surrender in all theaters of the war. In Bremen there had been fighting until the last minute to preserve the city. My father had been instrumental in preventing the blowing up of the three main bridges crossing the Weser. Risking his life, he had stood with others in front of German tanks that had orders to demolish the inner city. This order was part of Hitler's plans to annihilate Germany. Hitler's "Scorched Earth" idea had been to leave an absolute void for the enemy—no buildings, no life, a great nothing. Many brave men had helped to reverse this last frustration of a madman.

Already on the following day, Nazi Germany ceased to exist. In the city hall "changing of the guard" took place. This time the Nazi senators and their Bürgermeisters went out through the backdoor and the old senate entered through the front. My father had his old office back, even his old secretary. There were some new members in the senate now, because twelve years of Nazi regime had taken its toll on some of the old gentlemen. One of the brand-new senators was André Bölken, under whom I had worked during my *Pflichtjahr*. One of the two *Bürgermeisters* was replaced by a very capable former stone mason, Herr Kaisen. The other one was my parents' old friend, Dr. Spitta, father of my classmate Paula. Every year on January 5, Dr. Spitta, whose birthday was the same day as my mother's, came to the Richard Strauss Platz to visit my mother to congratulate her, and every time she had a drink ready for him.

So, it was at Parkstraße where I found my parents on the top floor under the slanted roof after some neighbors on our Platz, who still lived in the remains of their house, had told me where to find them. Again there was a happy reunion and this time I promised not to leave my parents, at least not for a while. From the dates in some of my records, I know that this promise was kept until April of 1946, nine months after I had come back from southern Germany.

My Stay in Bremen: I remember having contradictory feelings during this time. I really wanted to help my parents. My mother, who had frail health as long as I can remember, developed a heart condition after the bombing of the house and had to rest for about two hours every day after the noon meal. Formerly, it used to be just a one hour nap. Not aiding this condition were the two flights of rather steep stairs that had to be climbed. Since the upper story where we lived had no bathroom, we always had to make an additional trip to the second floor and up again.

When, towards winter, Frau Ruth Löning, Dr. Grischow's daughter, a widow with two teenaged children, moved in and occupied the second floor, it came to frictions in the now overcrowded house that was built to shelter just one household. The kitchen was in the basement and the food had to be carried up to the higher floors. Our host had a cook for himself and his daughter's family, who cooked and served them in the dining room on the ground floor. In order to be independent from the others in the house, my parents had installed a little cook stove, called *Hexe* (witch), in the large attic that was our activity room. A long stovepipe had to be installed through the slanted skylight. We observed that, in spite of all the care while cooking, that the room was always smoky. I had to sleep in that room because there was no other room in the apartment. The two other rooms were the tiny living room and the parents' bedroom. In the meantime my other sisters had moved to Blumenthal on the Lower Weser; Rohlands because Wulf was now director of the wool treatment plant there and Christoph Kulenkampff had found a job with the *Ammies* (Americans).

Cooking was a great problem. First, because there was precious little food available, and second, there was nothing to make a fire with. Gas and electricity were out for more than half a year after the end of the war. We had kerosene lamps and our *Hexe* to cook and warm ourselves. I had already had experience making fires with very little fuel from the times in the *Arbeitsdienst*. For hours I looked for bits of coal on huge piles of coal dust at a shed in town and for kindling. The others and I went into nearby brushes to gather twigs. Forests like the one in *Hänsel and Gretel* were not near our city. It was strictly forbidden to take any wood from ornamental bushes in our parks, but nobody enforced this law. We managed somehow. When, towards the first cold day of November, electricity came back, we could use an electric hot plate for cooking and felt like kings. *What* to eat was also a big problem. The allotted amount of food for our *Lebensmittelkarten* (food stamps) was just enough for a week but had to last for a month. For instance, I remember having one loaf of bread per person per month and one eighth of a stick of butter. We, who had always indulged in fresh vegetables and fruit from our *Parzelle,* now had to stand in long lines at the grocers for a handful of what was available that day. The *Parzelle* could not be leased anymore since the land was needed to build new houses for all the people whose property had been destroyed.

It was the same for dairy products and meats. We craved to have fat in our meat portions because we got so little fat elsewhere; even the milk was skimmed.

Everybody became thin in those days. One staple that was always available in any quantity was *Wrucken*, yellow beets that were used for everything by inventive cooks: *Wrucken* stew, *Wrucken* salad, *Wrucken* jam, cake, cookies—you name it. I could not stand the penetrating smell of boiled *Wrucken* anymore.

Immediately after the end of the war, the Red Cross arranged a wonderful service called "Care Packages." Relatives and friends of Germans who were living abroad were allowed to either purchase already assembled packages and have them sent to their starving people overseas or pack and send them off by themselves. My sister, Cornelie, then living with her family in Mt. Gilead, a small town in Ohio, was very concerned about us and sent us care packages of every kind, as much as she could afford to do. This was not easy for her as she had to raise four small children, Walt, Barbara, and the twins, Phyllis and Madeline, and had a tall husband who liked to eat. When these packages came, often including gifts such as books, materials for dresses, dolls, and toys for the children, we had a joyous holiday. The whole family, including my sisters' families stood around these wonderful packages and felt like in fairy land.

I liked the pre-packed parcels especially; they always had cigarettes, and while none of us smoked, these cigarettes were valuable bartering chips on the quickly developing black market. I was soon a very shrewd bargainer who tried to make the most out of our Camels and Lucky Strikes. My father, who considered himself a dutiful servant of the city, rejected the thought of using the black market and refused to eat anything that looked too luxurious or plentiful to him, and he forbade us strictly to go through unauthorized channels. He was imagining that a normal person could live off of the food stamps! But he had to deal with my mother and me who did anything short of robbery or murder to get a decent meal on the table. My father was getting very thin and he had more frequent temper tantrums and we were really worried about him.

At this time we had a wonderful person in our house. Her name was Helene, Freifrau von Hundt. She belonged to the nobility class, a lady who had lost not only her huge property, but also her husband and two sons in the war. She was one of the many refugees who had fled from the Communists and had come from East Prussia with her two remaining sons. My mother had met her at her bank in town where Frau von Hundt was employed as a cook for all the employees. My mother convinced her to give up that job and work for our family as a housekeeper. I was very relieved to know my parents were in her capable hands and began thinking of pursuing my long-hatched plans to go to a university.

University Years in Hamburg

Studying begins: After Christmas, in the beginning of 1946, I started searching again for a goal in life. I felt that my real destination was going to a university and so I started to send for application forms to various places of higher learning. Filling out all these forms and sending them out took a great deal of time. Most of the better known universities sent negative responses: my education so far was too sporadic, my *Abitur* not adequate, they were overcrowded, and so forth. Only one university responded positively, the University of Hamburg. They told me that space was available and I would be welcome at their campus as of the beginning of the semester of 1946.

One of the reasons they accepted me was that Frau Löning, our host's daughter, knew the botany teacher, Professor Dr. Mövius in Hamburg, through her late husband, Dr. Löning, and could help me by sending a personal letter to this professor. Also, this university was relatively young and had been almost completely destroyed in the war. Most classes were taught in make-shift buildings, "Nissen huts"[1] (metal sheds), even ruins. They needed money. Anybody who could pay was welcome. An advantage of Hamburg was its closeness to Bremen.

The big problem was to convince my parents of the necessity to start a long study time at my age. They had to help me. My father's income as senator was limited, how well I knew that! In the end, my parents, who did not want to make the same mistake of denying me education twice and who must have admired my determination for higher learning, gave in and proposed to give me one hundred marks per month for the duration of my studies. This was all the money they could give me. It was too much for them and not enough for me. With this money I had to pay my tuition, my books, my lodging, and my food. So it took a lot of balancing my budget to make it work.

But I was happy as a clam when I set off to Hamburg in the first week of April in 1946, with a backpack containing the bare necessities of life and one hundred marks in my wallet.

The first thing I had to accomplish in Hamburg was finding a place to live. For years after the war, there was a fiercely hated system ruling the choice of shelter for everyone who did not own a house: the *Wohnungsamt* (office for housing).

---

1. The Nissen hut is a prefabricated shelter that consists of a sheet of corrugated steel bent into half a cylinder and planted in the ground with its axis horizontal. The open ends are closed with masonry walls. It was developed for the British military by the Canadian engineer Peter Norman Nissen in 1916. Later it was replaced by the Quonset hut. Wikipedia

When I boldly entered the building of the *Wohnungsamt*, after having stood in line for hours, visualizing a long list of pretty apartments to choose from, I was told coldly, "Single persons are only entitled to rent half-rooms. There are no half-rooms available." Confronted with these two premises, I concluded that there were no rooms for me at the moment. Not giving up the fight, I asked a friend of my family to give me shelter for at least one night and was given a sofa to sleep on for one night, as I had requested. People in Hamburg did not readily open their arms and houses for people from Bremen, I learned.

Next day, I stood in line again at the *Wohnungsamt* and got the same response. "No half-rooms. All rented out to students. Come back in six months."

That night I slept on a park bench.

I decided to look for a room without the *Wohnungsamt*. This time I was in luck. I found a half-room (just big enough to place a narrow bed and a table, fortunately also a small stove) that proved to be available. The former renter had just moved out and the landlady, Frau Baerer, had not had enough time to go to the *Wohnungsamt* to offer her room to the housing market. She liked me—it really didn't matter whom she had as renter next and she straightened things out for me at the Wohnungsamt. The price was forty marks. That represented two-fifths of my monthly allowance. I accepted enthusiastically and even succeeded in persuading Frau Baerer to reduce the price to thirty-five marks. "But not a penny less, and take good care of the room," she added.

Later she softened up and even offered me dinner sometimes when there were leftovers. I also proved helpful to her for answering questions for a game called "Toto." If you could answer all the questions correctly you got food stamps or even some money. The questions were not hard for me and I gladly helped Frau Baerer this way, the least I could do to show her my appreciation.

Now I had a roof over my head—a rather dark little room with something like a view when you would bend your upper torso out the window. Normally, I just saw the other side of the street.

The next problem was registration at the university. While I stood in a long line at the registration office in a bombed-out building, I had to make up my mind *what* to study. The obvious choice for me would have been biology and related subjects like husbandry and agriculture, both offered in Hamburg—but that would have been too easy. I knew all that stuff already, or so I thought. I decided to start studying mathematics and physics, the so-called exact natural sciences, subjects that I had liked in upper school and that I thought presented more of a challenge. Moreover, my great-grandfather had been a natural scientist. These subjects were of a completely abstract nature and presented more than enough challenge. But I didn't know that when I registered for five difficult subjects that day. The tuition nearly wiped me out. The registration fee was a flat twenty marks and in addition I had to pay over seventeen marks for my five subjects. I had already spent more than one half of my monthly allowance!

Next I had to think of transportation and food. The former was easy to solve; I walked. Later I would bring my bike from home. Food was more of a challenge—I needed at least one mark each day to still my ever-nagging hunger. It was a great help that the cafeteria of the university offered extremely cheap, even edible food, to the students. So I got along, at least for the first month, with a small amount of money for food.

One more problem remained, books. That was solved easily. Books were rare because of paper shortages, so that the university gave out photocopies on recycled paper to each student. It was a little difficult to read these sometimes dark and muddled pages and the books were bulky—but we managed. We were all in the same boat except for those who had rich parents who still could afford to buy real books.

In this way, five and one-half months went on, interrupted only by three weeks of summer vacation and several weekends for visits at home. There are no tests given in the German higher education system. Instead, one grade is given for each field of study at the end of the university years. No credits are given in this system, and records consist of nothing but a receipt for paying the fees and the signature of the professor having given the course of study. Actually, the student does not know where he stands scholastically and if and when he is ready to take the big final exam.

I did very poorly during my first semester but did not realize that As experienced educators would have told me, I was ill prepared to take the most difficult courses and something had to give. The subsequent courses became more frustrating with every new semester, and I started to fall back in my homework. Writing notes in classes and lectures without understanding what I had recorded and then having to depend on them was frightening. I started dropping out of courses and repeated others with the same result—I didn't get it. Before going deeper into this miserable experience, caused by my own short-sightedness, I will first write about my life in Bremen during vacations with my parents.

Life in Bremen After the War: After the last bomb fell onto our house; after my parents had miraculously survived, and after they had found a shelter at my father's colleague's house, they started to make daily trips to the demolished house with a little wooden handcart; the same one that had been used to carry home the bounty of the *Parzelle* that did not exist anymore because of urban sprawl. My parents crawled on their hands and knees through the rubble and retrieved some of their belongings, piece by piece. My father was mostly interested in saving his books before the fall rains set in, my mother wanted to salvage everything possible. When the little cart was full, they trudged home and carefully cleaned everything before it went up the two flights to their roof apartment. About seventy percent of all the books were thus saved. Some of the books still today smell like rubble and even contain mortar dust between their pages. Many invaluable memorabilia and useful things were salvaged. For bigger objects like carpets, furniture, and appliances my parents hired help and many things were repaired and either put in storage or immediately used again. Needless to say, I pulled many a load through the streets of Bremen when I was still at home.

My father had simple bookcases made that stood on every free wall of the small roof apartment. They housed his favorite books that were used constantly. Whenever I came home from Hamburg, there were new things that had been restored. In fact, later one of the two double beds of my parents stood in my own room in the newly erected house on Richard Strauss Platz.

Finally, after heavy rains set in, my parents called it quits. The days were getting too short anyway, the rubble beginning to decompose, and weeds starting to come up. We were happy and sad at the same time that one of our favorite apple trees in the backyard was still, although barely, alive and even produced some blossoms the next spring, and consequently fruit in the fall of 1946.

I did not tell my parents about my scholastic troubles. They had enough troubles of their own.

Switching Course of Study: After two years of taking mostly difficult courses of a mathematical nature, I began to take a good look at my futile efforts and decided to change the field of my studies. In Goethe's *Faust* Mephistopheles says to the student who is undecided about his choice of study:

"My worthy friend, gray is all theory; the verdant Tree of Life alone is green."

I had enough of theoretical subjects and wanted to taste Life.

Instead of the heavy math and physics courses, I registered for biological sciences and geography. If I should fail in math, my major so far, I had two minors now that gave me pleasure.

While still in my second year of studies at Hamburg, we had to fill out a questionnaire about our plans for the future. This important question had been asked before, when the application for admittance as a student had to be filled out, but that only had been a vague statement of objectives. Now we had to commit ourselves. The theory behind this demand to focus on our goal was built on the premises to let the student roam around at first to try several fields before settling down to narrowing the scope of course selection to the required subjects in a chosen field. Since most other students opted for the teaching profession at elementary or upper schools—in order to teach at universities one needed the doctorate—and though I could hardly visualize myself as a teacher, I marked the slot on the questionnaire for "teaching upper school" with math as major and physics and chemistry as minors. Stating these lofty goals, I also had sporadic visions of becoming a second Fräulein Dr. Ruschmann and inspire young people to love sciences as I was inspired.

So I nailed my own coffin, because shortly thereafter I realized that I would never confront an exam in any of my first chosen fields, and that I would have to drop them.

This meant starting completely over in other subjects and needing five to six years instead of the usual four. In addition I now had to take classes in philosophy and pedagogy in order to submit to a pre-exam that every student of the teaching profession had to pass. In my fourth semester I added these preliminary courses to my already crowded course list (twenty-five units altogether with the math-related courses). I wanted to do at least all the required classes, just in case I flip-flopped again! Looking over the pages of my *Studienbuch*, (a thin booklet containing the titles and instructors of all classes with a signature of the professor after completing the course), that was my sole record for all my activities at the university, reveals to me now how overloaded my schedule must have been. It was an average of twenty-two units per semester, and a whopping thirty-five unit schedule in the sixth semester. Things got much better when I had fully transferred to geography and biology. Fewer classes and lectures had to be taken. The tedious philosophy and pedagogic classes were under my belt.

I took the pre-exam in 1949 and passed it. I remember writing a paper about the oldest Greek philosophers who tried to understand how the world was created and how it worked. Some of their basic ideas are still in vogue with modern scientists.

Lab sessions and excursions were interesting and fun. The students in the humanity disciplines, which included life science and geography were different. In 1951, I took only a few classes because I had to write my thesis and prepare for the big final exam.

There were no counselors at our universities. A young person (and I was older than most students) was supposed to be mature enough to make his or her own decisions, for better or for worse. Anyway, both of my newly chosen subjects had the same very attractive serendipity—both required field trips and excursions. Biology, which was divided up into two subjects, zoology and botany, also relied heavily on lab courses.

Since I was feeling more relaxed, I started to live a more normal life and developed some relationships with other students.

Social Life

<u>Alfred.</u> In the beginning of my studies I met a very studious young man, Alfred Strübing. This young student (almost everyone was younger than I) attended the same beginning calculus class as I did. But in contrast to me, *he* understood what he was doing. Our relationship started when I felt him staring at me before, during, and after classes. At first I tried to avoid him. He was not my actual dreamboat. I was attracted to tall men and he was barely taller than I. I liked sporty clothes and his were very old and baggy. No, he was not my type, and I let him know this by disappearing into the crowd after class. But one day he bumped into me and I could not avoid speaking to him. He asked me if he could accompany me to my apartment and I hesitated until he insisted.

The relationship got a little friendlier when he discovered that I had not understood the class work and he offered to help me. I accepted and now we started a teacher-pupil relationship. He invited me to his apartment where he lived alone with his mother. His father, who had passed away, had been a teacher and Alfred wanted to follow in his footsteps. I began to admire his organized study habits and his well-kept notebooks. If my note-taking skills were that good, I would learn too!

Alfred's mother did not like me and suspected the worst. I did not like her and knew that she suspected the worst. I was under the impression that I had done Alfred a favor by starting a friendship with him and thought that it was very one-sided. I thought that only he was involved because he had pursued me, and did not realize that, though against my own wishes, I too, got involved.

When, almost overnight, Alfred took sick with pleurisy and the doctor ordered that he had to stop studying for one year and prescribed a cure that included a stay on one of the North Sea islands, I noticed that I missed him very much.

The disease had changed Alfred's entire outlook on life. He now hated everyone including me and himself and almost forbade me to come to the sea resort to visit him as I had proposed to make him happy. This was what I wanted to think but really I pressured him because I was now drawn to him by an invisible force.

Now *I* became the pursuer and *he* tried to avoid me. I did visit him on the island and he tried to look happy, but I felt that this was a façade. We took a long walk into the low-tide *Watt* (shoals) with the horizon stretched into infinity out in front of us and no sound to be heard but the screeching of the seagulls. "I really loved you," he said, "but I am a sick man now and that is all I can think about. Go back and live your own life."

I believed him then and saw the uselessness of my pursuing him, went back, and tried to find someone else.

Michael and Fräulein Schmidt: I met two students in zoology lab. One was a young man named Normann Michaelsen who sat on one side of me and a young lady named Edith Schmidt who sat on the other side. Herr Michaelsen was a tall, good-looking, blond-haired, blue-eyed man who dressed in casual sports clothes and was my type exactly. Fräulein Schmidt was a petite, highly inquisitive woman who struck me as somebody striving for knowledge in the same way that I did.

My change to the life sciences from the highly theoretical natural sciences might have also been triggered by the loss of my boyfriend, Alfred. Now I had new things to learn and met new friends. There was an instant attraction between Herr Michaelsen and Fräulein Apelt. We all said *Sie* and addressed each other by last name unless we had offered each other to become real friends—over a glass of wine—and address the other with "Du" and first name. Relatives, of course, always said "Du". And Michael and I—we were in love.

While Herr Michaelsen had nothing to do with Fräulein Schmidt, I got entangled with both of them. Michael, as I addressed him fondly after a few encounters, was, as I learned to my dismay, engaged to a beautiful young lady, as blond as he and working as a pharmacist for a drugstore. When I saw both of them together they struck me as the most perfect couple. Nevertheless, during the day, when the fiancée was safely tucked away at work, Michael was mine. We studied together, walked in the park, and went swimming at the beaches of the Elbe River. Michael never let me forget that he really belonged to this other girl and I accepted the situation. I think she did too.

One event proved to be the apex of our relationship. Our zoology department was giving its yearly costume party in the spring of 1949. This event was unique, and only zoology students were invited. Michael could not (and as I hoped did not want to) invite his fiancée to the party. It was not really a party for couples. You just came and had a good time. Both Professor Klatt, a jolly overweight married man, and his racy assistant, Fräulein Dr. Oboussier, came as Antonio and Cleopatra—he chacing the young girls and she cavorting with good-looking male students of any age. I forgot what Michael was wearing—but I was the *Ratten-fänger von Hameln* (Rat Catcher of Hamelin), in a tight-fitting, rose-colored satin outfit, with gray ears and a long tail, lent to me by my landlady. We danced together all night and walked together in the park during the upcoming morning hours, forgetting the world around us. It was the night of nights for us and will never be forgotten. Everyone should have at least one night like this one in one's memories!

When I was not busy working with or talking to Michael in lab class, as we were dissecting our rats or other animals, I turned to my other neighbor, Edith Schmidt. I had met Edith first in the cafeteria of the university, where both of us were waiting in the line for food. We started talking and soon found common ground. She took biological science courses with the option to achieve a doctorate in this field. It strengthened our friendship to find out that both of us took the same laboratory classes. She was slightly built, always simply but stylishly dressed, and always eager to learn and engage in new endeavors. Nothing ever looked dull to her. Unlike me, she was already successful in her studies and even had a paying job working for a professor of our faculty. She told me about her family, how they had fled from Poland, barely saving their lives, how the whole family had found each other in a small town in the *Lüneburger Heide* (Heath near Celle), and how privileged she was to be able to study here in Hamburg. "I *have* to earn money," she confessed. "My family cannot pay everything for me."

As Edith talked about herself and her family, I found myself admiring them more and more. While we were working on our cadavers, I admired her toolbox and she told me that her brother, Leo, now living in America, had made it for her. Little did I know then that she was talking about my future husband.

Developing Triangles: A strange twist of fate took place after Alfred returned from his exile, cured and anxious to pick up where he had left off a year ago. He realized that I was otherwise engaged now, had made new friends, and had new interests. But when all of the students went to a big party given by the faculty of our department, I saw Alfred dancing with Edith. This surprised me. I talked to him during a pause between dances and asked, "How did you meet Fräulein Schmidt?"

"She is my student," he answered, "and I think she is the most desirable girl I have ever met."

This barb was taken by me with a grain of salt. I asked Edith about her new friend (without letting her know about my bumpy relationship with him) and she told me that she needed a course in applied physics to complete her studies and that Alfred, taking the same course, had offered to help her. "He is a very good teacher," she said, "but *nothing* more."

So that's where things stood, and I only hoped she would not fall into the same snare as I had.

Gertraude: During the final phase of my study years, I met a very unusual female. She happened to be in most of my classes and lectures and took part in our wonderful excursions. She must have been very attractive to men because I always saw her surrounded by male students, like bees around the honey pot, though I could not understand what her secret was. She was not pretty at all; tall, heavy, with strange hair, dark clothing, and piercing eyes that looked straight through you. Maybe it was those penetrating eyes, maybe the way she talked, very softly and drawling like a slowly flowing brook. She had a mysterious aura around her, like a member of some ancient cult. Along with these attributes, she was extremely intelligent and seemed to possess the gift of total memory. Her name was Gertraude, an unusual name, even for Germans. Gertraude and I started to become friendly. She even invited me to her house, where she lived with her family, and helped me with my cramming. *She* definitely did not need help. She became the only graduate that I had met, with a flawless *sehr gut*.

If Gertraude was weird, so was her house. I was only allowed into her living room, and she told me that only her very closest friends were invited to enter the sanctuary of her bedroom. My conclusion from this was that I did not belong to her exalted circle. Neither did I particularly crave to see the bedroom—the living room was enough for me. It was always in a chaotic state, with books, musical instruments, clothing, even underwear all over the chairs, sofas, table, and floor. To be able to study, Gertraude nonchalantly cleared the table by wiping off all the stuff with her arm, did the same thing with two chairs, and invited me to sit down and get out my books. Together we went over all the notes collected over the years, and if I had not understood or grasped important details, she explained, filled me in, and then drilled me in these matters. Even today I can recite the twelve cranial nerves forward and backward and could tell you the functions of every one.

In Gertraude's living room, the walls were filled with white butcher paper showing huge gourd-like creatures in gloomy colors, purples, dark reds, navy blues, and blacks with centers like nuclei or pits in a fruit. "That's me," she told me when I inquired who had done these abstractions and what they meant. "That is my own self, do you see a resemblance?"

She nailed me with her eyes and I had a creepy, eerie feeling that almost resembled fear.

"I think it's very good," I replied dutifully. "It looks very much like you!"

I even got bolder and asked her to draw a picture of me, but she dismissed this request with the mysterious sphinx-like smile of a Mona Lisa.

I was caught in her net like a fly and let her completely influence me. This odd relationship lasted only for a few months. We drifted apart as soon as the exams were over.

My Last Years in Germany

Back to Bremen: In Bremen, meanwhile, things were changing. My parents found it increasingly difficult to live in Dr. Degner's house. They planned to move into a rented place. I fully agreed with them—the overpowering presence of Frau Löning didn't allow my mother to feel like being in her own home. So, with my help, they found a flat in a nice area of town near our *Bürgerpark* Citizens' Park) and we moved everything from Parkstrasse to the new apartment on Schwachhauser Ring. This must have been during one of my vacations. But my parents did not like this new place either. They moved two more times until finally, in 1950, my brother-in-law, Christoph Kulenkampff, took matters in his hands and presented us with a plan.

"You really want a house of your own again," he told my parents, "so this is what you should do. The lot at Richard Strauss Platz is very nice, in a good neighborhood, and belongs to you. We shall have the rubble cleared away, hire an architect, and have your own new house ready in a short time on your old familiar lot. I will lend you the money and you will make payments until it is paid off. Should you pass away before the house is paid off, my wife and I will take everything over and move into the house ourselves."

How could Christoph make such a generous offer? Before the war he had been working as a partner in the wool merchant firm that his father had founded. Kulenkamff und Konitzky was at a low point financially during the war, like all other enterprises in Bremen. Christoph did not have enough work in his own firm that had been barely held together by two relatives. That's why he had worked for the Americans for a while. Kulenkampff and Konitzki began slowly picking up trade after the war and as soon as Christoph saw fit to work again as the owner of the firm, he quit his job with the Americans, from the start considered temporary, and worked for himself. Four years after the war, trade all over Germany had picked up and the capital was there to help my parents. It was a wise investment, because though my father died in 1960, my mother lived on and was able to pay off the house fair and square. In fact, she lived so long, that

Christoph and Julie did not move into the house on Richard Strauss Platz until she passed away in 1982. It was now her house and in her testament she declared us four children as heiresses. This document, a second testament, overriding the first, which had declared Julie and Christoph as the owners of the house, led to some unpleasant rifts in the family.

My parents liked Christoph's plan and wanted to build right away. A cleanup crew removed the rubble. A good architect drew several plans, and we had to decide which one to choose. Since I was going to live in that house too, during vacation and after my studies, I had an impact too. In the old house there had been a balcony from my bedroom that I wanted to have again. However, I was talked out of the idea of having that luxury.

In many ways the new house was to be more practical than the old one; there was, besides the basement, the ground floor with living/dining room, the parents' bedroom, kitchen and a half-bath, the second floor with three bedrooms and a bathroom, and a small attic. There was no little cubicle for my father, so the living room was sunny and light, and the old-fashioned heating system was replaced by a clean modern central heating device.

The building itself went ahead quickly, and already during the spring of 1951 we could move into *our* house. There was so much to do now that my mother didn't even have time to feel sick anymore. My parents were happy to have three of their daughters still living near them. However, not for long.

Rohlands Move to Argentina: In 1948, my sister Dorothee and her husband, Wulf Rohland, decided to follow a business proposition that included living in Buenos Aires. My brother-in-law had been director of a *Wollkämmerei* (factory for treatment of wool) in Blumenthal, the same job he had in Bunzlau since the war ended and was looking forward to do similar work in Argentina. So the whole family—meanwhile a baby boy had been born and a sixth child was on the way—embarked for South America and left a big gap in our family. For my parents it was especially hard to now have a second daughter move to a different continent.

I remember meeting the Rohlands at the Harbor in Hamburg, from where their ship embarked, and being told by the oldest daughter, Julie, that I would never see them again. This turned out not to be true—the Rohlands returned to Germany after the war and only the second daughter, Regula, decided to go back to Buenos Aires and get settled there. I am in contact with her through email and she, working now for a university in Buenos Aires, is sometimes sent overseas to speak about Spanish literature to interested audiences. Whenever she is called to conferences in New York, she visits Doris and Charlie, and thus our families stay connected. Her oldest daughter, Cora, has visited California for several months and stayed with our family for a while. She, like our son Marty, is interested in mountain climbing, and both of them have done excursions together. Everybody in our family had found their niche and was settling down comfortably.

Stabilizing German Currency: The economic situation in Germany looked up too. Until 1948, the old *Reichsmark* had been devaluated by a terrible inflation that made prices go up sky-high overnight. Merchants were hiding their wares under the counters since money was almost worthless. So everyone was very relieved when the government stabilized the mark and distributed even portions to every person. Everyone had the right to forty deutsche marks, an average amount for one pair of shoes.

However, experiences showed that not all men are alike. Though all had equal amounts of money, next day already some were broke, some had gained and some had not touched their money. On the same day the *Währungsreform* (stabilization of currency) became implemented, all the hidden goods appeared on the counters and the economy soon awakened from its doldrums.

Our country was now divided into four distinct sectors: the northwest occupied by the British, with the exception of Bremen, which was an American enclave, the southwest by the Americans, the northeast by the Russians, and the southeast by the French. Later on the English and the French withdrew their claims, and after the Iron Curtain was erected in 1961, the east of Germany became a different country under Communist rule. It would be hard for families who had members in the other part of Germany since the border was closed hermetically. Of our family only my aunt Thilde lived in East Germany, and my sister Julie was making the effort to visit her several times. When she passed away, Julie crossed the border once more to be present at her funeral and also to settle her estate—not an easy task. I had been in America for almost ten years then, and was too busy with my growing family to attend her funeral. She had been my favorite aunt and I missed her very much.

The Toedtmans: During 1948 we met an interesting American couple and their nine-year old son, John. The Toedtmans were sent to Bremen to supervise the cultural development of the city after the war and my father, who was the president of the Kunstverein (society in charge of arts) and so influential about decisions made in lieu of the Kunsthalle, our art museum, had to work with Mr. Toedtman. They were given one of the big mansions in the suburbs to live in. I knew this house well, a friend of mine used to live there, and the family had to give it up and move elsewhere. We should have hated the Toedtmans for this, but they could not really help it; after all, the Americans had won the war. They were extremely nice people, and soon it was discovered that they came from Dayton, the same city my sister had moved to! The Ernsts and the Toedtmans became good friends subsequently, and I stayed in contact with them as long as they lived. John was starting to play the piano while the family was living in Bremen. I was amazed at his talent when he played for us during occasional visits. I would see more of the Toedtmans after I had moved to the United States.

My Last Three Years at Hamburg University: For me, it was a big decision to face my mentors for the final exam. I had dallied long enough. In 1952 I had six years of studying under my belt, and was told "enough is enough." I was thirty-one years old and did not have much to show for it.

The years from 1948 to 1951 were relatively happy years. I especially loved the zoology classes. Professor Klatt was a brilliant lecturer and his lessons on hormones are unforgettable to me. For the first time I really understood that the difference between male and female is merely a matter of hormonal balance, a fact that explains many problems that plague mankind since the beginning of human life. Botany, which really is a subject I should have enjoyed, was taught by a dried out, older man, Professor Dr. Mövius, who was the one who recommended my admittance at the university because of Ruth Löning. He was close to retirement, and did not inspire me. I dutifully learned all the vast material we were supposed to know, but at the exam, I failed because I could not remember details about one of Dr. Mövius' sacred cows, an ancient tree, *Ginkgo Biloba*. (Today I have one in my backyard.) This indicated to him that either had I been absent-minded in class or even worse, had not attended the day he elaborated about his favorite tree. I was not prepared to know what the professor wanted to hear! I got a miserable grade for botany, and only my good grade in zoology (thanks to the tutelage of Gertraude) raised my average grade for biology to *genügend* (satisfactory).

I really liked geography. After stumbling through the exact sciences, mostly unsuccessfully, I relished in the warm, human endeavor of looking at other countries, people, customs, and ways of life. I loved excursions and went to many places in Germany and even saw Italy. There were several excursions offered for both disciplines of biology too, and I took advantage of everything that was offered.

These excursions were expensive and in order to participate I took a job for the weekends. I did yard work and babysitting for a family living near Hamburg where I spent whole weekends, including the nights from Saturday to Sunday. I got paid well and even had free meals; this was a good deal. I was grateful to the family and tried hard to please them. Only after the wife observed her husband fondling my legs while I was picking apples, I was dismissed. I also copied papers for one of the professors on my typewriter and made some easy money this way. Also, I did some house cleaning for single, working women.

Romances, as have been told before about my friends in zoology classes, did not happen in my geography classes—here I was friends with everyone and did not isolate myself with a few selected friends. Several professors taught us. Everyone was friendly and humorous and there was much laughter.

Italy: One of the excursions was especially interesting. I did not have enough money to pay the two hundred marks for the proposed trip to Italy. My parents refused to pay, so I took the courage to ask Christoph. He talked it over with Julie and both of them thought that it would be a good experience for me. So I got the money and signed up for the trip.

We traveled in Italy for four weeks. For this trip a bus had been chartered that took us first across the Alps over the Brenner Pass into northern Italy.

The first night we camped at beautiful Lake Garda and got initiated into the "on the road" style of living that we would be engaged in for the following four weeks. We had a primitive kitchen on board of our bus and bought whatever we needed at our rest places. Every night around six o'clock we had to start looking for a suitable place to spend the night; it had to be flat enough to sleep, it had to have water, and we had to get permission to camp. Once we were established we cooked, ate, cleaned up, and sat around a camp fire talking and singing, until it was time to stretch out on our ground cloth and sleep. It was summer, the nights were balmy, and we were young; we had no problem falling asleep after all the wonderful impressions and experiences of each day.

After Lake Garda we went on to Venice, Ravenna, and along the East Coast through Rimini, Pescara, and Bari, where we observed an ancient shipyard, to southern Italy, crossed the heel to Tarent, and drove through old Mediterranean forests to Reggio on the tip of the boot.

Here we crossed the Strait of Messina to Sicily, where we stayed for three days. First we explored the northern coast of this island, that is positioned like a football on top of the tip of the boot of Italy, drove through luscious orchards of oranges and lemons, then examined ancient temples on the west side of Sicily, and on the third day visited Mt. Etna, the giant volcano which was getting ready to explode shortly after we were home again safely. We were able to climb over the rim of the main crater and look into several smaller craters that were bubbling with a yellowish witches' brew, emitting clouds of acrid vapors, stinging our nostrils and blinding our eyes. We heard a subdued rumbling and felt a slight tremor beneath our feet. We were glad when we had crawled back over the rim again and felt solid ground under our feet. On the way down from the top we observed wide beds of crystallized lava and remnants of buildings partly covered with the dark substance. We drove back to Messina and crossed back to Italy's mainland.

The trip north on the western coast brought us to Naples where we visited the Island of Capri and the Blue Grotto. We also climbed on top of Vesuvius, a volcano quite different from Etna with only one giant crater, and saw the unfortunate cities of Pompeii and Herculaneum, taken by surprise by sudden lava flows from Vesuvius. Here we ladies of the tour had a discriminating experience: when the tour guide proposed to show us a public bath where men were caught masturbating, female students were not allowed to go.

We went on to Rome, where we stayed for four days in a real hotel, a great experience after weeks of camping in fields. After a stint to Florence, our bus took us back to the coast to Genoa, not to forget Pisa and its slanted tower, then to Milano and home to Germany over the St. Gotthard Pass, through the Gotthard Tunnel, and back to Hamburg.

The Final Exam: After this enriching excursion we were ready to face the big exam. We were examined by representatives of the Hamburg School Board, since most of us would end up teaching in Hamburg, and not by our professors who represented the university. This sounds like a contradiction to what I mentioned about Professor Mövius—but I think now that he must have had dual status and wore two hats, one for the state and one for the university. Professor Kolb, my geography teacher, was not involved in my examination. During the geography exam, I was asked a strange question: "Define the meaning of *Heimat.*" (Some place where you feel at home?) This is a word that does not even have a clear translation into English. I was baffled and started stumbling over my own words, telling the gentlemen that I thought *Heimat* meant the place where someone has been born, but that obviously was not the right answer, and I met with elongated faces. So all I could show after twelve semesters of studies were two mediocre grades of "genügend." I thought this was very unfair.

To be tested in math, I had not dared—all those efforts seemed to be down the drain. For months I had been working on a thesis for geography and had received a good grade for this. It was titled *Die Bedeutung der Baumwolle für Bremen* (The Importance of Cotton for Bremen). Preparing the paper had given me many happy hours of collecting my material and putting it together into an informational, useful document.

I had chosen the field of cotton for my thesis because of the rich opportunities that were offered in Bremen to study the import of cotton to Bremen and also because cotton is one of the commodities that comes chiefly from the United States. America was still looming in the back of my mind and lured me with an invisible pull.

With my father's help, I was introduced to cotton firms, where I learned to touch and examine many different strains of cotton, and to the powerful Cotton Exchange. My father personally introduced me to the huge machinery that processed incoming cotton bales in the port. I studied about the history of the cotton trade and why Bremen, and not Hamburg, had conquered the cotton market. The main reasons for this were the special human and business relationships that Bremen had been able to form with American firms. Hamburg was more oriented toward trade with South America. I also learned about the geographical reasons why, though all cotton came through Bremen in the north of Germany, spinning mills and weaving factories were all located in the south. This also had a historical reason, since Bremen never had started the development of manufacturing and it had been well established in southern Germany for centuries. This fact had led to Bremen's exceptional position during the American occupation after the war, when all of southern Germany had been under American rule and northern Germany under English jurisdiction, with the only exception of Bremen, then called *Enclave*, in order to facilitate the trade between the United States and Germany, and enable cotton to be sent to the factories that were located in the South…

I enjoyed all the personal contact with experts on cotton in my hometown and made many new friends. The actual writing of my thesis took about one year. I even engaged a professional draftsman to do the charts and maps, had typed everything to perfection, and had it bound professionally. All this evidently did not count—it was a requisition every candidate for the state exam had to sweat out. The original copy was filed away in storage places and probably never looked at again.

Afterward, I remember coming down in the elevator of the building where the exam had taken place and wishing to continue descending to the center of the earth. But I also was relieved that everything was over now, and that I was free again.

Looking for a Job: I now tried to get a teaching job. The *Schulbehörde* (Board of Education) in Hamburg told me in no uncertain terms that they had no room for me in their district (because of my poor grades). They thought maybe in Bremen it would be easier to get a job, since expectations might be less stringent than in Hamburg. They were so sorry!

In Bremen, the response was lukewarm. It was not overwhelming, but they would take me under one condition, that I would eventually add a third subject to my state exam. I realized that with only two minors and mediocre grades, I was not very marketable, so I was glad they took me and looked forward to begin work at the *Studienseminar* (study seminar) in my hometown in April of 1953. This study seminar was a course to initiate young rookie teachers into the intricate world of teaching. You had to teach a class, but you did not get paid. It is comparable to our student teaching, but is done *after* the state exam and presents another year of no income. But that did not ruffle me. Now I had ten precious months before me to do what I wanted.

First there was the option to finish my third subject for teaching. Since I had started my studies with math and physics, I decided to try my luck at math and use the short year I had available for this to prepare myself for the exam in this field. I went to the authorized professors in Hamburg who greeted me very coolly and unfriendly, since they had not seen me for several years in their classrooms. The same thing happened: the aloofness of the professors, the difficulty of their requirements, and the abstract nature of the subject matter intimidated me. I was repulsed by the thought of taking up the study of math once more. It was déja vus all over again. So for now I pushed the intent of working on the third subject back in my mind.

Secretly I wished I had not chosen the career of a teacher, but had taken the direction toward achieving the doctorate, which had nothing to do with the state and only required a thesis, not a state exam. One could not teach with the doctor's certificate, but then, did I *really* want to teach younger people? I could use my cotton thesis that had given me so much pleasure, as basis for a doctor thesis. At least one could teach at the university with the doctor title. I was so undecided that I let others decide my life for me. I even had asked the rector in Hamburg not to take me off the list but just grant me vacation for one year. I had applied for a teaching job in Bremen, had been accepted, so now I had to do it, but more and more, the idea to prepare for a doctor's thesis took roots.

Leaving the Old World Behind: Another idea to use my free time was to see my sister in America. I had not seen Cornelie in seventeen years; when would there be another chance like this? I decided that I might combine these two ideas: to visit the United States and to work on my doctor's thesis.

But first of all, I wanted to get away from it all, leave Bremen, Hamburg, lovers, and study seminars behind me and get on with my life! I decided to go to America to visit my sister!

PART II
The New World

4

The 1950s

The Trip to America

Preparations: To have the desire to go to America in 1952 was one thing. To actually make it happen was another. The first step was to figure out a way to combine my two goals: to travel to America *and* to prepare for writing a doctor's thesis about cotton. Maybe I could collect material for this thesis in the United States?

I went to the Institute of Geography in Hamburg. Unfortunately Professor Kolb, the head of the department who had already offered to be my mentor for a doctor's thesis, was on a study trip in Australia. His substitute, Professor Brünger, showed much interest in my idea, but could not help me since he did not want to infringe on Professor Kolb's territory. He advised me to take the trip anyway and get in contact with Professor Kolb through correspondence.

When I told my parents about the travel plans, they were rather skeptical at first. My parents had me back home, did not have to subsidize my studies anymore, liked my willingness to work hard around the house, and were not in favor of having yet *another* daughter cross the big ocean. But they also thought that it would be only temporary, just for half a year, since I had to be back for my assignment at the school system in Bremen. They could not give me much money, and they did not want me to cause any expense to my sister and her husband. The only thing that my father could do for me was to secure a free passage on a small freighter of the Norddeutsche Lloyd [1]. Even though the source for financial support for my plans was still rather unclear, I was now determined to go on this trip. I did not want to lose anymore unnecessary time. Therefore I started getting my necessary papers, which included applying for a visitor's visa and securing recommendation letters from the business friends I made during the time I had worked on my cotton paper for the state exam. I also wrote to my sister Cornelie, now living in Dayton, Ohio, with her family—and made plans to find some money for the journey.

When searching for money I was lucky. A friend of my father, Dr. Wagner, the director of the *Überseemuseum* (Museum exhibiting trade with America), located close to the train station in Bremen, wanted to create a new display of cotton raising and processing and asked me to bring him illustrative materials and pictures from the cotton belt. He gave me two hundred marks for this purpose and even lent me his camera. My father made good on his promise and secured for me a free passage on a little freighter, the *Magdalene Vinnen* (named after the wife of the owner of the ship). When I asked Mr. Vinnen when we would leave, he told me that the next departure was set for July 26. After that I would have to wait until some time in November. Since that later date was too late for me, as I intended to stay at least half a year in the States and then return for my *Studienseminar* (student teaching) before April of 1953, I had no choice. The date now was June 20, 1952. I had only five weeks to get ready.

To get the visa presented a challenge. For the regular visitor's visa one needed an affidavit from a United States' citizen to be accepted. My parents did not want to bother the Ernsts with this and I had to find an alternative. By applying for a study visa, which I was eligible for, still being a student, I did not need an affidavit. It worked and I actually received the visa in ten days.

My sister Cornelie was delighted that I intended to visit her and wrote me the most welcoming letters. She and her family were looking forward to having me as a house guest for as long as I pleased.

The *Magdalene Vinnen* was a small cargo ship of six thousand tons that was scheduled to go to Antwerp empty, load some goods there, and then sail to the United States. It was not built for passengers and only allowed to take on two passengers without charge. In this way my passage was all taken care of.

---

1.   Lloyd's is an insurance society popularly known as *Lloyd's of London*. It originated in the coffee house of Edward Lloyd in about 1688. Its newspaper, *Lloyd's List and Shipping Gazette,* founded in 1734, is the oldest newspaper in London. In the 1900s Lloyd's partly or completely insured property lost in the San Francisco earthquake and fire in 1906, the sinking of the *Titanic* in 1912, the airship *Hindenburg,* which burned in 1937, and many hurricanes in the United States. In 1856 the *Norddeutsche Lloyd* was founded in Bremen, named after the British insurance society. It later merged with HAPAG, *Hamburg Amerika Packetfahrt Actien Gesellschaft.* In both world wars the Norddeutsche Lloyd lost almost its entire fleet, which was subsequently restored again. Wikipedia.

I also prepared for my trip by visiting all of the cotton firms that I was acquainted with and asked for letters of recommendation to American firms. These were given to me in the most accomodating way. I had a set of my own business cards printed so that I would appear more professional. In this manner I received letters to Anderson, Clayton & Co., Grunow & Co., I. H .Bachmann, Carl Albrecht & Co., Otto Goedecke, and other firms and tycoons in the world of cotton. The Bremer Baumwollbörse (Bremen Cotton Exchange) gave me a blank recommendation to anyone I would find useful to be introduced to.

Preparations for my wardrobe took the least of my time. Since I intended to travel much, I only took just a small suitcase and a briefcase. Only the most necessary items were packed.

Farewell to Bremen and Voyage to New York: On July 26 I was well prepared when I took leave of my sick mother and my sister Julie, along with her four children and got into my father's car. His chauffeur drove us to the ship that departed from Brake between Bremen and Bremerhaven, because the harbor in Bremen was still partly in shambles from the war. It was a cool, rainy day, weather that made the parting a sad event.

On the ship we met my travel companion, Fräulein Elisabeth Lübke. This lady—a singer from Hanover, who had been brought to the ship by her boyfriend, and I were the only passengers on the *Magdalene Vinnen*. Since some repairs had to be made before departure, the captain invited us all into his cabin for a hot cup of coffee. Then the company had to leave the ship and the anchors were lifted. Slowly the freighter went down-stream and the waving figures on the shore became smaller and smaller. I would never see my father again!

We left the rail and went into our cabin to unpack. We had been given the pilot cabin next to the pantry. It was rather narrow, and I was happy not to have so much baggage since Fräulein Lübke had definitely a large wardrobe. A great disadvantage of our cabin was the fact that the exhaust pipe from the kitchen was directly in front of our door; therefore we had the smell of used cooking oil in our room constantly.

I started to realize then that nothing in life is free. It was a three-week long, bumpy ride, and I was seasick almost the entire time and became as thin as a match stick, hardly able to walk when we arrived in New York. The captain of the little ship was a very cynical man who made fun of me and Elisabeth, who had a better stomach than I but could not get used to the primitive lodging that the vessel offered. Since it had not been the purpose of the freighter to take passengers on board, there were no such accommodations as showers or flushing toilets. In fact, we had to share the common latrines with the crew. Our tiny cubicle was windowless and we had to shut the door because of the fumes. The *Magdalene Vinnen* was definitely not a cruise ship!

Meals were taken at the captain's table, but since I was always sick and could not stand the captain anyway, I hardly ever sat at that table. Elisabeth, my companion, had a healthy appetite and endured the crude meals. She told me afterward about the jokes the captain had made at our cost.

The vessel had left Brake at five o'clock in the afternoon of July 26, passed Bremerhaven after about two hours, and reached the German-Dutch border at 10:30, when the German pilot left us. He must have been given an even more primitive quarter since we had *his* cabin. During the night and the next day we went alongside the Dutch coast and around midnight the Belgian pilot came on board to guide the vessel into the Schelde River.

Antwerp: A landing in this Belgian port had been planned, and goods were to be loaded on. How long we would stay in Antwerp was uncertain since it was not clear how much cargo there was. I had known about this stay in the Belgian port and had also prepared for this visit by securing a written introduction from a Bremen cotton firm to a business friend in Antwerp. Two lucky circumstances coincided to insure me a gracious welcome in Antwerp. First, the mayor of Antwerp had visited Bremen recently and had been received very warmly, so that he remembered Bremen and also my father, who was in charge of the visitors' mansion for the senate, in the best possible way. Second, I had had the opportunity to meet Mr. Grisar (in Belgium it wasn't "Herr" anymore), in Bremen at his hotel. He would be my personal guide in Antwerp. Mr. Grisar, owner of a large shipping firm in Antwerp, had done business in Bremen with Herr Fürst, owner of the cotton firm Fürst, Koch & Co. When I asked Herr Fürst, who was a friend of my father, if he might know anyone in Antwerp who could show me the city, Herr Fürst sent me right away to the hotel where Mr. Grisar was staying, and I was received in the friendliest manner.

Since I had sent a telegram to Mr. Grisar telling him about the date of the departure of the *Magdalene Vinnen*, he was expecting me. I even received a welcoming telegram on board on the evening before my arrival that helped me to forget my seasickness for a while. When I woke up the next morning at five o'clock, we had already gone up the Schelde River a long way. The vessel was gliding very quietly, so I dared to climb to the upper deck and enjoy from there the beautiful passage through the turns of the meandering river. In the morning dusk the silhouette of Antwerp arose, vanished again when the ship went into another curve, and appeared again in enlarged form. About 7 o'clock we entered the harbor and docked on the pier, where we would stay for as long as it would take to load the ship.

I had a fantastic time in Antwerp. Not only was I escorted to all the sights within and without of the city; I was also wined and dined and entertained every minute of those fun-filled days. It was not possible for me to lodge in a hotel since my time of departure was uncertain. Every morning I was picked up by a limousine at the ship and brought back every night. One day Mr. Grisar even took me to Belgium's capital, Brussels. I was amazed at the ease with which most Belgians spoke several languages including German. I was never treated so royally in my life! After three memorable days in Antwerp our vessel left Europe for good, and life on board, including the sea sickness, soon took over again.

Arrival at the New World

New York: In New York, where we landed on August 17, 1952, it took almost an entire day before Elisabeth and I could get off the ship. The night before, our rude captain had threatened us with the possibility of having to undergo a long investigation on Ellis Island, and we had almost believed it until we learned from a crew member that this sort of thing was not done anymore to immigrants with legal passports. So, after waiting seemingly forever, I was actually standing on American soil—wobbly on my legs, but very happy. While I was looking around, a middle-aged man approached me, asked my name, and introduced himself as Mr. Molson, representative of the New York branch of the Bremen cotton firm I. H. Bachmann. He spoke in German and I felt very relieved to find a little part of home in this vast new country.

Mr. Molson must have noticed how exhausted I was, because he took me and my baggage without ado to a taxi and brought me to my lodging. That was a house where young people lived together for an affordable price, and I was invited to stay there for the week I had earmarked for New York. During my preparations for this trip, I had carefully planned my itinerary in America and had written letters to all the firms that I had connections with through my field-work for the university thesis. In New York it had been the firm of I. H. Bach-mann that represented Bremen's cotton trade and Mr. Molson was the man in charge. I had written to him that my intentions were to do preparatory work for a doctor's thesis on cotton and would be interested in staying for at least a week in New York. I would be interested in visiting the Cotton Exchange, the harbor, and the facilities there, and also seeing the sights in New York City.

Mr. Molson knew when my ship was arriving and he had made all the necessary arrangements to accommodate me. After all, he wished to remain in good standing with the senator for the port in Bremen. I got the royal treatment, was picked up by limousines, had appointments all over the financial district, and was escorted to the Cotton Exchange, where I was amazed by all the hubbub of voices, ticking machines, and brokers crowding around the visual displays of prices flashed onto huge boards. In the evenings I was wined and dined in luxurious restaurants. I clearly remember an evening when Mr. Molson himself took me for the first time to the Waldorf Astoria Hotel for a fabulous dinner. A fortune teller came to our table, looked at my palm, and predicted that I would be married that very year and have three children subsequently. This prediction almost came true—I met Leo that same year, though I married him the next year and had not only three, but four children. After dinner and fortune telling, Mr. Molson took me up to the Rainbow Room in the Rockefeller Center, where we had a cocktail and we sat by the wide window overlooking the sparkling city. What a sight!

I also took a trip up the Hudson River by myself. The large riverboat glided under the Washington Bridge, past the black palisades of Newark, New Jersey, and lovely hills still covered with gorgeous fall colors to Poughkeepsie, where I ate at a restaurant directly on the river.

Another time I visited the just-completed house of the United Nations with its glass façade and crescent construction overlooking all of New York City. Then I was escorted back to the harbor and again met with the colossal lady greeting all immigrants and visitors, the Statue of Liberty. It had been cloudy when we arrived on our ship, and I had been feeling so wretched that I had missed the spectacular view. But now the weather was perfect, a clear crisp day in late August.

Philadelphia: On August 26 I was brought to Grand Central Station by Mr. Molson and headed for Philadelphia. All my expenses in New York, including the train tickets, had been covered by the I. H. Bachmann firm, and I had felt very secure in their care. Now in Philadelphia, I was on my own. I did have references and went to one office that was connected with Bremen trade, but I did not receive quite the overwhelming reception I had received in New York. Philadelphia is not the hub of trade that New York is; it is a government-oriented town by nature. I found my own accommodation in the center of town and looked up the few contacts that had been given to me in Bremen. In one of the offices I was given a guide to show me the city; a young clerk who was happy to have the day off with all expenses paid. The two of us had a great time visiting all of the historic sights in the oldest part of the city: Independence Hall, the Liberty Bell, the Atwater Kent Museum, Benjamin Franklin's grave, and even Betsy Ross's humble home with the same chair she sat on to sew the first flag for the young nation. After lunch in Bookbinders, we visited the art museum and the aquarium. The day was topped off by a drive through the then new part of the outskirts of Philadelphia and dinner in the park restaurant. Then my guide brought me to the residence of his boss, where we all spent a wonderful evening with the family and enjoyed the nice garden in the calm, balmy summer night. My escort brought me back to my hotel, and next morning I continued my journey to the nation's capital, this time on a Trailways Bus, again prepaid by my gracious host from New York.

Washington DC: It took about one and a half hours to get to Washington DC. I was picked up at the station and brought to the International House, where I would stay for three days. I met with many interesting young people from all over the world. I also had my first proposal of marriage in this institution. A very persistent, fat, short lawyer, Dr. Hertz, whom I found repulsive, glued himself to my side, declared himself my personal tour guide, and when I meekly accepted his offer to go sightseeing with him, he boldly declared that he had decided to marry me. It did not matter that I was not Jewish and he was.

I was disgusted and tried to get rid of him, but to no avail. So I had to cut short my last day in Washington DC and thus avoided having to consider his offer to take me to Jefferson's Monticello in Virginia. Consequently I missed out on Jefferson's estate and on a husband. Little did I know then that there were four more such proposals to follow this one, including the last one by my future husband! I must confess that the idea of finding a husband in America was not something I did not anticipate subconsciously, especially after the revelations of the fortune teller at the Waldorf in New York. But it had to be the right man!

In spite of everything, I managed to see all the important sights in Washington DC: the White House, Jefferson Memorial on Tidal Basin, the Reflecting Pool leading into the mall from Lincoln Memorial to the Washington Memorial and further to the US Capitol, even a glimpse of the Pentagon across the Potomac River. I spent beautiful hours by myself in the great museums lining the Mall on both sides.

On the last evening, my admirer, Dr. Hertz, succeeded in taking me to a theater nearby, where Luise Rainer starred in *Biography*. I just couldn't resist that offer, but when he proposed to pick me up the next morning for a trip to Monticello, I was ready to bolt. Having already purchased a Greyhound ticket to Dayton the day before, I left early the next morning, standing up my pursuer.

Dayton, Ohio: I arrived in Dayton on September 1 at 11 o'clock at night and was greeted by all the members of my sister's family. The children had one more week of vacation and were as excited to meet their aunt as I was to meet my nieces and nephew. My sister Cornelie and her husband Walter lived in a handsome house in Dayton, where they had moved with their four children from the little town of Mt. Gilead. Walter's profession as a mechanical engineer, specializing in patents for hydraulic machinery, had given him more work opportunities in the much larger city. Their oldest child, Walter Jr. or Walt had come to Bremen once as a two-year old. So I had met him fifteen years ago, but he did not remember me. He was our little *Wützchen* then, and I had taught him his first Latin words! He seemed to follow in his father's footsteps—when I arrived I saw his antique cars and other mechanical projects all over the place. He was in the process of upholstering an old Model T Ford and a baby blue Model A with bright red seat covers for his transportation. Barbara, the fifteen-year-old, was a busy teenager, very popular at school, and between boyfriends at that time. The twins, Phyllis and Madeline, were long-legged eleven-year-olds, who were eager to devour their newly found aunt. I was thirty-one at that time but I felt like one of them. I slept upstairs together with the twins. We all slept in one bed as I remember. This could have been very cozy had I not had the bad habit of reading until about 1 o'clock every night. The twins soon started to complain that they could not go to sleep; therefore I moved into the hallway, where I could read to my heart's content.

We did many activities together. Cornelie took the girls and me to the school football game where Walt played his clarinet in the band and Barb was a cheerleader. Three of the Ernst children are very good musicians. Because he showed much promise to become a good musician, Walt had a private teacher come to the house. Barb was a natural talent: she insisted on playing the piano when only five and played with enthusiasm and vigor. One of the twins, Madeline, chose the clarinet as her main instrument because her brother was playing it, while Phyllis preferred sports, mainly tennis. The musical talent in the Ernst family stems from Walter's mother, Luise von Benda—also known as Lilli—whose ancestors were great musicians, one of them playing first violin in Friederich der Große's (Frederick II's) private chamber orchestra. Unfortunately, the musical talent has not yet manifested itself in the next generation of Ernst descendants.

We also visited the apartment house in the city then owned by Walter and Cornelie and took me there to work in the garden. We saw a Shakespeare play in a barn near Dayton—I think it was *Romeo and Juliet*. All of us went to a fruit farm and gathered baskets full of ripe peaches. I took the twins to the local fair and won a big teddy bear for them by tossing balls into holes on a board several times. Walter and Cornelie took me to a concert at the symphony hall. A few times we ate at the Executive Club for Engineers. The twins and Barb invited me to visit their school where I was amazed at how effectively the teachers had prepared their lessons. During the second week of September, a heat wave set in and the children and I went swimming in a nearby pool.

Always before dinner—a new custom for me, who was used to eating the main meal at noontime—when Walter came from work, the two of us had a Manhattan cocktail with a big red cherry. Cornelie did not join us. She did not drink any alcohol—she said that she needed to have a clear head for all her chores. Cornelie never had a maid or other help. She preferred to do everything herself. I, who had been used to helpers in my parents' household, found this very commendable. I decided never to have anybody in my own household either, should I ever find a husband.

All four children were excellent students at school and were popular. Barb later was chosen to become May Queen, a great honor, and she filled her position with poise and grace. At a young age both Walt and Barb were often asked to perform on their instruments at various events. Both of the older children had friends coming and going and the telephone was always ringing. Two cats, Sammy and Oscar, played a big role. It was a typical American household with teenagers and pets, and I was happy to be part of so much life.

But I was planning to move on. I had promised Dr. Wagner that I would get cotton material for him, and I wanted to see the United States as well. For this I needed money. My sister and brother-in-law had their hands full with raising their four children and had nothing to spare. My brother-in-law had a friend who had just lost his wife and needed a housekeeper. He came to the house often and obviously admired my sister. When he met me, he could not suppress his delight. "Another Cornelie," he drooled. "How delightful." Evidently, German girls were in high demand in those days for their domestic qualities. His name was Walter Lippman, affectionately called "Lippy" by us. My sister suggested that I should work for Lippy to earn some money. I agreed and applied for the job.

I was enthusiastically accepted. Lippy had three children, two boys of eleven and eight and a five-year-old little girl. The girl was with friends in Louisiana, where Lippy had lived before with his family. The two boys were constantly fighting and used to grab each other by the front of their shirts and rip off all the buttons, taking the buttonholes with them. On the first day of my employment, I opened a closet door and out fell dozens of damaged shirts, all waiting for someone to fix them. So, whenever I could spare some time between cleaning the apartment, cooking for the "men," and giving the place a homelike appearance, I sat down and mended shirts.

Lippy was very pleased with all this, took me out to dinner, and paid me well. He even proposed to me (my second offer). But he was Jewish and made it very clear that he was not changing his faith and that he did not want more children. I declined. I *wanted* children and wanted to keep my faith (though it was not a driving force in my life), and I told him that I did not love him.

After I had earned enough money, I started my big journey on October 21. On the Sunday before I left, my sister, as well as Lippy and his sons, took me on a trip to Ohio Caverns. It was a sparkling cool Indian summer day, and we explored the ancient American Indian mounds that were all around the cavern.

For my trip to cotton country in the Deep South, I had purchased a round-trip Greyhound ticket through Memphis, New Orleans, New Iberia, Houston, and Dallas. That was all I could afford. My original wish to go to California seemed unattainable. My sister brought me to the bus station and told me to come back anytime I wanted to.

Memphis, Tennessee: I had references to cotton firms in all the cities I visited. The management of these firms in Memphis, especially that of Anderson, Clayton & Co., bent over backward to put together a rich and informative program for me. Most of the bigger cotton firms are located on one street close to the Mississippi River, appropriately called "Cotton Row." Looking over the notes I took then, I am amazed at what a variety of activities was laid out for me. There were visits to cotton firms, cotton gins, and cotton fields. I was given chances to take pictures of blacks working in the fields, even given my own gathering bag and the opportunity to try the picking myself, alongside a tiny black girl. She picked much faster than I.

There were trips to neighboring sights such as Presidents' Island, Native American graves, and Pickwick Dam, a project of the Tennessee Valley Authority, a topic I had written a paper about during my study years. I was given many brochures and illustrative materials and took candid pictures with Dr. Wagner's camera. I was even presented with rolls of color film, a new invention at that time. From time to time, I packed all my material and sent it to my sister's house in Dayton and to Bremen, because it was too much to carry with me.

I had been given a room in a private home with a Mrs. Morris, who took very good care of me. On the morning of October 29 I felt feverish and asked Mrs. Morris to call a doctor. She not only did that, but she nursed me back to health for two days. It had been a bad cold, aggravated by exhaustion. No wonder, I had been going without a free moment for eight days and needed bed rest. On Halloween, the Anderson family, owners of the big cotton firm whose guest I was, invited me to see the movie *The Snows of Kilimanjaro*, running at that time at the theaters. I felt much better thanks to Mrs. Morris's good care.

November 4, 1952 was Election Day. I had been informed already in my sister's home about this important event and all of Dayton and Republican Ohio had rooted for Eisenhower.

I had heard the twins constantly singing "I like Ike" and "I like Adley badly." So I was glad when the radio and newspapers announced that Eisenhower had beaten Stevenson. I did not know much about politics back then, especially those of America. Television was just starting in 1952. The Andersons were one of the few families who owned a television set. They invited me to watch with them in the evening when we were not going out. My impression then was that advertising played a big role, that the shows were mediocre, and that children seems to be glued to the screen, no matter what was playing. But, of course, I could not tell that to my hosts.

New Orleans, Louisiana: I left Memphis and continued my journey to New Orleans. The bus went through Stoneville, where I briefly interrupted my trip to see several cotton facilities and, among other things, an experimental laboratory where they had bred *colored* cotton. Unfortunately, this promising experiment never proved profitable in the industrial world—it must have been more advantageous to use dyes in the traditional way.

On November 7 I got as far as Jackson, Mississippi, and stayed there overnight. Very early the next morning, my journey went on through interesting bayous and swamps, past Lake Ponchartrain to New Orleans. Here I had lodging of my own, because Lippy's parents lived there and were glad to let me stay with them. Lippy must have told them that he wanted to marry me, but he had failed to mention that I had refused, so I was closely scrutinized. They speculated that I would become their new daughter-in-law and did not seem to know that I did not intend to marry their son. They would not have been able to understand how someone could not want to do that. Lippy's parents informed me of several undesirable traits in Lippy's former wife, how extravagant a woman she had been, how ill health had interfered with her raising her children, how she had hated housework, and so forth. I had the feeling that was a lesson about how not to behave as Lippy's wife. I agreed to everything and did not have the heart to tell the truth. I also did not want to lose free lodging.

I stayed in New Orleans until November 19. The weather was hard on me. It was humid and sticky, almost like the weather in New York in August. It was almost winter time and felt like hot summer! Again, I had many cotton firms to visit. Here in New Orleans there were mostly shipping companies like Lykes Brothers who had secured my ticket for my return to Bremen. All had received my letters and treated me royally. I enjoyed the quaint inner city and the surrounding parks with trees hung with moss. I was taken to The Court of Two Sisters and heard Louis Armstrong play original jazz music. A voyage on a huge steam wheeler up the Mississippi was included in my entertainment.

In contrast to the red carpet treatment from American cotton moguls, I was received almost with contempt by the German consulate in New Orleans. I had wanted to make a boat trip through the bayous and inquired at the consulate as to how to go about this. I was rebuked by the unfriendly answer, "We do these trips for groups of people, but not for only one person."

When I told them that I would gladly join a group, they just shrugged and told me, "There is no one going this week."

I recognized that this was not cotton producing or cotton trading territory. I was a *nobody* tourist in their eyes. My negative feelings toward Germans (except my family) and my love for Americans were fortified by this experience. I also realized that I had become accustomed to being spoiled and some day had to get back to reality. Had I possessed enough money I could have hired a guide through a travel agency to tour the bayous—but my money had been spent for the Greyhound ticket back to Dayton and was only taking me as far as Dallas. So I was dependent on people to feed, house, and entertain me and had to relinquish all hope of seeing the mysterious bayous. At least I had the good judgment not to mention this wish to my cotton-mogul friends.

My command of the English language in those days must have been adequate but flawed, though people kept assuring me that I had a charming accent. (They still do, but now they don't pull the wool over my eyes anymore.) The Americans, as I found out later, are trained from youth on to say what the other person wants to hear, while Germans blubber out what they think: *they* would have said, "Your accent is awful," and been closer to the truth, but they would also have aroused a defiant feeling in the other person. Of course, whenever Germans met with countrymen in America, they conversed in their own language and uttered their remarks in their mother tongue.

It was apparent that the streets of New Orleans were layered like a *Schichttorte* (layered cake) of my youth; rows of houses with black people were interspersed with rows where only white people were living. Evidently, there were no strict housing codes in this city, but still, birds of a feather stuck together. Lippy's folks lived, of course, in a white street, but they had black neighbors across the street and in back.

On November 19, after a great time in the unique city of New Orleans, I left for Houston. I had visited all my cotton acquaintances once more, had announced my coming to Houston by telephone, had said good-bye to the Lippmans, and then set off on the Greyhound.

New Iberia, Louisiana: The Lippmans had insisted that I interrupt my trip at New Iberia to visit Lippy's five-year-old daughter Tanya, their granddaughter. So I got off my bus in this charming little Louisiana town between New Orleans and Houston and was picked up by Mrs. Marie, who took care of Tanya.

Mr. and Mrs. Marie owned a beauty shop and were an outstanding couple. They loved Tanya like their own child and had only one complaint: they did not like any of the other Lippmans, especially the grandparents in New Orleans. They, too, must have thought I was the future stepmother of Tanya and did everything to foster bonding between us two. They had us sleep in one bed and kept saying, "We are so happy that Tanya will have a *real* mother soon!"

I felt cramped and left after one night, but not without accepting a free haircut.

During my stay in New Iberia, I took a bus ride to Avery Island where I had hoped to see the famous salt mines, but, as in New Orleans, came to find out that without the mighty assistance of King Cotton I was powerless—one had to pay an exorbitant price or no entrance to the mines was possible.

Houston, Texas: So I went on to Houston. I arrived there on November 21 and was housed at the YWCA, a new discovery for me. It was comparable to the youth hostels in Germany, only a little fancier. In Houston, my fairyland style of living was resumed. Several cotton firms competed to give me the time of my life. I was taken to every place of importance; was shown around factories, fields, and museums; was wined, dined and entertained at night, and met the nicest business people. Connections to Bremen and my father's reputation did wonders. And in Texas, everything was done with extra flare.

One of my hosts, Mr. Biehl, owner of the cotton firm Biehl & Co., had planned an unforgettable excursion. In his private jet he took me to Galveston, circled over the island to show me the sights of the island with rows of bordellos on the coast and then, when I became airsick, went down and let me rest at his own house. On the way to his house he told me about the terrible hurricane that had destroyed his parents' house at the turn of the century. He was very young at that time, but he would never forget this storm. Mr. Biehl was superrich; he owned three mansions in Texas and kept keys to these houses jingling in his pockets. When I felt better, he showed me one of the most productive oil fields at Baytown, and then he took me for dinner at the Jacindo Hotel and offered me a drink at the Shamrock—at that time in the outskirts of Houston. On the way back to the center of town, he even gave me a driving lesson in his fancy car and had me steer the car on the then empty highway. (It probably was around midnight.) He seemed to own everything! In one of his houses lived his family, who must have been the happiest people on earth, or so I thought in my innocent frugal way.

Dallas, Texas: On November 27, Thanksgiving Day, I was scheduled to be in Dallas for dinner with a family from Bremen representing the mighty cotton firm of Albrecht & Co. Young Mrs. Albrecht had recently come from Germany and was giving her very first Thanksgiving party. I was introduced to, as I was told, a traditional turkey feast with all the trimmings, seven different vegetables and mince pie as side dishes, and pumpkin pie with whipped cream for dessert.

The Albrechts lived in a charming house in the suburbs of Dallas, complete with a brand new baby, and had to put up a glamorous front. This they did, and when, after all the guests were seated around the lavishly set table and looked expectantly toward the big sliding door to the kitchen, the young wife appeared holding a huge platter bearing the perfectly roasted bird, we all exclaimed "ahhh", and we felt that this was what the pilgrims must have experienced. All the guests were German and not yet used to Texas-American grand style.

In Dallas I was invited to stay at the mansion belonging to Mr. Molson, my generous host from New York. His firm, I. H. Bachmann, had branches all over cotton country. He had a steady housekeeper to keep the house going and lived in it whenever business called him to Dallas. His ex-wife, who was also rich, as I was told, lived in the house when he was not around. When I came, she had just arrived and had been given orders by her ex-husband to treat me well. I was given a beautiful airy room that had belonged to one of their children and cared for by the housekeeper. The ex-Mrs. Molson had a wing for herself and invited me sometimes to her elegant boudoir to chat or just lounge. Until this day, I cannot understand how a divorced couple can still share belongings—but it seemed to suit both of them.

On the Sunday after Thanksgiving, I was invited to yet another firm representing Bremen, Grunow & Co. I must have mentioned to someone that Dallas was my turning point and that I could not afford to get to California, my long cherished dream. That evening at the dinner table, I picked up my napkin and found, to my great surprise, a one-hundred dollar bill hidden underneath in a white envelope labeled "For your trip to California." I was stunned and thought it was too good to be true.

As I found out later, there was a string attached. The Grunows had a branch of their firm in Fresno, California, which was managed by a young man from Holland with a questionable reputation. In the days following they told me:

"He is a very good man and headquarters in Germany recommended him highly. We would prefer to see him married and settled down. So if you could do us this favor, meet the young man and possibly get him to marry you. We would be very much obliged. Of course, if it does not work out, we will give you the trip anyway."

That was Bremen for you. I was being used for business purposes. Gritting my teeth inwardly, I thanked them, assured them that I would do my best, and went to the bus depot the next morning to change my ticket. One more sight-seeing trip to the huge tower of Nieman Marcus, where an ordinary winter coat cost six hundred dollars (a high price in those days), a farewell party at the Molson's, Elisabeth going about inviting young people for me, one more look at vast cattle ranches and rich estates, and off I went to go further west.

Phoenix, Arizona: It was December 3 and I spent the following twenty-eight hours on the bus. The journey went through El Paso and Superior, where we could see the copper mines of a huge copper company from the bus. At noon time the next day, we arrived in Phoenix, Arizona. This was another cotton town and I had references to a few firms. A delightful young couple, the Simpsons, picked me up and showed me around. Phoenix was a fast-developing new town then, completely depending on irrigation. It was my first experience with desert country and I loved the purple and orange hues of the landscape around the city, interspersed with huge dark green candelabra cactus. After the crowded and over-built cities in Texas, Arizona seemed almost void of people. Irrigation canals not only made planting of cotton possible, there were also orchards of every kind of fruit, even oranges. I saw genuine Indian Hogans and could take pictures to my heart's content.

In the evening, the Simpsons took me to the fanciest restaurant in town, just opening to upcoming trade and industry. It was named Green Gables and had not been tried by the Simpsons, who were given an allowance for this lavish treatment of me, as they innocently told me. "We could never afford something like this," they confessed, probably thinking I was connected with some business moguls back in Europe. They did not know that my assets consisted of a Greyhound ticket and a twenty dollar bill. My bus was scheduled to leave the next morning, so they graciously had me stay for the night in their little house.

The Grand Canyon: I was determined to see the Grand Canyon. Previously in geography class in Hamburg I had learned about this unequaled phenomenon and could not pass by without at least seeing it. My ticket included the route over Flagstaff, and for a few dollars more I caught another bus to the South Rim of the Canyon. We arrived late at night and I was lucky to get a small room at the lodge for two dollars (unthinkable nowadays).

The next morning (it was now December 7) there was snow on the rim—in fact, all the upper plains around the big gap in the ground were covered with the white stuff. I walked around and went into a gift shop to acquire a tiny brooch made by the local American Indians, little shoes dangling from a pin. Later I wore this pin often to the delight of my children. Then I came to a stable that advertised mule trips down into the canyon. I inquired what such a trip would cost me and was told: "Ten dollars for the day trip, twenty-five dollars if you stay overnight." Since I did not have twenty-five dollars, I chose the day trip and was instructed to be at the start of the mule trail in one-half hour.

There was only one other person going down that day, a German baron, Herr von Rittershausen. Slowly, the three of us, the guide and we two tourists, had the mules carry us down the narrow, winding path along the reddish stone walls, about two thousand feet down into the canyon. The weather became warmer the lower we went, and on the bottom it was spring-like, with flowers blooming and soft green grass bordering the narrow band of the Colorado River. We saw the majestic formations of multicolored layers of sediments and rocks rising above us and were absolutely overwhelmed. After a lunch break that the guide had prepared, we mounted our faithful mules again and slowly went up. It was evening and almost dark when we came back to the South Rim.

Herr von Rittershausen also wanted to go to Los Angeles by Greyhound, so we both took off to the bus station to catch the shuttle to Flagstaff. At the Greyhound depot, we learned to our dismay that the next connection to Los Angeles would leave at 6 o'clock the next morning. We both decided it was too late to look for a shelter and stayed on a bench at the Greyhound station. No wonder we were sleepy when the bus took off next morning. We must have slept all through the marvelous pass by Hoover Dam and woke up in California!

California, Here I Come!

Los Angeles: It was an unforgettable ride through the "Purple Mountain's Majesty." Herr von Rittershausen told me all about his unsuccessful past and how he longed to settle down with a nice German girl. He expressed the wish to see me again and pried my address in Lodi from me—although I did not really know if I would ever make it to Lodi; time was running out for me. I still wanted to see San Francisco and then be back in Dayton before Christmas. This encounter could have led to marriage proposal number three had I been more cooperative. He tried one more time, though, by writing to me in Lodi. By then I was engaged to be married soon. Poor Herr Baron!

In Los Angeles there was another branch of Anderson-Clayton cotton, but here the red carpet treatment was fading. I was getting further away from Bremen and people did not seem to have time to impress visitors. However, after having been lodged comfortably at a YWCA in Santa Monica (at their expense), the secretary at the firm told me that Mr. Cleveland, her boss, was not available, but that his daughter would show me around. This daughter, with the masculine name of George, was the youngest of three daughters and, as she had been supposed to be a boy (a fact I could sympathize with) was dubbed "George" after her father. George was a little younger than I, was impeccably dressed, and drove an expensive big car. She was friendly and professional, a typical Californian business woman destined for a promising career.

She showed me, among many other sights connected to cotton, the Grauman's Chinese Theater in Hollywood, where I could touch the footprints of famous movie stars, and the Rose Bowl that everybody in America would give their right eye to see, except me, who had never heard about it and wasn't interested in football. Then she drove me to Pasadena and showed off their family home. In the evening Mr. Cleveland had come back from his business trip and invited us two girls to see a movie with him and have dinner at the Tallyho. After that I was brought to my hotel and spent the next wonderful day by myself at the beach.

Fresno: On December 10 I went on to Fresno, where the young man from Holland was expecting me. He had a sullen look on his face and I disliked him the minute I saw him. He was supposed to take me to dinner but asked if I would like to come to his room instead. He probably wanted to check me out. But I thanked him politely for his offer and said that I was expected in Lodi that same evening and better be on my way. He seemed bored with me anyway (most likely

I was not the first girl his firm had sent out west to make him settle down) and left me alone.

I had been only half truthful when I had insisted on being expected in Lodi; the Schmidts did not know that I was coming and I decided to spend another night on a bench at the depot. But just in case, I wanted to let them know that I was in Fresno. When I reached the Schmidt residence on the pay phone, Father Schmidt answered, seemed a little baffled and handed the phone to Mother Schmidt, who could not suppress her enthusiasm: "Ach, Fräulein Apelt, we knew from Edith that you would come. You *must* come and stay with us. You absolutely have to come. My husband and son will pick you up." Who could resist such a fervent invitation?

And so I came to Lodi, the small city in the fertile Big Valley, where I should meet my husband and live for the next ten years.

The Whirlwind Marriage

Lodi and the Proposal: My bus pulled into the Lodi bus station at eleven o'clock that night, and there they stood, my future husband, Leo, and his father. But, of course, none of us knew that then, only Mother Schmidt knew!

So, close to midnight on December 12, I was received at the house of the Schmidts on Eden Street in Lodi with open arms, a delicious meal, and a comfortable sofa to sleep on. I was so tired from all the previous adventures that I slept without interruption that night. I had arrived on a Friday and the next morning everyone was at home. I got up at eight o'clock—late for me who usually gets up around 6 o'clock—and found the family already at breakfast. I was introduced to the second son with the words, "This is our son Dagobert. He is *engaged* to a girl in Germany." Leo just smiled at me and all of them invited me to sit down and eat. Then Father Schmidt said, "And what are we going to do today?"

It appeared that Father and Mother Schmidt had a previous engagement and Dagobert had to work on his car; so that left Leo and me to "do something." Leo suggested a trip to Yosemite and I agreed enthusiastically—I had heard so much about this beautiful park. In class in Hamburg we had studied glacier formations, so I was all prepared scientifically and mentally to visit Yosemite.

Leo drove on back roads and over the old covered bridge near Copperopolis that was demolished shortly after our trip because it was unsafe and repairs were too expensive. Then we drove through Chinese Camp on Highway 120 into the park, spent the whole afternoon there, saw Mirror Lake still intact, and the fire fall from Glacier Point. This, we learned later, was discontinued soon after we saw it. Finally we came back to Lodi around midnight. That night I had a visitor on my sofa!

The next day we went to San Francisco, which had been my secret dream since I was young. When we drove over the Bay Bridge on that clear sunny Sunday morning, the bay shimmering, the city glowing in the morning sun, I was absolutely happy and could not wait to see all the wonderful sights waiting for me. It must have been a great satisfaction for Leo to make somebody so radiant. Leo gave me the royal tour. First we went to Golden Gate Park, where I mostly remember an exhibition about Leonardo da Vinci, which interested both of us: Leo was fascinated by the intricate models of machines Leonardo had invented, and I marveled at the wonderful art of Leonardo, the painter. After a stroll through Chinatown that had been my secret goal since I was a little girl, we had a good meal at one of the restaurants on Fisherman's Wharf, walked by the bay, drove across the Golden Gate Bridge, and had one more look onto the fabulous city from Vista Point. On the way back to Lodi, Leo asked me if I would marry him.

I was stunned, though after all the other proposals during my trip, I should have been prepared for this. I was not ready and did not accept then and there. "But I hardly know you," I must have said, "and I want to go back to Dayton and spend Christmas with my sister's family."

Leo accepted my answer and said that he understood. He thought that I would learn to love him in time. In order to get better acquainted, he suggested that I should spend a few more days with his family and then go back to Dayton. This I agreed to and stayed in Lodi until December 20.

Those five days from December 15 to 20 went by fast. The men were working during the day, and I had time to get to know Leo's mother who told me about their life in Poland, their flight to Germany in 1945, and their years in the heath near Celle in northern Germany. "We always had the family together," she told me, "and the most wonderful thing is that we are now together here in California." Then she added with a sad smile, "I only wish Edith were here too." I was amazed at how she looked like her daughter, almost like a replica of my friend in Hamburg.

I asked her about Leo and why he had been so young when he became a soldier. Leo had mentioned that he was just seventeen when he was drafted to fight the Russians. She started to tell me his story.

"Before he was drafted Leo had gone to business school, which he left when he was fifteen. Then my husband wanted him to go to college and become an engineer, but Leo did not want that; he wanted to be a farmer. So, in 1941 my husband sent him to a farm not far from Großneudorf (near Bromberg in Poland, then a German town), where the family lived at that time. He stayed there until 1942 and then had to go into the *Arbeitsdienst*. After that he was drafted into the war and was training to be an officer. He became a *Junker,* the first step toward the career of officer. At the end of 1944 he was sent to Kurland in Litauen (Lithuania), then to Ostpreußen (East Prussia). There he served at the front. After one year serving there he was supposed to go to military school."

I interrupted her, "Weren't you worried about him being a soldier so close to the front?"

"Yes, terribly," she said. "I hated the idea of him being a soldier in combat. The Russians were coming closer and closer. At one time they were only a few kilometer away from the German front and their rockets were flying all over our boys. Fortunately he wasn't hurt. He was so lucky.

Leo left the front in 1945 and was on the way to military school when the *Rückmarsch* (retreat) started. The Russians had broken through the front line. We were so relieved when we heard that Leo had already left and was now in Danzig, where his sister was working as a nurse. But they could not stay together, Danzig was taken by the Poles, and Leo had to retreat farther west. We did not know where Edith went. Waldemar, my husband, decided to flee from Großneudorf to Germany, which turned out to be a trek from hell. We—Waldemar, Dagobert and I—ended up in Müden an der Aller in the region of Hanover, where we stayed until 1950, when the entire family was together again, and we crossed the big ocean to go to America. We are very happy here and think we could not have chosen a better country to live in."

All this was told in almost one breath, and I was fascinated by her story. Now finally I had a chance to cut in.

"How did Leo and Edith find you in Müden?"

"That is another story," said my future mother-in-law. "Leo was dismissed from the army after the war ended and starting looking for his family, first for Edith who had to flee from Danzig and then both together found us with the help of an organization that helped all the *Flüchtlinge* (refugees) to find their folks. Maybe Leo will tell you how lucky they were to bring us all together again."

Leo later told me how he pursued every lead, how he went to many places and central organizations and finally found Edith in the center of Germany. I realized that we could have met already then, in 1945, when I was traveling in Germany too. But fate (my "Guardian Angel?") had a different plan to bring us together.

Toward the end of the day, after work, which consisted of hard, physical labor in an iron foundry, the men washed up and we had dinner together. Then Leo and I went out, seeing friends, dancing, or joining other young people in the basement of the Lutheran Church where Onkel Roleder was the pastor.

Reverend Emil Roleder had been married to Leo's father's sister Selma since all of them had lived together in Sokolov in the Ukraine. They were descendants of a group of Germans who had been homesteading along the Volga, since the time when Catharine the Great had invited them to cultivate the land about two hundred years ago. At the end of World War II, the Roleders had immigrated to Canada and later moved to Lodi, where Leo's uncle became the minister of the Lutheran Church. He had sent his affidavit to the German offices for immigration to America and had thus made it possible for Leo and later for his parents and Dagobert, to come to Lodi.

On the morning of Friday, December 20 I was ready to go back to my sister in Dayton.

Back to Dayton: Leo had asked me graciously if I needed money, but I assured him that I had my bus ticket and a few dollars and that was all I needed. This turned out to be a fallacy. The bus got into a snowstorm when we were on the pass over the Rockies and the trip took three full days. I lived on hotdogs and pleasant memories and arrived stiff-necked, hungry, dirty, and dead tired in Dayton, one day before Christmas.

Here I found my sister and her family in a flurry of Christmas preparations. We had a wonderful celebration on Christmas Eve, the traditional German Holy Night. Cornelie had outdone herself by having an abundance of gifts for everyone, including me. We had stayed in close contact all the time and she had expected my coming.

After the holidays, when all had calmed down, I confided my great news with all my doubts to her. She was very excited with the prospect of having one of her sisters on the same continent with her. "Now let's make lists of what you like about him and what you don't," she said in her practical way.

My list of good attributes run like this. "He is nice, I like his eyes, he works hard, and he has a wonderful family. He likes to go on trips, he is a good dancer, he owns a car, and above all, he lives in California, and he wants children."

"Hmmm," my sister said, "how about things you don't like?"

I counted, "He is not very tall, he smokes, and he is younger than I."

"Is that all?" Cornelie asked. "That's *nothing*. I think he sounds wonderful. Go ahead and do it. Why not?"

Armed with this approval, I decided to "give it a try," picked up the phone and sent a telegram to Lodi that I would be back on December 31.

Leo probably had made a similar list as I, that I was too tall, too old, and so forth. This time I chose to go by train and my sister bought the ticket for me.

Back to Lodi: It was a long ride but not as long as the bus ride before Christmas. I had a few hours between trains in Chicago and explored Michigan Avenue and the shore of the big lake. Back at the station I boarded the City of San Francisco train and had a pleasant ride west. The train had a glass dome and I remember sitting in the upper deck, looking onto the moonlit desert of Utah. What a strange, beautiful, vast country!

I arrived in Sacramento as scheduled on the morning of New Year's Eve. To my dismay, there was no one to meet me when I scrambled off the train with my suitcase. What was I to do? Go back to Dayton? Just as I was thus debating, I saw a somber Leo slowly coming toward me. I was very relieved to see him, but thought he might have changed his mind.

"Did you get my telegram," I asked foolishly—how could he be here otherwise?

"Oh, yes," he said. "It's nice to have you back."

This did not sound too enthusiastic, but there was no choice. I was there, so Leo picked up my baggage and brought me home to his parents. Everybody was there waiting, and I got a warm welcome and my old place on the sofa. Leo and I went to a New Year's Eve party at one of his friend's, and then we talked for the rest of the night together. Leo had thawed and was his old self again. Next morning we told the family that we were *engaged*. Everyone acted very surprised, and we celebrated by having a scrumptious breakfast and going to church.

Four weeks Between Engagement and Wedding: Now the courtship was over and we settled down to reality. I could not very well stay with Leo under one roof, at least so the parents thought. So Leo offered to ask the two sweet old ladies who had been his landladies before his parents arrived in April of 1952, just eight months before I appeared, to let me rent his former room in the old water tower on Hutchin Street. These wonderful people were so delighted that *their* Leo had found himself a girl that they not only offered me Leo's old room, but they also told me to feel free to use their whole house and garden whenever I wanted. The house was the oldest building on Hutchin Street and had been outside the original city limits of Lodi when constructed by the grandfather of one of the ladies. My room was above an old water tower and had everything I needed.

On January 6 I moved to Hutchin Street and stayed there until August, when we rented a house. The tower room was connected to the house by a narrow staircase that led through the kitchen and living room of my landladies; so inventive Leo, who did not want to disturb the ladies, Blanche and Nelly, put a tall ladder to my only window and came to me at night like the prince to *Rapunzel* in the fairy tale. Rapunzel had been put into a high tower to keep her safe from men, but the prince, her lover, had put a tall ladder up to her window so that he could climb up and visit her at night. When this was discovered and the ladder taken away, the prince told Rapunzel to let her hair down, and down came the beautiful long tresses, strong enough to let the prince climb up to her. The ladder Leo put under my window was close by, not for engaged lovers, but for the three cats the ladies owned to make it easy for them to climb up to the roof and down. The cats did not tell anyone, so nobody took the ladder away. That was good for us, since my hair would not have been long enough to hold my Leo.

The three cats were treated like children and I became good friends with them. Blanche and Nelly could not assure me enough that Leo was a wonderful young man, polite and considerate, and that he could fix anything around the house.

While still in Dayton, I had written my parents about the new turn my life had taken, told them about my fiancé and that I would not return home unless I absolutely had to. I also wrote to the school board in Bremen and asked them to take my name off the list of candidates for student teaching. My parents were happy for me but very sad to lose a third daughter to a faraway continent: my sister Cornelie in Ohio, Dorothee in Argentina, and now their youngest daughter in California. Only one daughter, Julie, had stayed faithfully in Bremen. The parents' letter did not sound too surprised, however. Cornelie had already written to them after I had left Dayton. I held back on writing to others because we had not set the wedding date yet. Both of us agreed it should be soon. Both of us were ready, so why wait?

What about my cotton thesis and the doctor title I had inspired for earlier? All that was replaced by the present events and would be dealt with later. I find among my correspondence two letters from Professor Kolb in Hamburg: one addressed to Fräulein Mathilde Apelt with plans for my thesis, and the other one to Mrs. Leo Schmidt with congratulations for making such a clever move. Of course, the second letter arrived after my marriage.

On January 7 our pastor, Uncle Emil Roleder, and his wife, Aunt Selma, were invited for dinner at the Schmidts' to get acquainted with me. Uncle Emil asked who my parents were, where I had grown up, how long I had been in the States, and so forth. And then came the big question, "When do you plan to marry?" When we told him that we wanted to get married as soon as possible, maybe next Sunday, he seemed shocked, looked at his wife and Leo's parents, and said, "But you two don't know each other yet. Wait at least one year."

We persisted in spite of this advice, and finally we all agreed that January 30 was the earliest possible date, that there was so much to prepare for a wedding, and that the vows had to be printed in the church bulletin.

Our Wedding: The end of January was only three weeks away and I had my hands full with selecting a gown, writing invitations to Leo's friends and relatives, planning the menu together with Mutti, as Mother Schmidt suggested I call her since "Mutter" was my own mother at home (now my own daughter Doris is calling me "Mutti"), and preparing myself mentally to get married. I also wrote many letters to let my friends in Germany and in America know what I was up to.

I also had to go to the immigration office in San Francisco to get my visa extended. After all, I had sworn solemnly in Bremen that I would return after half a year, because my visitor's visa only allowed for that. This meant that by law I had to return to Germany on February 17, exactly six months after setting foot on American soil, or get an extension for six more months because of extenuating circumstances. This was granted to me, but I was told that they gave such extensions only once. August 17, 1953 would be my deadline to leave the country and go through legal channels in Germany to apply for immigration. Only in very exceptional cases would it be possible to fill a "hole" in the quota, if someone had given up his or her place on the waiting list.

We were happy to have at least one extension and did not worry at this point about the future. Leo also wanted me to take the written test for a driver's license at city hall in order to get a permit so he could teach me how to drive a car. I shopped for a wedding gown and found a beautiful one for only fifty dollars, which made Leo happy. The rings were also inexpensive; two single wedding bands at twelve dollars each. My ring is still on my finger. The menu for the reception consisted of turkey, potatoes, and vegetables, followed by the three-tiered wedding cake that I baked myself, covered with royal frosting and a multitude of multicolored gumdrops.

And so the big day dawned, a lovely Friday morning with brilliant sunshine, birds singing, and spring bulbs beginning to push through the ground. We had rehearsed the wedding procedures on the night before and were ready for the important event. The wedding ceremony took place at Leo's uncle's Lutheran church, and it was filled with friends and relatives. However, none of my own family was present—the invitations had come too late. My sister in Dayton was too occupied with her own family and knew I was in good hands at the Schmidt's. Bridesmaids and ushers were friends of Leo. I had no way of telling if it was an elaborate wedding—I had never seen anyone get married in America before. Now I know that it was all very simple and modest. One of the two ushers (he had nothing to do because the bride had nobody to be ushered) doubled as the photographer and did a fine job.

After church the wedding party, about twenty-five people, went to Eden Street where the whole house had been turned upside down to accommodate the guests. It was a roaring reception party with wonderful food, nice presents—most of them I am still using—and dancing to phonograph music. At midnight we slipped away and drove to Sacramento where we had a room reserved in a fancy motel—our only extravagance—where the ceiling and the shower were covered with mirrors! In the middle of the night, though, the bed broke down, two twin beds that came apart, and we fell into the crack. We could watch ourselves in the mirrored ceiling after Leo had turned on the light.

We had some legal business in town and left for the ocean in the afternoon. The rest of Saturday and Sunday was spent at the beach, relaxing after all the excitement we had behind us. On Monday our brief honeymoon was over. Leo had to be back at work.

The First Years of Married Life

The Young Family: I felt wonderful in my little cubicle high up in the water tower, with real men's clothing hanging in the makeshift closet next to my skirts and dresses. The tall ladder leading to the window was not needed anymore—it was given back to the cats again. Leo could legally enter through the door, and I was Mrs. Leo Schmidt.

I had arrived. A new chapter of my life had begun. The time that followed now was so different from what I had ever experienced in life. For the last months, before marriage, I had led a turbulent life with nonstop activities, taking in cities, sights, landscapes, and meeting new people everyday; so I never really had time to absorb it all and think. There was also the feeling of homesickness and the guilty conscience of having left my parents, who had done so much for me, so abruptly. Here is an excerpt from the letter I wrote to my parents on Dec. 26, telling them for the first time of my plan to marry. After a detailed description of Leo and the Schmidt family I wrote:

...Now you see what purpose all my studying had; without it I would never have met Edith and never have come to Lodi. Even though the studying is not directly useful to me, it is so indirectly. Besides, I didn't really study to become a teacher, but for the purpose of having studied. I am now so satisfied with my life, it could not at all be better!...

I wrote this right after I had decided to marry, and I have never regretted that decision, but everything happened so fast that it took some adjustment.

Now I started a stable, almost monotonous life, with an abundance of leisure during the day. All I had to do was straighten out our little room after Leo had left for work, read or write letters, walk to Eden Street to keep Mutti company, and wait for Leo to come home. We still had most of our meals at Eden Street. I decided that a young wife should cook for her husband. So a few days after our wedding I went shopping and cooked in the ladies' kitchen what constituted my favorite meal: chicken and rice. The butcher had sold me an old hen—it was the cheapest meat available and I had cooked it for only half an hour, not knowing that such an ancient bird needed at least two hours to soften up. Leo was very proud of me for inviting him to our first home-cooked meal, but he soon changed his mind when he could hardly bite the tough fare. "Is this what I will get from now on?" he growled. "You better take some cooking lessons." I tried to explain that it was entirely the butcher's fault, but to no avail. He never in our married life forgot that first unsuccessful meal. I was more careful after that and in time learned to please him.

We had many enjoyable weekends, visited Big Trees where Tobogganing Hill was still in operation, went fishing in the Delta, saw gold-digging mines in the foothills (now abandoned), went to the beach, and one time even drove to Lake Tahoe with brother Dagobert, where we did some dancing and gambling in casinos. During these trips I had ample opportunity to look at my new homeland. The immediate surroundings of Lodi are as flat as the landscape around Bremen, and instead of green meadows dotted with cows, there are vineyards that change constantly with the seasons. But the hills and mountains that I so craved in my youth were just a few hours by car away from us; we could visit Big Trees on a Sunday afternoon and even cross the entire Great Valley from foothills to coast range and back comfortably in a day.

Surprising to me was the absence of trains and train stations, such a vital part of commuting in Europe. What I liked best was the weather. I enjoyed more sunshine during the few weeks I had spent in California than I ever had before. Of course, century-old buildings such as those I was accustomed to in my hometown were not to be found; if I wanted to see them again, I had to visit Bremen.

One day the mailman brought me two unexpected letters, both addressed to Fräulein Apelt. One was from Michael, whom I had not written, but who had gotten my new address from my mother in Bremen. He wrote me that his fiancée had broken up with him and married someone else. Therefore, he was free now and if I would reconsider and marry him (Mother must not have told him that I was Mrs. Leo Schmidt now), he would be happy. I tore up that letter then and there. The other letter was from Herr Baron von Rittershausen. He excused himself for getting back to me so late. He finally had been granted a divorce from his wife and was ready to marry me now. What an avalanche of proposals to a former wallflower!

Michael's letter hurt me more than I would admit—he kept cropping up in my dreams with his six foot, blue-eyed, blond frame, looking sadly at me. I realized, though, that he would not have made a good husband. He was too weak and too easily swayed. This was probably the reason why his fiancée had left him. Leo and I had agreed not to talk to each other about former entanglements, so I spared him my unhappy feeling. Time heals everything and I had much to be happy about.

At the end of February, I found myself pregnant and started to see Dr. Hoff, the family physician of the Schmidt family. I had been slightly anemic when leaving Germany in July of 1952 and was supposed to take iron to boost my red blood count. Somehow, I had forgotten about this, because of my antipathy to taking medicine. Later on I would regret this neglect, because my first baby was extremely slow in his development.

But right now Leo and I were deliriously happy about the prospect of becoming parents. We were a little worried that Leo's wages at the foundry were not enough to raise a family and I decided to help.

Looking for a Job: At first I found a job transplanting seedlings at a local nursery. That was work I had done in my seed breeding years and also in Strasbourg, so I was familiar with it. First a wooden flat had to be filled with good dirt, then the dirt was evened with a flat dowel, then a grid was pressed into the dirt and into the crossing points little plants from a seed pan were planted with the help of a pencil-like planting stick. After the flat was filled with young plants, it was marked and carried to the corner, where all the flats were stacked. This was piecework. The faster one could finish the flats, the more money one would earn. I liked this work because it introduced me to many different kinds of plants, and I was free to take leftover seedlings home with me. Since Nelly and Blanche had given me free reign in their backyard, I had dug up a parcel, prepared it for planting, and put all my little treasures in, carefully labeling them. That summer we all enjoyed the wonderful flowers and vegetables from the garden.

After all the transplanting was done and the nursery had no more work for me, I looked for a job at the packing sheds. Spring had turned into early summer and fruits of all kinds were being shipped from the rich San Joaquin Valley to Lodi to be packed in big sheds for distribution all over California and beyond. There was a constant need for packers. The pay was adequate and the work not too demanding, or so I thought. Full of expectations, I signed up for work in my fourth month of pregnancy. We had to pack cherries at that time. Wagons loaded with fruit were hauled into the shed where the workers stood at long tables with bins of cherries in front of them, which they had to pack into flats with twelve baskets. We were told to fill the baskets first with medium-sized fruit, and then select the biggest cherries and arrange them neatly on top.

I learned then to always turn a cherry basket upside down and to inspect the bottom before I buy it! We received a standard wage for each finished flat; I think it was twenty-five cents. It took me about one hour to finish four flats. It was not so easy to make a dollar in those days!

When the cherry crop was finished, so was I. My fellow workers continued with strawberries, then peaches, then grapes; but I had had enough and quit.

First Pregnancy: In the beginning of my pregnancy I had not noticed unusual fatigue, but the closer the actual date of birth came, the more tired I got. When the heat of summer began in late July, I started to take regular naps every day. Those naps grew longer, the weather became hotter and Lodi can be very hot during the months of August and September.

In August my visa was running out, so we had to do something about this. I was in no condition to go back to Germany now. Armed with our doctor's statement that my confinement was due at the end of October, we went once more to the immigration office in San Francisco to ask for an extension of the visa or, even better, for permanent residence. You can imagine our elation when, after hours of waiting, we were told that I did not have to go back to Germany, but because someone had given up his or her place on the waiting list, that I now had legal alien status along with the coveted green card, and that I could apply for regular citizenship in three years together with my husband who by then would also be eligible to become a citizen. The whole family celebrated that night. Later I learned that the real reason for granting me to stay was our little bundle of joy. Our baby was going to be born in the States and become a natural citizen!

Now I could really enjoy the last weeks before that big event. This took place on October 24, 1953, around midnight, in our local hospital. We had a little boy of average weight and height and named him Leo Hermann, after his father and grandfather. He was the first baby in the family and soon became the center of attention. When, in November, Dagobert's bride arrived from Germany and the wedding was celebrated on Christmas Day, there was no end to happiness. I had been in Lodi for one year.

However, a few clouds were rising on the horizon. Leo Hermann was not developing as normally as we had expected. His teeth grew in late and he rolled over and sat up slower than the average child. He was a fussy eater and weighed less than he should have. He cried often and seemed to be in pain. He did not gain enough weight. Dr. Hoff told me that all was well, that thin babies were healthier than fat ones, and that all mothers of first babies tended to worry too much.

When I noticed one evening that Leo Hermann's earlobes were completely bloodless, I got alarmed and took him to the doctor's office the next morning. When Dr. Hoff again told me that nothing was wrong, I had had enough. Against the wishes of the family, I took the baby to another doctor, who checked his blood and noticed a deficient blood count. "Your little boy is anemic," he told me. "He has to get iron shots and has to be put on regular medication."

Soon after the iron treatment had started, Leo Hermann ate better, gained weight and cried less. I never went back to Dr. Hoff. I was now almost certain that the anemia, which he must have inherited from me, was the culprit for Leo's slow development, and I stopped worrying. I felt better during the summer of 1954 and was ready for a new venture.

Looking for a Career: Two months before our son was born, we had moved to a little house on Redwood Street very close to Eden Street. We rented the house from a lady who lived in a bigger house facing the street, while we lived in back of her. The house had a living room and one bedroom, a tiny bath, kitchen, and service porch. The space was just enough for the three of us and the price adequate. Leo had a rule of thumb for his finances: housing should not be more than one-tenth of the income, if one intended to save. We definitely wanted to save money for a house of our own. This little house was rented to us for thirty dollars, which was about one-tenth of Leo's income at that time, so we could afford it. For the first time in our young marriage, we could entertain guests, not lavishly, but comfortably. We invited Leo's family, the Roleders, friends and neighbors, usually for tea and cookies. Leo Hermann's playpen stood in the middle of the living room, and we sat around him on second-hand furniture.

Our aspirations were to buy a house, and that took more money than just the little savings Leo put aside every month. We all agreed that my working in packing sheds or nurseries or even cleaning other peoples' households was out of the question. "Why don't you teach school," Leo suggested. "You certainly had enough education in that field."

I agreed and made appointments with several principals in Lodi schools. But I was very disappointed when I was asked to present my credentials.[2] I assured the questioners that I had gone to a university for six years and felt confident that I would be able to teach. "In California schools teachers need California credentials," was the stern reply. "Inquire at an accredited college and complete the requirements for the credential. Then come back to us and we might be able to use you. You seem to have had an interesting background. It was very nice meeting you. Good-bye."

After half a dozen of such meetings, I got the picture. To be able to get a coveted teaching position, one had to have the magic key: credentials. So Leo took me to the University of the Pacific in Stockton, at that time called College of the Pacific, or C.O.P for short, the school closest to us with a program to train for the teaching career. I was received politely, my papers were evaluated and I was told that I should start taking classes as soon as the beginning of the spring quarter in February. With enough dedication I would be able to finish the required courses for an elementary credential in about one year and could do student teaching in nearby schools during the spring quarter of 1955. I would receive my certificate in time to start teaching in the fall of 1955. Then I got a breakdown of registration and tuition fees and a list of required courses and was dismissed.

I had mixed feelings when I told Leo, who had waited outside in his car, the news that for one year I would not make money but spend it. I would also need transportation to and from Stockton and a babysitter for Leo Hermann. After thinking long and hard, my husband decided that if I really wanted to do it, he had nothing against my plans.

The money would be there, because he had applied for a job as a mechanic in a local factory that fixed up used tires. At Supermold, as the factory was named, he would get a higher wage than he did at the foundry, so instead of buying a house right away, we would have to pay for my teaching preparation.

As to transportation, we decided that I had to work on my driver's license immediately. The permit had come in. I now needed driving lessons, which Leo gave me. After many frustrating hours, for me as well as for my husband—one

2.   A credential is a certificate that allows teaching at public schools. It has to be earned at accredited colleges or universities. Most private schools do not require a credential. The California Commision for Teaching Credentials, CCTC, sets the standards for obtaining credentials.

time landing in a ditch on the side of the road; another time I was caught making a U-turn on the freeway—I was finally declared fit for the driver's test and passed it fairly well. We decided that I would take Leo to his job at Supermold and pick him up after work. I would have the car all day.

The third problem was to find a reliable person to be in charge of Leo Hermann. I did not want to ask Leo's mother. The parents had expressed vehement opposition to our plan. Though Leo's mother had been a teacher herself, she did not see any reason for her daughter-in-law to do likewise. "The woman's place is at home," I was told in no uncertain terms. "You don't need to have a job. Leo will always provide for you."

Things looked grim, but an easy solution was found when Leni, Dagobert's wife, offered to take care of "Schnucki-pucki," as she called the baby fondly. Dagobert had been drafted to do military service—first in Monterey, then in Atlanta, Georgia—so Leni was by herself and said she would love to be occupied with Leo Hermann.

On a beautiful morning, I set off in our Plymouth to start my college education in Stockton. At least all my university work in Germany had qualified me to be an accepted student at C.O.P. (College of the Pacific).[3] Everything went smoothly after that, and I would have been able to fulfill all the requirements for the credential in the allotted time had not another event prevented me from finishing up my year in Stockton. I became pregnant again in the fall of 1954 and was unable to complete the second part of my student teaching, which was scheduled for the beginning of April to the end of May of 1955. Even I saw the necessity of interrupting my plan. The family came first.

Rifts are Appearing: Leo's parents had nothing to do with this decision. They had problems concerning their two other children. Leni had become more and more distraught about the absence of her husband and toward the end of 1954 she declared categorically to all of us one Sunday morning, "I am going to Georgia to be with Dagobert."

The parents were perplexed and wanted to persuade her that it would be much better if she stayed with them and could find a job. They pleaded with her not to go all across America to Georgia. But Leni had already written to her husband about her intentions. He had agreed, so there was nothing Leo's parents could do.

---

3.   Later on C.O.P. became U.O.P., University of the Pacific at Stockton, following the trend of upgrading titles of schools.

Leni left, leaving a void that was soon filled when Edith arrived. She had stayed in Hamburg, had continued working for the professor who had engaged her before, and had decided to marry a young docent at the University of Hamburg. The parents now concentrated on making Edith forget about those plans. They wanted her to drop everything and come to Lodi to be with the family. Edith had finally given in to their pleading, had cut all ties with Hamburg, and had broken off her engagement. She appeared in Lodi just after Leni had left. It was an emotional reunion of the Schmidt family and Edith was amazed to find one of her brothers already with a complete family. Of course, she knew about our marriage but up to now she had been skeptical about its working out.

Edith also was not pleased about the fact that Leo and I had managed to learn the English language and were using it to talk to each other. She wanted all of us to converse strictly in German. She had a lot to learn. What she did not realize then—what I had experienced frequently—was that Germans sometimes were not looked upon favorably in postwar America. It was wise to learn to speak English as soon as possible to avoid unpleasant confrontations. However, Edith was strong-natured and demanded that in her presence only German was spoken. The elderly Schmidts spoke German anyway, but Leo and I had worked hard to learn fairly fluent English and were not going to give this up. Later Edith mellowed out in this regard.

As was to be expected, Edith, who was used to being active, could not sit around doing nothing for long, and she soon started looking for work. She had done some nursing before in her life and found a patient, a young man stricken with polio who needed constant care around the clock, which required her to move to the house of his parents. After this patient died, Edith was at loose ends again and decided to move to Sacramento to work on her teaching credential. One of her professors became interested in her, took her out a few times and she decided to marry him. Peter Deuel was Jewish, and Edith knew that this might present a problem with her parents. She was right, for as soon as the parents found out that their daughter was dating a Jewish person and even intended to marry him, they objected strongly. In spite of this, Edith and Peter got married in 1957. Only my husband attended their wedding. I was occupied with my small children and had to stay home. Neither Leo's parents nor Dagobert and his wife made an appearance, though they had been invited. This very unhappy situation lasted into the 1970's, and only Mutti's pleading for peace in the family before she passed away in 1977, made Father Schmidt reconsider. The two children of the Deuels hardly knew their grandfather. Edith was very disappointed at her parents' aversion toward her husband. The elder Schmidts were wrong in assuming that Peter would exploit their daughter—he was a wonderful husband and father.

Our parents were alone in the house again and Mutti especially could relax after the tumultuous times that had passed. Leni and Dagobert were in Georgia, Edith lived at her patient's house, and later in Sacramento. Father Schmidt and Leo were working and I was at my home with Leo Hermann. We often visited each other and discussed our problems. I had taken evening classes during the few weeks after Christmas of 1954 into February of 1955 to get as far in my preparations toward the credential as I could, but I could not finish the student teaching. Leo took care of the baby on the evenings I was gone and I did my homework whenever I found the time.

The visits with my mother-in-law became increasingly strained when she realized that I was still not giving up college completely. Looking back, I must say that I can understand her point of view now, but nobody then tried to understand me and my drive for striving to complete my education and being able to earn money. Therefore, rifts appeared and this led to unpleasant scenes between the parents and me.

I did, however, indirectly gain several advantages from the incomplete studies in Stockton. I learned to drive a car and had an opportunity to further my knowledge of the English language. I also had made new friends. In the summer of 1954, my head teacher at C.O.P., Mrs. Pease, had invited all her students with their spouses to her estate in the Sierra foothills. She owned a spacious cabin there between Murphys and Arnold on Highway 4, with a few acres of land that included a tumbling creek on which we could float on inner tubes of car tires. Our little boy was nine months old, and he was praised by everyone for being such a good and quiet baby. He could sit up then and looked around with wide eyes—he seemed very pleased by all the happy noises. My husband and I had a wonderful vacation day at the lovely place and started dreaming about having a cabin like this some day in the future ourselves. Little did we know then that this dream would come true about twenty years later.

The Family is Growing: Our second baby was born on May 4, 1955. It was a little girl this time and was named Doris Jane; Doris after Doris Day, my husband's favorite actress and Jane after one of my nieces. We wanted short names that were used in English as well as in German.

Doris developed much faster than Leo Hermann and had an outgoing personality, while Leo Hermann could sit still for hours and observe the world around him. Doris could never sit still and flew into vehement rages when things did not go her way. I was reminded of my father's temper tantrums. She used to get fiery red in her face, kicking her little legs, screaming at the top of her lungs, but quickly calming down when she got what she wanted. She was a very friendly and gregarious child, making friends easily. She and Leo Hermann were wonderful playmates. I was happy and fulfilled with my two children.

During this time I met a German woman who had three little boys. She lived close by and we became good friends. Her husband was a butcher by trade, but he wanted to farm, and soon the Dosterts moved to the country and grew grapes and raised cows. We were often invited and the children loved to go to the country, learn where the milk came from and ride on real horses. Tante Hilde, as we called her affectionately, taught me how to bake bread, and I have not stopped baking my own bread to this day. Later the Dosterts would have one more boy and would move to Oregon, where we would see them one more time after a trip to Yellowstone Park. We phoned each other once in a while and then drifted apart.

Our little house on Redwood Street soon became very crowded. We had to move Leo Hermann into the service porch, where his crib stood next to the washing machine and under rows of canned fruit. We looked for houses and found exactly what we needed on a quiet little street close to Lodi Lake. This house on Howard Street became our home for the next eight years. Leo was even able to pay off the loan on the house in a few years, so it really belonged to us. The house was ideal for the four of us. We had a little ivy-covered entry porch leading into the spacious living room with a dining corner, an adequate kitchen with a service porch, two medium-sized bedrooms and a small den that had French doors leading into a lovely backyard. The house had one bathroom, enough for us then. The one-car garage was detached from the house. A wide driveway led to the garage and was a wonderful playground for the children. Our car was usually parked on the street in front of the house so the children could play on the driveway unobstructed. In the yard we soon installed swing sets and a slide, and Leo built a beautiful patio for outdoor living. The front of the house had a well-kept lawn, rose bushes, and a tulip tree.

We had lovely neighbors, all young couples with small children like ourselves. Two houses from us lived the Feltons. Mr. Felton's father was a restaurant owner in town. Nick Jr., the son, was the manager. They had two children about the ages of ours. Leo Hermann played with Stevie Felton and Doris grew up with little Liza. Both Beverly and I were pregnant with our third child. Across the street were the Buchanans, Pat and Duncan, who so far had one child of Doris's age and also another one on the way. We had our babies almost at the same time.

Since there were so many young mothers, we formed a babysitting club that worked on the premise that for each hour of free sitting for one couple an equal amount of work had to be donated by that couple. A secretary, whose job rotated, had to keep scores of plus and minus points so that the nonprofit business worked smoothly. We did not go out much, but sometimes we liked to spend an evening with our parents without the children, so we used the club sparingly. When it was my turn to work, I was glad to learn how other parents managed their children.

We also enjoyed each other's company by visiting for coffee, giving birthday parties, and playing badminton in the street. Howard Street consisted of one block and since almost all the inhabitants were in the game, we blocked off the street with saw-horses. I still have the poles that held the net. Leo had welded them for us from pipes and they are now used as lamps in our cabin in the Sierra.

When our daughter Barbara Ann was born on March 3, 1957, I had three children in diapers. Leo Hermann, being late in most areas, was just being trained. He still had little accidents. Doris was beginning training and, of course, Barbara was an infant. I used cloth diapers—disposable ones had not been invented yet. All my available clotheslines in the garden were filled with diapers, as we did not possess a clothes dryer. I sometimes imagined all the diapers I had ever washed in a straight line reaching to New York. But I was happy and would not have changed places with anyone in the world.

Barbara proved to be a wonderful baby. While I was nursing her I was reading some of the great books by Pearl S. Buck and somehow my love for these books was transferred to my baby; she also loved them when she grew up.

When Barbara was about eighteen months old we had an epidemic of chicken pox. The two older children contracted them but had only slight discomfort, while Barbara was very sick and suffered a severe outbreak of blisters all over her body. The doctor told us to give her frequent baths with baking soda solution; this helped a little to relieve the terrible itching. We were afraid that she might have some permanent skin damage. For a long time she had scars on her face that must have contributed to a feeling of self-consciousness, but in time these scares faded away and became hardly visible.

On May 27, 1959 Leo and I took the U.S. citizen exam in Stockton. We had prepared for it carefully and had attended night school together for half a year. Before the important event, we tested each other frequently and also talked with other naturalized citizens about the kind of questions we might be asked. Both of us did well, and we were now legal citizens of the United States.

As soon as it was possible, we went to church with our children. Sunday morning was always a festive event, everyone in his or her finest clothes, even the baby. All three children were baptized a few weeks after they were born, and each of these baptisms was celebrated by inviting relatives and friends for coffee and cake. Leni and Dagobert, who came back from Georgia when his service time was over, as well as Edith and Peter, now married and living in Sacramento, had a little girl.

We were growing into a large family and could hardly fit less than one roof anymore. Leo's father now became Opa, the German word for "Grandpa," and his mother was Omi now, the German form of endearment for "Grandma." Opa's brother, Alex, and his wife, Anna, who did not have children, had bought a roomy house where we all spent happy hours, playing croquet outside or Monopoly and Yatzee inside. Alex, like Leo, had served time at the German front against the Russians, but he had had the bad luck of becoming a Russian prisoner of war and almost starved to death before he was released years after the end of the war. Alex had met Anna who had been raised in South Dacota and always spent the winters in Lodi because of the climate, and they were already married and settled for half a year, when I arrived on the horizon. Anna had been raised to be a devout Christian and was very adamant about our attending church regularly.

When Leo Hermann was four years old, we bought our first television set, black-and-white, as colored ones were yet not available in 1957. He instantly liked to watch and could sit for hours in front of it. Much later we bought a color television set to replace the old black and white one but never had more than one set. Though I now appreciated some of the programs, for instance the news, I never could quite get used to spending whole evenings in front of that strange contraption. One good thing was that we now were tuned in more to the events around us and knew what was happening in the world.

Political events like Russia's Sputnik in 1957, Khrushchev's visit to the United States in 1958, presidential elections, and so forth, were hardly noticed by us—we were too busy with our lives. However, with television now in our house, at least we heard about it. We had, of course, newspapers, but I must confess that I did not read them too diligently.

Worries About Leo Hermann: Leo Hermann had worried us lately. He had uttered his first words at the age of two and a half but did not seem to progress. We first thought that he was just a quiet child, but when Doris started talking fluently at the age of two, and even Barbara said a few words at one, we became worried and had him evaluated. The result was that Leo Hermann was tested and found to be highly intelligent but hard of hearing. The reason for this was not clear. We immediately took our son to an ear specialist in Stockton, who discovered a build-up of mucus in his ears. After removal of this glue-like substance, Leo Hermann seemed to hear better. He started talking and we were relieved. However, the doctor told us that Leo needed constant observation so his hearing problem would not worsen. Little did we know then that our son actually suffered from a permanent hearing loss and would have to rely on hearing aids all his life.

But all during his school years the brave little man tried to get along in spite of his handicap. There were no special classes in those days. Unfortunately, Leo Hermann was born in October, which made him one of the youngest students in his class. When kindergarten started for him in September of 1957, he was not even five years old. I explained our concern to the school principal and asked if we could hold our boy back for another year. "Absolutely not," I was told. "It would not be fair to the taxpayers."

Though we did not quite understand this, we obliged and sent Leo Hermann to kindergarten. Since we lived close to Woodbridge, a small community on the other side of Lodi Lake, Leo had to go to the school there because not enough schools had been built in Lodi in 1958. It was definitely too early for Leo Hermann to be in school. He was very immature and seemed unhappy. I wondered about the Readiness Theory we had been spoon-fed in college, that it is unwise to send a child to school before he or she is ready. Definitely there is a difference between theory and practice when it comes to school politics! As for the argument that the taxpayers might revolt: we paid taxes too and had rights to raise our little citizen correctly as well as we possibly could. We wanted to do what was best for *him*, not for the government.

Leo Hermann struggled through two more years of school. When, at the end of second grade, he received such low grades and poor assessments that I had had enough. I went again to the principal's office. In the meantime, a new school had been built close to us in Lodi and our children now went to this school, Erma B. Reese. The principal of that new school was a very understanding woman who listened to me and agreed that it would be better for Leo Hermann to repeat second grade.

My decision did not meet with understanding in the family. Even my husband thought that I had overreacted and had deprived Leo Hermann of one year of his life. It was also very hard to make Leo Hermann comprehend why he had "flunked" and had to let all his friends go on to third grade. I was alone but was convinced that it was the right thing to do. The teacher in Leo Hermann's second year of second grade was a wonderful woman, and soon Leo Hermann was an average student with good grades. He made new friends, even had his first girl-friend. The family eventually came around to agree with my decision and did not bother me anymore with accusations that I had been too hasty.

Doris, who had been two years behind Leo Hermann in school, was now just one year behind him. This did not make any difference in their relationship. I think that Leo Hermann always appreciated that his sister was a faster learner and he admired her for that. The two of them were always good friends. However, it was harder for Leo Hermann to get along with Barbara, who was four and a half years younger and interfered with his activities. He was heartbroken when he had worked hard to put a model airplane together and the toddler came and broke it to pieces with her inquisitive little hands. "She wrecks airplanes," was Leo's evaluation of his younger sister.

For three years we had three young children and thought that this was a good-sized family. However, during the fall of 1959 I became pregnant once more, and Leo and I braced ourselves for the future.

5

The 1960s

Last Years in Lodi

Marty's Birth: So far the predictions of the fortune teller in New York had come true. I had met my husband in 1952 and we had three children. Would it be possible to override the predictions and have another baby? Would another baby disturb the balance of our perfect home life? I had been one of four children; my sister was happy with four—why not me? Leo thought that three children were enough for him, but it would be nice if there was another boy for Leo Hermann. In any event, our youngest son took matters into his own hands and made his appearance on June 10, 1960. We all were overjoyed with the happy event.

We named this baby Martin Walter, another German name that both of us liked. The other children were proud of their brother and called him "Marty." Had there been a girl, we would have named her "Julie Alice" after the two mothers, Leo's and mine. But we all agreed that this little boy made our family complete. "There are now two boys and two girls in our family," the children proudly told relatives and friends. Leni and Dagobert had a little boy three months later and Edith and Peter's little boy was born in 1965, eight years after his sister Carol Ann. So the elder Schmidts had eight grandchildren, four boys and four girls. The grandparents would have liked to see them all grow up around them, but the Deuels (Edith's family) lived in Sacramento and our family would soon leave Lodi and move to the Bay Area. Unfortunately the strain between the Schmidts and the Deuels threw a shadow over the otherwise happy family.

My Father in Bremen Dies: In 1960, the year of our son Marty's birth, my father in Bremen passed away after a very successful career as senator for the Bremen port and railroads. His death came very suddenly and unexpectedly. The night before, he had gone to a crowning event in his career, the opening of a lock in Hameln (Hamelin), upstream from Bremen. The new lock would enable ships up to a certain tonnage to bring goods deep into our country and would help the economy of Bremen considerably. When he was brought home that night by his faithful chauffeur, Herr Ahrens, everything seemed normal. My mother, who was always ailing, had already gone to bed and my father joined her, happy with the successful evening. At about four o'clock in the morning, my mother was awakened by a loud scream and my father convulsed and fell out of the bed. Shaking all over, Mother contacted my sister Julie right away, and an ambulance was dispatched at once. Upon the arrival of the doctor, my father was pronounced dead. His death was caused by a heart attack. It was a terrible blow for my mother and she never quite recuperated from it. On the following day my father's body was laid out in state in the great hall of the *Rathaus*, an honor well deserved for his life-long services to the city.

I was not able to go to Bremen to attend the funeral. All the work at home tied me down. It was a severe loss for me, and I gave myself the solemn promise to travel to Germany to see my mother as soon as possible. But first we had to move to Castro Valley in the Bay Area.

Move to Castro Valley: Leo had joined the work force at Supermold in Lodi a few years after his brother Dagobert. When the company started having financial problems in the year 1962, Leo was one of the first workers to be laid off. This presented a severe blow to our growing family—we had four children now. The house on Howard Street was getting too small for us and we needed more, not less, money to go on with life. Leo tried to find another job in Lodi, then in Stockton, but he did not find anything for his line of skills. He had acquired the license to work as a tool-and-die maker[1] while at Supermold and had passed a special exam for this in Sacramento.

In order to find work as a tool-and-die maker, he had to go to the Bay Area. There would be ample opportunity to acquire a good position with enough pay. The Bay Area is an ever-expanding metropolitan region in the coast range near San Francisco, and we studied brochures of the residential areas. We liked Castro Valley for being our future home since it was a smaller community on the outskirts of the vast industrial area. Originally there had been separate cities distanced from each other, like Hayward, San Lorenzo, San Leandro, and Oakland, but they all tended to grow together into one big complex, the Bay Area.

---

1.   Toolmaking or tool-and-die making is a craft that makes tools and dies (forms, molds) used to make other parts for industry. Tools used by the toolmaker include lathes, milling machines, grinding machines, and boring machines. However, the toolmaker still does much of his work by hand, particularly the finishing stages of the products.

Since most of the industry is located in San Leandro, Leo went there first and soon found a job on Doolittle Drive with a tool-and die maker firm called Kaiser. They were looking for workers with this special skill. He rented a small apartment on 164th Street, where he stayed during the week and came home to Lodi every weekend. In his spare time, he looked for a residence for all of us in the Bay Area. We at home tried to sell our house on Howard Street. The house had to be looking perfect at all times for potential buyers, not an easy task for a single mother with four young children.

In the span of half a year, Leo had found a suitable house for us in Castro Valley, which had been our choice anyway because of its lovely hills, on Walnut Road, originally a canyon with rather steep slopes on each side. So from living horizontally in Lodi, we would live vertically in the future. But our house in Lodi had not been sold yet. We talked to the real estate agent and agreed to move anyway; he would keep the house on his list and let us know when it was sold. Nothing now stood in our way to relocate, and on June 10, 1963, on Marty's third birthday, the family moved, complete with a winter's firewood supply and our cat, Blackie. We used the Mayflower Moving Company and also our two cars, my Studebaker station wagon, and Leo's Ford Falcon to transport our belongings.

The night before the move we had taken leave from the family in Lodi, which was not easy for any of us. We had been used to being surrounded by our family and would have none of the relatives in Castro Valley. Friends and neighbors would also be missed; school and church were part of our life. All that we would find in Castro Valley, too, but nothing could substitute for the family. So we went with mixed feelings, bemoaning the loss of the old and anticipating the new life in Castro Valley. On the other hand, we now had fewer tensions and didn't have to suffer daily criticism from the family. We were on our own.

Leo had taken me to our new home once before so I could measure the windows for curtains, decide what furniture to take, and also what to leave behind. I also had had the chance to look at the school for our children. I was very pleased with everything. The house was situated in a good neighborhood on the sunny side of the canyon and had enough space for us. The only drawback was that it was on a street noisier than we were used to in Lodi. The driveway was very steep, but Leo already had plans in his head to remodel it. The big backyard was a great feature, though it needed a lot of work. The school was in walking distance, just up the street, and looked pleasant and promising to me. Since we moved at the beginning of summer vacation, there were three months ahead of us to get acquainted with the new surroundings and prepare the children for school.

The weather seemed to be more maritime and balanced—influenced by the closeness of the Bay—than in the Great Valley; we did not have the excessive heat in the summer or the severe cold in the winter.

Life in Castro Valley

Swimming: We moved to Castro Valley at the beginning of summer in 1963 and school would not start for three months. During that first summer in Castro Valley, we joined a private swim club that was close by and served as a substitute for the wonderful lake in Lodi where we had spent many happy hours. Before we joined the club, I had taken the children to a swimming lagoon on the other side of Castro Valley, but this had proved unsatisfactory. It was too far away from our house and did not provide for the swimming lessons that were needed for the children. Our club was filling all those needs; it was in walking distance and provided swimming instruction as well as a complete social life for all of us. I still communicate with friends from that club.

There is a picturesque lake located between Castro Valley and San Leandro, Lake Chabot. However, in 1963, when we moved there, it was not available to the public. Lake Chabot was strictly used to store drinking water for the community. Only in 1967 would the local water district—East Bay Municipal District or "East Bay Mud"—as we called it, build a marina for boats and a small restaurant and prepare trails for hiking. Fish eggs were planted and later people were allowed to fish, provided they had a license. Swimming in the lake was never allowed.

Our swim club soon became our home away from home. Many other young families belonged to it. We were always surrounded by friends. All our children learned to swim and many Sundays were spent with swim-team events.

Scouting: That first summer also we became involved with Scouting. Leo Hermann had already been a Cub Scout in Lodi and was ready to become a Boy Scout. There were enough boys in the neighborhood to form a sizable group, but no one wanted to be the leader. So my husband volunteered to be a Boy Scout assistant leader and I volunteered to be a Cub Scout den mother if a trained leader could be found. Soon such a man evolved, and our Troop 733 was started. Leo Hermann loved Scouting and even attained highest honor—he became an Eagle Scout in 1968. Much later three of our grandsons also achieved this goal.

The girls had started in Lodi as Bluebirds, a division of the Campfire Girls organization. Girl Scouting was not available, at least not while we were living in Lodi. I had built up a nice little Bluebird group of about eight girls, who came to our house once a week, sang, danced, acted out little skits, and even sewed little Bluebird aprons with my help. In Castro Valley, our girls, then eight and six years old, wanted to continue this activity, but there was no Campfire group in our neighborhood. A strong troop of Girl Scouts had been built up by one of our neighbors on Walnut Road, Mrs. Grant. But no mother was willing to take on the younger girls, or Brownies, as they were called because of their brown uniforms. So, if I wanted my girls to be active in Scouting, I had to become the Brownie leader. A few other mothers who were willing to be assistants and I formed a fine group of Brownies who, in due time, went "across the bridge," symbolic for crossing over into Girl Scouts, over a little wooden bridge made by my husband. Since Mrs. Grant was retiring, I followed the girls and became a Girl Scout leader.

All these Scouting activities were not only great fun; they reached over into the next generation. Three of our grandchildren became Eagle Scouts and their parents devoted leaders and helpers.

My assistant was a young mother of four children, Shirley Kuller. I had met Shirley before when school had started in September and Leo Hermann had come home excitedly, telling us about this neat new friend he had made, Lester Kuller. Lester was the Kuller's oldest son, and the boys' friendship led to a wonderful relationship between our two families that has continued through the years. The Kuller's only daughter, Loanne, was of the same age as our Doris, so Shirley and I had a mutual interest in forming a Brownie group.

Shirley became my good friend. Though she is about seventeen years younger than I and quite different in many ways, we liked each other instantly and did many things together. She told me about her interesting background. Both of her parents were deaf and had met each other in the deaf community. She and her sister Diane were born with normal hearing and, in order to be able to communicate with their parents, learned to use sign language at the same time that they started talking. Their parents were able to speak, but could not hear. All of the five grandchildren, Kullers' four children and daughter Diana's little girl, have normal hearing. Shirley does not know if the cause of her parents' hearing problem is hereditary— so far it does not seem to be. Shirley has a wonderful mature outlook on life and is in spite of many hardships in her life, a basically happy person. This is probably the reason for our mutual attraction.

Church also enriched our lives. We were used to going to our Uncle Roleder's Lutheran Church regularly in Lodi, partly because everybody in the family did and also because our uncle was the pastor. We joined the Faith Lutheran Church on Redwood Road in Castro Valley, and not only did we go to church every Sunday and the children to Sunday School; we all participated in church activities like Bible study courses, picnics, and parties. When it was time to prepare our growing children for conformation, all of them went to church school for that event for two years. Once they were confirmed, they had to decide for themselves if they wanted to continue to be good Christians or find other ways to worship God.

I must confess that church was never a driving force in my life. I had my own private philosophy about religion. God represented a very remote personality for me and I had fabricated a female version of invisible helper, my own Guardian Angel, who took care of me through all my life.

My First Visit to Germany: In 1963, just after we had moved to Castro Valley, we met a delightful German couple with an eight-year-old daughter whose name surprisingly was Doris. The two Doris's became good friends, and their parents began visiting each other. The In der Schmittens (a long name meaning "in the smithy") had a contract from a German engineering firm to work in the States for one year. They lived in an apartment close to our house, and we exchanged babysitting services. The following year my mother would be eighty years old (on January 5, 1964), so I asked my husband if he would let me visit my mother for two weeks, from Christmas until after her birthday, if we could persuade the In der Schmittens to baby-sit for us during the day. At night Leo would be home. Leo agreed that I should go, since it had been ten years that I had not been home and had lost my father already, so it was settled. The In der Schmittens were very happy to help, little Doris was delighted to be part of our family, and nothing stood in the way of my departure.

The trip to Bremen was a complete success. All my relatives and friends came to see me. I was happy to be in my old home again, at least for a while. My mother was ecstatic and my sister Julie proudly paraded all her children in front of me. Two of them, Christine and Charlotte, had been born after I had left Bremen. My mother enjoyed being the center of attention and felt well enough on her day of honor to be a most gracious host for all her guests. My sister Julie had helped with the preparations, and we had a wonderful party.

I must add that this was my very first airplane ride and I was very impressed how much faster it went than my freighter *Magdalene Finnen*. I came back home loaded with presents for my family and the In der Schmittens, and felt like a newborn person. With renewed vigor, I threw myself into all the work of a wife, mother, and Girl Scout leader.

Teaching German at the Adult School: However, this busy, active life still left a void in my life. My hunger for knowledge started to nag again. We had a very good evening school in Castro Valley, and I enrolled in a course in Conversational Spanish. After having taken a quarter of this class and having observed the teacher carefully, I decided that I could do just as well as he did by teaching my native German. I went to the principal of the night school and asked if he could use my services for the coming school year. Not only was I given the job, but he was delighted to add German to his curriculum. All I had to do was to submit an outline of my classes and to state my intent to take proper classes at a nearby college for obtaining an adult teaching credential. "But you don't have to do this now. Do it whenever you have the time."

I was very proud about the prospect of teaching and even receiving money for it. Leo was a little skeptical at first but soon got accustomed to my leaving home once a week in the evening. My teaching was a great success, and I taught Conversational German at Castro Valley Adult School for twenty consecutive years. I should have been happy and content with this endeavor, and for a while, I was.

One political event in that time stands out. The sudden death of President Kennedy on November 22, 1963 was announced over the television when I was ironing stacks of laundry and was casually listening to some program.

"The President has been shot!" was the shocking news.

The children were sent home from school early that day and all of us grieved together.

Our Four Children Develop: Meanwhile, family life went on. Leo worked his eight hours as a tool-and-die maker, occasionally working overtime on Saturdays and even Sundays. The children went to school. Until the school year 1965/66, all our children attended the same elementary school, Parsons. Leo Hermann was in sixth grade, Doris in fifth grade, Barbara in third grade and Marty in kindergarten. After elementary school we experienced junior high school, then A.B. Morris School, which has now been replaced by a housing tract. Parson's Elementary has been turned into a playground, Parson's Park, which opened in 2003.

After that, it was Castro Valley High School, which all the children attended and finished in due time. In spite of the same upbringing, the same education, and the same environment, our four children developed entirely different personalities. Very much like my father compared my own sisters and me with the four Greek elements, I find it possible to draw the same analogy to our children. Leo was like the air, always there but hardly noticeable. Everybody loved him and he did not stir up trouble. Doris had a fiery temperament and could blow up at any time, much like my father. Barbara was the good earth. She loved to putter in the garden and her hands were always busy with things to do. And Marty, like me, the youngest, was always on the go, always finding new things to do, like the water that never rests. If I had to find one adjective for each of my children, I would say that Leo Hermann was the steady one, Doris the inquisitive one, Barbara the practical one, and Marty the adventurous one. Of course, this characterization is grossly simplified. All of our children also have many things in common. They all love nature, all are honest and dependable, all love their family, and all honor their parents. We can be very grateful for each and every one of our children.

A few nice little stories arise from the ocean of memories that flood over me when I think back to the happy years when the children were still with us. Many happy moments occurred when the summer vacation allowed all of us to participate in activities together.

Leo Hermann was working on his Boy Scout merit badges and chose, among others, to try rabbit raising. We studied up on the requirements for the badge. We needed a female rabbit, one that was fertilized by a buck, and a cage. Leo and Leo Hermann worked on the cage, and then Leo Hermann and I acquired the future mommy rabbit. We called her Genie, after the mysterious demon on Leo Hermann's favorite television show *I Dream of Jeanie*. I liked to use the spelling "Genie" after the spirit from *A Thousand and One Night* (Arabian Nights). Leo Hermann took his little brother with him when we took Genie to the buck (fortunately there was a rabbit farm close to our house). He did not allow his sisters to go—they found this very discriminatory and mean. Properly fertilized, Genie just sat in her lovely hutch and ate all day, but she refused to produce babies, or so it seemed. One day, I had had enough of this lack of fecundity. I asked Leo Hermann to hold his pet and I dumped out the cage. To our great surprise, out fell not only lots of hay, rabbit raisins, and debris but also four tiny perfectly formed baby rabbits. All's well that ends well! Leo made his badge and each one of the children had his or her own rabbit. Genie went back to the rabbit farm, and everybody was happy.

We used to go to a nature center in Hayward where pet animals could be rented for a week. Besides guinea pigs and hamsters, the children also chose rats and liked them so well that I had to *buy* some rats—usually considered pests rather than pets—that summer. I remember the girls sheltering the rats in their long-sleeved blouses, having them walk back and forth along their arms. When they arrived at the wristband of the blouses, they stuck out their little noses, sniffed the fresh air, and turned around into the warm sleeve again. Our cat did not touch those rats. They must have been too domesticated for him.

We also had little turtles. There were always two of them, and we named them Romeo and Juliet. Sadly, they never made it and had to be replaced every summer. Another pet was a parakeet that never sang and produced much dirt in our kitchen.

Leo's Role in the Family: My husband, Leo, had been laid off his job at Kaiser a few years after we had moved to Castro Valley and had found a much better work place at a small company called Manor Research. It was a highly challenging, interesting job that allowed him to use his skills optimally and to develop more knowledge in his field. He is now eighty years old and still works for the same company. In recent years the company has been bought out by another one, Ilmberger Tool & Die, and all the workers were invited to stay. Three of our four children earned their first spending money at the shop, doing menial jobs and getting their first taste of work.

My husband was always very interested in the development of our children. Not only did he participate actively in Scouting; he played games with them, worked with them, and provided wonderful outings for the whole family. Also he had the entire family working at landscaping our big garden.

One project that was done with the help of all of us was the creation of our backyard. When we bought our house in 1963, the land behind it could hardly be called a garden. It was a raw hill, a big slope consisting of clay, rocks, and weeds. The first thing Leo planned was to build several retaining walls on the hill to create terraces. We now have five distinct plateaus that are partially cemented and partially made into flower beds and vegetable gardens. On one terrace stands a little playhouse for the children with a luscious lawn in front of it, even sporting a fishpond for guppies and goldfish. The retaining walls are built of cement bricks and all of us helped mixing and pouring the cement for the foundations. When, after a long day of work he finally called it quits, Leo took us to Foster Freeze for an ice cream cone. How all of us were looking forward to this treat!

Trips: As soon as Marty could walk, we started going on trips. When he was only one and a half years old, in the fall of 1961, my sister Cornelie visited us in Lodi. Her husband Walter had to go on a lengthy business trip and she used this time to come to California. Her children are much older than mine and had already left home at that time. We all picked her up in Sacramento and she was treated like the Queen of Sheba. Leo and I slept on the sofa in the living room and Cornelie had our bedroom all to herself.

One Saturday Leo took us all to the mountains to show my sister how big and beautiful California is. He had selected Big Trees Park as our goal, and Cornelie was extremely impressed. She could not believe the height and majesty of the red-wood giants. What was even more astonishing was that our little Marty, barely seventeen months old, walked all of the North Loop by himself, holding on to a walking stick his father held out to him. He was not even tired when we returned to our car.

Another trip took place in 1963, when we had just moved to Castro Valley. We went to Big Basin and stayed there overnight in two tents. All the children, including Marty, did very well and loved it so much that they wanted to do this every year from then on. In fact, all through the years from 1964 to 1974, we made at least one family trip a year, mostly backpacking and "roughing it." Over the years we traveled to Yosemite Park, Mt. Lassen, Yellowstone Park, and Mt. Diablo. On each camping trip, we learned new skills and strengthened our family ties. Those family trips were done in addition to Scout camp-outs and school events.

One of these trips to Yosemite is worth writing about. My husband arranged the preliminary preparations by taking a one-week vacation and laying out the route of our hike. I was in charge of food, clothing, and the bare necessities of life. We had been very careful not to bring too many things since everything had to be carried on our backs. We were going to tour the three Dog Lakes at Yosemite Park. After we had parked the car on the parking lot at the foot of the trail to Dog Lakes we took our backpacks and started the rather steep way up to the Lower Lake. The three lakes are on three plateaus of different altitude. We arrived at Lower Dog Lake toward evening and set up our two little tents. It was the end of summer and the night proved to be rather chilly. When the children, who had been swimming in the lake and had hung up their bathing suits on a makeshift line, came out of their tents, they found those suits frozen stiff! Leo built a nice little fire; we had a good breakfast, and packed up.

Middle Dog Lake is much higher up and we had to climb up the trail for many hours. When we finally arrived, we decided to stay there for a few days since we found a comfortable cave to sleep in and had a lovely view of the lake. The children were brave and swam in the lake, but only for a short time because it was ice-cold. We explored the surroundings of the lake, which were only sparsely covered with bushes. We had left the dense forest around Lower Dog Lake behind us and had settled close to the tree line. We also hiked up to Upper

Dog Lake, which is above the tree line and has only rocks and a thin cover of Alpine vegetation. We even found snow around the lake. When we returned to our little settlement, consisting of two small tents and the cave, we spread out my old pink robe—the only luxury I had brought—and played cards. We also had books and could read until the sun went down. We all did the cooking together and sat after dinner around our campfire to talk and have fun. After three of these busy days we had to think of going home, so we packed up and descended to our car in just one day. It was so much easier to go down than up, and the packs were much lighter. To top this event off, Leo took us to a nice restaurant on the way back and let everyone choose what he wanted.

We would continue these back packing trips with or without visitors from Germany until 1976, when we bought our cabin in the Sierras.

Music and Sports: I always loved music and wanted the children to enjoy it too. Unlike the Ernsts' children, none of ours had a talent for singing, though we sang during Scout events and also in church, but the children's school offered a wonderful opportunity to learn an instrument from the time a child entered the fourth grade. Leo and I agreed that it would be good for our children to learn to play at least one instrument and play in the orchestra or band. The three older children chose string instruments. Leo Hermann picked the viola, Doris the violin, Barbara the cello, and Marty decided to play the clarinet. Lessons given by the music teacher were free, and we had many occasions to hear our children play in school concerts. Orchestra and band were also instrumental in the performance of the yearly school musical that ranged from *The Sound of Music* to *Annie Get Your Gun*. We also bought a piano so that I could accompany each child when he or she practiced. I had learned enough from my own piano lessons with Frau Marshall to do that. When both girls showed an interest in playing piano, they received lessons, for which we had to pay. I found that the money was well spent. Doris still plays both instruments, violin and piano, while Barbara's life is so busy that she had to give up her musical aspirations. But she appreciates music very much. The boys did not show too much interest in the piano, but they kept their instruments. They preferred sports.

All the children had ample opportunity to participate in sports like baseball, soccer, swimming, and running, just to name a few. Both girls loved swimming and also became very good in gymnastics in high school. Barbara especially showed great flexibility and excelled in dance exercises. She is still able to perform the Chinese splits with ease and sometimes regrets that she did not study ballet.

Our membership at Chabot Swim Club made it possible for all four children to learn to swim well and participate in the events of the swim team.

Visits and Visitors: The first visitor from Bremen was Christoph Kulenkampff. In 1957 when we had only two children, just days before our Barbara (named after Barbara Ernst, my sister's daughter in Dayton) was born, we received a telephone call from New Zealand that my brother-in-law Christoph was coming to visit us for three days at the end of February. Barbara's birth was due at the beginning of March, so I was very unsightly and heavy on my feet. But nothing mattered. We were overjoyed having a visitor from Bremen. Christoph had been in New Zealand and other wool-producing countries to buy wool for his company, Kulenkampff & Konitzky. He had to examine the wool on the sheep for this purpose. Having finished his business, he decided to visit us on his way back to Germany. He was the most wonderful guest. All of us were spoiled by him. He took us shopping and had everyone choose what he or she wanted. The children had toys, I a pearl necklace and the whole family a grocery cart full of delicious food. Unfortunately, the weather was awful. It rained heavily during the entire time of Christoph's stay, but it did not matter. We had an unforgettable time.

Cornelie's visit in 1961 has already been mentioned; it was followed by the visit of her daughter Barbara in 1963, just before our move to Castro Valley. She was a young bride and on the way to pick up her husband, Jim Allen, who had been on a business trip to the Bay Area. Both of them were on their way to Las Vegas for some fun before going home to Dayton. Barbara stayed with us for about a week and was a wonderful house guest. We even took her to Castro Valley to show our new house to her. She approved and thought it was a great house. Barb was very elegant; especially her hair looked extremely chic. She inspired me to do something about my mousy, straggly looking hair and from then on I had my hair tinted and cut regularly and started looking more decent. I still have pictures of me from those years before "something was done" to my hair—I look like my own grandmother in them.

My sister Cornelie had friends living in Dayton, John and Margaret Toedtman, whom I had actually met before she did. As told previously, John Toedtman was assigned to head cultural development in Bremen after the war. Since my father was the president of the arts council and at the same time my mother was very active in the management of the symphony hall, it was only natural that John worked closely with both my parents to redevelop and further the fine arts in Bremen.

We also became socially involved after Mrs. Toedtman and my mother conversed at a party and the topic turned to Dayton, Ohio. Margaret had just told my mother that she and her family were living in Dayton, Ohio. "My oldest daughter Cornelie is living in Dayton. They must be very happy there," my mother told Mrs. Toedtman.

"But isn't that a happy coincidence," she replied enthusiastically.

When Bremen ceased to be a besieged city and the Toedtmans went home again, Margaret contacted Cornelie and started a long lasting friendship with her.

When I came to Dayton in 1952, the Toedtmans gave a party and invited us all. It was there, at this event, that I met Ethel Slaggie for the first time. Ethel's friendship with Margaret went far back in time, and now she became my friend, too. Ethel was a widow, and at that time she must have been about fifty-five years old. She worked at the municipal office for insurance and handled claims. She was a unique person, petite and graceful, extremely well-bred and the most considerate conversationalist I have ever met. She was a wonderful listener and made it a pleasure to talk to her.

Shortly before we moved to Castro Valley, Ethel's office transferred her to California, where she settled in Albany, close to Berkeley. We picked up our relationship again and visited each other a few times, and Ethel became acquainted with our four children. She loved them and was extremely interested in their development. After we had moved to the Bay Area she became the grandmother figure to them that they were missing. We saw each other frequently, because it took only about twenty minutes to get to each other's houses. Today the traffic through the Alameda Maze is so congested that commuting time is unpredictable.

When I was teaching German at the adult school in Castro Valley (I did this from 1964 to1984) Ethel came to my class for many years, since German was one of her favorite subjects. It was a pleasure to have her as a student. She learned extremely quickly and showed great aptitude for my native tongue. We lost Ethel in 1979 when she had overexerted herself caring for visitors from Germany and simply collapsed at her kitchen table. All our children mourned her death as they would have for their own grandmother.

The Toedtmans remained my sister's friends. Even after John's death, Margaret and son John kept up the relationship. They visited us in Castro Valley on their way to Banff, Canada. In 1968, I visited my sister with my youngest children, Barbara and Martin. Margaret gave a party in our honor and invited many other friends. I never had experienced such hospitality. She must have cooked for days to produce so much wonderful food. Needless to say, my ever-hungry children loved it. John Jr. developed into a fine musician and is now the proud owner of a well-known music school in Cincinnati. Margaret passed away in 1992.

The family from Lodi was invited regularly and they admired our nice house and garden. We lived close to the edge of the city and could take the family on pleasant hikes in the neighborhood. The closeness of beautiful Lake Chabot offered opportunities for boat rides and picnics like those in Lodi.

My sister Julie sent her eighteen-year-old daughter, another Julie, to stay with us the entire summer of 1967. The highlight of that vacation was a trip to Lake Tahoe, where we camped right on the shore of Emerald Bay. Unforgettable for me was the ride back home when the generator of my little Carmenghia Volkswagen gave out and I had to drive nonstop for four hours because, if I stopped, I wouldn't be able to start the car again. I had Julie with me, while Leo had our four children in his Falcon. We had just bought my little second-hand car because the old Studebaker station wagon had given up its ghost. During the last ride in it driving through Castro Valley with a load full of Scouts, the horn had gotten stuck and we had aroused the attention of the whole town!

For the entire trip from Tahoe to Castro Valley, I sat as tight as a ramrod in my driver's seat, treating the transmission like a baby, praying that the motor would not die, while stoic Julie sat quietly next to me, giving me wonderful support by praising my fledgling driving skills. She was just in the process of learning to drive in Germany and admired anybody who could drive a car, especially one with a faulty generator.

Two years after Julie's visit, we had another visitor, Rainer Kohlrausch, also from Bremen, who would become Julie's husband a few years later. Rainer was working at his father's shipping agency and had business in San Francisco. He stayed at our house and commuted daily to the city in a rented Volkswagen beetle. He was a wonderful house guest, full of humor and always friendly and helpful. Rainer loved the idea of sleeping in the bed Julie Kulenkampff had occupied two years before because, though she was only eighteen years old to his twenty-four, he was determined that she was the one for him. He had only one vice; he loved to drink beer.

A drastic thing happened when Rainer left in the fall. On the morning he was scheduled to fly home, we discovered that his little rented Volkswagen that was parked in front of our house had been rammed by another car and was undrivable. That morning I had to drive Rainer to the airport—Leo had already gone to work—and fight the thick traffic between Castro Valley and San Francisco. We made it in time to the airport, the demolished Volkswagen was being picked up by the rental company, and I could rest on my laurels for having been indispensable. Rainer visited us several times thereafter when he had business in the Bay Area or Los Angeles. But never for a long stretch again as in 1967. He and Julie got married in 1969.

The Busy Summer of 1968: From July to September that summer, we sent our two oldest children to Germany to meet their grandmother and all their relatives in Bremen. That was the first time we let our children go so far away by themselves, and both Leo and I had mixed feelings. Leo Hermann was barely fifteen and Doris was thirteen years old, and both looked so young and vulnerable when they disappeared into the gateway of the big jumbo jet. We had made arrangements for Christoph Kulenkampff to pick them up in Frankfurt. Christoph was a little late and found both of the children asleep on a bench at the airport. They were overjoyed to see him. They remembered him vaguely from his previous visit in Lodi. In order not to upset Grandmother's household in Bremen too much, the Kulenkampffs took one of the children to their house while the other one stayed with Grandmother at Richard Strauss Platz. This arrangement was altered every few days by exchanging the children, so Grandmother had the chance to get to know both of them intimately. My mother was then eighty-four years old and could still enjoy the children to the fullest. Had Leo and I known then that my mother would reach the ripe old age of ninety-eight years, we would have waited for that visit until the children were older.

While our two older children were visiting in Bremen, I took the two younger ones to Dayton to visit my sister Cornelie and her family. We got acquainted with all four of Cornelie's children, who had grown up and had children of their own. We especially liked Phyllis, who had married Don Kreider, a mathematician, who worked as an actuary for a large insurance firm. The couple had a one-year-old son, Alex, whom our Barbara loved to baby-sit. Alex was then the youngest grandchild of the Ernsts, there being three older children of Jim and Barbara Allen. Later Alex had a younger sister, Johanna. It so happens that Kathy, my sister's oldest granddaughter, is slightly older than Marty, my son. Kathy, who is logically one generation below Marty, teased him by calling him "Uncle Marty," which he resented. This mix-up of generations is due to the fact that my sister—eleven years older than I—married relatively young, whereas I was rather old when Marty was born. So Marty is my son and Kathy is my sister's granddaughter.

Both girls, Kathy and Johanna, regular cousins, got married in due time and gave the respective families the opportunities to stage a great wedding party, Kathy's in Dayton in 1988, a few years before Walter Ernst died and Johanna's in

1993, which was attended by Cornelie's sisters, Dorothee and me. Julie could not come because she had just lost her husband, Christoph. We will always be a closely-knit family.

The Toedtmans invited us all for an overwhelming party at their plush residence in Kensington, one of the wealthy areas in town. That party has been mentioned previously, but it merits to be mentioned twice. Margaret had overdone herself with cooking and preparing. Johnny remembered me well; he had grown into a nice-looking young man. He had improved his piano playing considerably and intended to make music his career. Cornelia and Walter had decided to stay home and could not believe it when they were told about all the food we had been offered.

Unfortunately, at the beginning of the third week of our stay in Dayton my Barbara got the mumps and we had to leave Dayton earlier than planned. It was really my own fault. Marty had just recovered from the mumps before our trip to Dayton and I did not realize that the incubation time for this disease is so long.

After Leo and Doris came back from Germany, very fulfilled with all the new experiences that had impressed them, and even speaking a little German, we had yet another visitor, Carol Ann Deuel, daughter of Edith and Peter Deuel, who stayed with us for two weeks. Also Dagobert's daughter, Susanne, visited us over several weeks. Those were busy summers!

6

The 1970s and 1980s

The years flew by and before we knew it our three older children were approaching the end of their high school days. In 1972 graduations began, followed by their university years. One by one they left us, and we old ones were left behind and had time to enjoy each other.

Trips Without children

In 1970 Leo and I decided to take a European trip by ourselves. Our good friend, Shirley Keller, whom I had known from the time we arrived in Castro Valley, had a younger sister, Diana, who was willing to live at our house and take care of our children, who ranged then in age from ten to seventeen. Diana and her young husband, John, had just had a baby, little Chantal. They all moved in, and our children had a wonderful summer at home while we were gone for five weeks. When we came back from our trip, the children had learned to cook and eat Mexican food, had done arts and crafts with clever John, and had helped to take care of little Chantal. There was also a new cat in the family, another black one—the old one had run away soon after we had moved to Castro Valley and had not yet been replaced.

Bremen: That trip with my husband gave me a new perspective on life. I missed the children, but also found it very relaxing to be removed from the daily grind of doing household chores and having to meet deadlines. Someone else had to worry about making beds, dusting the house, and keeping the children happy. I discovered that my husband and I had interests in common that I had never thought existed.

Our flight to Germany was Leo's first airplane ride, an exciting event in itself. In Frankfurt we rented a car and visited our old friends, the In der Schmittens, whose fifteen-year-old daughter Doris had been joined by a little brother. After two nice days in their brand new house, we drove leisurely to Bremen where everyone was anxious to meet Leo. Except for Christoph, Julie, and Rainer, nobody in the family had met my husband yet. My sister Julie gave a big family picnic at their second home, an old farmhouse in Horstedt outside of Bremen, where we met the entire clan. Even my mother came to this party.

Leo and I had a little adventure before we joined the gathering at Horstedt. We had been invited to visit Jane Darjes, sister of Wolf Roland, and her husband Adolf in Weyerdehlen near Worpswede, a well-known art colony outside of Bremen. Here the Darjes lived in an old farmhouse, similar to the one in Horstedt. We were, as everywhere else, received like royalty and had been given a good noon meal, called *Mittagessen*, which is more than a lunch. Most people in Germany used to take a nap after this noon meal. Leo and I were not tired and decided to take a walk. "Be sure to take an umbrella," our host, Jane, warned. "There will be rain." We looked at the sky. It was a brilliant blue with just a few little clouds on the horizon. We thought that we would be back in a short time and did not bother to take any protection against rain. A lovely little path led us to a beautiful green meadow dotted with black and white cows, stretching to the horizon. We were strolling along a silvery brook when suddenly big clouds gathered directly above us. Rumbling of distant thunder was heard.

"We better turn around now," said practical Leo. We started to run toward the farmhouse when the first drops fell, and after a few seconds the whole sky seemed to come down. We arrived at the house completely drenched. There was not a dry fiber on our bodies. Our hosts had just gotten up from their nap and were sorry to see us in such a state. They hurried to get us into a hot bath and supplied us with dry clothes from their own closets. When, later in the afternoon, we arrived at the family gathering in Horstedt, we must have made a strange-looking couple in clothes too wide and too long. But my husband and I will never forget that walk on the green meadows in northern Germany.

Once we were dry and comfortable again, we sat around the fire in the cozy livingroom, and Jane, the oldest daughter of Milly Becker and Hans Rohland, and Adolf told us many things about the Becker family. Some of those stories I had know before, but my memory had faded, and I also wanted Leo to hear whose grave we just had visited.

Worpswede and the Beckers: Before we went to Weyerdehlen, where later on we would be surprised by a cloud burst, we had visited the grave of the artist Paula Moderson-Becker, Wulf Rohland's aunt, the youngest sister of his mother, Milly Rohland, née Becker. In my house in Castro Valley are several copies of pictures by this post-impressionist painter.

Paula's family was involved with our family in several ways, not by blood, but by intermarriage and friendship. Her mother had been an old friend of the family. Großmutter Becker, who lived in the *Knusperhaus* in Bremen, represented one of my first childhood memories. Her name was Mathilde, like mine, and I loved her—but she passed away when I was only a little over five years old. She had a large family, and several of her children became part of our family. Her oldest daughter, Milly, became the wife of Hans Rohland, a huge, good-looking man. They had four tall handsome sons and one daughter, Jane, our host in Weyerdehlen, where Leo and I had our adventure with the rainstorm. Peter, the oldest of the boys, had married first. Both of my sisters, Julie and Dorothee, were good friends with all the Rohlands, and once loved the youngest son, Hans, at the same time, which was the cause of some jealousy. Dorothee later fell in love with the two older brothers, Rudolf and Wulf—she could not decide which of the two to marry. She asked me—I was then about eighteen—which one I thought would be the better choice, and I responded that Rudolf was better looking and therefore would be my pick. When after a while Rudolf made other plans, there was only one choice left. If Dorothee wanted to marry a Rohland boy, it had to be Wulf, and Wulf it was. Dorothee was already studying medicine and was in the middle of her exams when the wedding took place in 1937 in Düsseldorf. Unfortunately I had come down with a bad case of the flu and my parents felt that I should stay home. But as soon as my parents had left, I started to feel better and, independent as I was, inquired about trains to Düsseldorf, scratched my savings together, and appeared at the reception hall just when dinner was starting. My parents had provided me with the address and phone number of the place where the marriage took place, in case something happened to me. I am still proud of myself for being so independent.

The effort was worthwhile. My sister and her new husband were overjoyed to see me as Dorothee and I had always been very close. She looked lovely in an informal blue gown, and the guests were in a happy state following such a joyful occasion. My parents, of course, were worried that I had gotten up too early and that I would give my disease to some of the guests, but that didn't happen and it was an unforgettable event for me.

Mother Milly and Father Hans lived most of their lives in Basel, Switzerland, and helped many Germans and the young couple during the war by smuggling food across the border between Switzerland and Germany. Smuggling, of course was not permitted. Travelers crossing the border were examined for taxable goods and, if they had some, had to pay duty. The story goes that Milly, who was rather stout, possessed several petticoats with large pockets, which she filled with goods that needed to be paid for with a hefty duty. She told suspicious customs collectors at the German border that she had nothing to declare and came to her friends and family loaded with good Swiss food stuffs. Unfortunately she was found out one time and so her smuggling endeavors had to be discontinued.

Two sons of Großmutter Becker also became close to our family. The oldest son, Kurt, became a doctor and had five children. He married Gertrud Sander, whose sister-in-law was the mother of Irmgard Sander, my classmate from upper school. Like Milly, he and his wife had four sons and one daughter. In order to be distinguished from other Beckers, he added "Glauch" to his name. The Becker-Glauch children were very close friends with us four Apelts, and we spent many hours together in our mutual houses. Uncle Kurt, the doctor, had a hip ailment and had difficulty moving around. He therefore had his practice in his large house in the center of Bremen. He and his wife raised their children very methodically and the story goes that none of the children could use more than one handkerchief during the span of one week. Once Elisabeth had a cold and asked for another handkerchief, though it was only Wednesday.

"But Elisabeth, a fresh handkerchief in the *middle* of the week?" she was scolded by her mother.

Three of their sons fell in the war and the two remaining children, Wulf and Elisabeth, both became doctors. Elisabeth never married and still lives in the charming little house, so much like the gingerbread house in *Hänsel and Gretel,* in the suburbs of Bremen.

Another son of Großmutter Becker was Henner, who later married Tante Lotte. She was my mother's sister who had first married the painter Anton Albers, with whom she had two children, Dirk and Susanne Albers. Thus, they were our cousins and we knew them well. After the painter's death, Tante Lotte married Henry Becker, who was affiliated with the Navy and ran a tight ship in his household. I remember that I was afraid of him. My mother loved to be invited by the Beckers because I always behaved well when Uncle Henner was around. They lived in Rönnebeck, a small village downstream from Bremen, where they had a house on the water. We enjoyed their private beach and rowed in their rowboat. It would have been like a vacation to be in Rönnebeck had it not been for Uncle Henner!

Tante Herma was Henner's twin sister. I forget the name of her husband, but she had a son named Peter with whom I had my first written correspondence when I was only six years old. That relationship was a platonic one.

The youngest member of the Beckers was Paula. I had never met her because she had already died in 1907 as a young woman, after she had given birth to a little girl. I had met this daughter of Paula, Tille Moderson, several times at the Kunsthalle, but had never made the connection between her and her famous mother. I admired Paula's art and tried to understand her highly unusual pictures. My mother rejected her paintings; I guess, Paula's art was too "progressive" for her conservative taste. Paula always had been headstrong and determined to become a painter. She studied in Paris, developed her own style and lived most of her young life in Worpswede where she and other artists had developed a famous center for contemporary art. Clara Westhoff, the sculptress, was a close friend of Paula.

Rainer Maria Rilke, the poet, visited Worpswede once to accept an invitation by the painter Heinrich Vogeler. He met the two female artists—the three of them being of the same age, about twenty-four—and fell in love with both of them. Although Rilke found the girls very different, Clara Westhoff was outgoing, exuberant, and full of life, while Paula Becker struck him as shy, thoughtful, and reserved. He could not make up his mind whom he liked better. He felt more drawn to Paula, his "blond" paintress, and had wonderful conversations with her. But Paula decided to marry the painter Otto Moderson, though he was considerably older and had a child from his previous marriage. So Paula solved Rilke's indecision, and he turned to Clara who accepted his proposal.

Paula never felt very secure in her marriage because she was struggling with unknown forces within herself that pulled her constantly toward an undefined goal for her painting. She knew what she wanted to achieve, but it almost seemed to be an unreachable goal. Spending some time in Paris away from her husband, helped her regain her stability a little. Her pictures became increasingly abstract, and she felt a growing chasm arising between her and her husband. To please him and to run the household became a burden, rather than a happy, fulfilled life.

In 1906 Paula suffered from a deep depression. She thought of dissolving her marriage. However, after living for a while by herself in Paris, she changed her mind and invited Otto to join her. In the beginning of 1907 she became pregnant and was looking forward to the birth of her child. However, only two weeks after the birth of her daughter, another Mathilde, she died of an embolism. She had never been able to adjust to married life.

She was buried at the foot of the only elevation in all of northern Germany, the Weyerberg, where a beautifully sculptured monument adorns her resting place. It was *her* grave that we had visited.

Somehow the artistic vein of the Beckers is still preserved in the daughter of Jane and Adolf Darjes, Hille, who is an actress, and in also Dorothee's son Wulf

Jr., who became a potter and, together with his Parisian wife, creates beautiful dishes.

My sister Dorothee, who lost her husband Wulf Rohland soon after the couple had visited us in 1988, and lived by herself in Kleve close to the Holland border until her death in 2004, remained a close friend of Wulf and Elisabeth Becker-Glauch. She owned several original paintings by Paula that are becoming more and more valuable for their everlasting quality. The Beckers' talent for art was continued in Dorothee's daughter Jane, who became a restaurateur of paintings and worked in this capacity for the art museum in Bremen. My father, who had always been interested in the development of the Kunsthalle, and was asked to decide what pictures to buy—he became the head of the Kunstverein soon after he had married, was instrumental in acquiring originals of the Worpswede circle together with other German, French, and Italian masters.

During the war my father managed to have most of the paintings shipped to different places in the East of Germany, hoping to save them that way from destruction. Some of these pictures came back after the war was over, some did not. It was hard to make decisions during those times!

My daughter Doris discovered the art of Paula Becker during her studies abroad and decided to write a paper about this distant related artist for a class at the University of California at Berkeley. I was amazed when I found two original paintings by Paula at the art museum in Berkeley. It shows that the interest in the northwest German art colony had reached across the ocean, even to the west coast of our continent.

So we had a good time talking about the Beckers and their descendents.

In the afternoon, after the showers had ceased, Adolf brought us to Horstedt where my sister Julie, my mother, and the other guests were happy to see us. Our wet clothes were dried in Julie's clothes drier and Adolf took his clothes, which we had worn when we came to Horstedt, back again to his home. We had a very informative time and had learned many facts about my family.

Müden: Between Bremen and Hamburg, on the outskirts of the Lüneburger Heide, (heath near Lüneburg), lies Müden, the little town where Leo's family stayed for several years after the war, before setting off to America. Leo and I visited Müden one day and I saw where he had lived and worked. It was heartwarming to see that many people there still remembered him, especially some pretty women. "Ach, der Leo!" we heard several times, which showed me how popular he must have been.

Leo also showed me the house where the family had lived for several years and their workshop, now an abandoned shed. We stopped by the house where our sister-in-law Leni had grown up and had a chat with Mother Herzberg, Leni's mother. It was moving to delve into the past of my husband's life, and I would love to plan a trip to the east of Germany with an excursion to Poland and the area where Leo had grown up. This trip would include a visit to Vienna and Berlin, both of which I had never seen. But somehow so far this trip has never happened.

The Rhine: After one week of being with family in Bremen, Leo had had enough and wanted to go on. We visited my sister Dorothee and her husband Wulf (whose sister had been our host in Worpswede) in Kleve near Düsseldorf close to the Rhine River. The Rohlands took us on a tour to Amsterdam, which was a great experience with its *Grachten*, canals within the city that give it the name "Venice of the North". We even took a boat ride on one of those waterways. We saw an impressive collection of Rembrandt paintings, now housed in a new museum of its own. The famous *Nachtwache* (Night Watch) was exhibited in a separate room by itself and impressed us much more than seeing the picture in an art book.

Instead of a tour *bus*, we took a tour *boat* in Amsterdam.

We left Kleve after a few days and drove leisurely up the Rhein (German spelling), taking in as many castles and ruins as we possibly could. "Just one more castle," was my constant plea (I was reminded of my father saying that in Italy when I was sixteen and had to trot along with my parents), and Leo had to admit that every one was worth the effort. About three hundred Burgen (castles) are said to be in this historic part of Germany, some so old that only an arch remains, the Rolandbogen, others still in good condition and inhabited by descendants of royal families. We saw three of all those old castles: the Rheinstein, the Harburg, and Ehrenbreitstein. The first is one of those well preserved tall structures, perched high upon a rock, visible from far and still maintained by the royal family that owns it. They don't live there; they rent some of the rooms out. We had to climb up many stairs to get to the entrance, so it was understandable that Leo had enough seeing just one castle.

However, after we had crossed the Rhein at Koblenz, we saw the mighty fortress Ehrenbreitstein, and Leo's interest perked up. "Let's see this one," he said and we parked our car on the right side of the Rhine and hiked up to the entrance. We were amazed when we saw the solid walls of this fortress. Some of them were six feet wide and the windows were like small tunnels. We saw canons and weapons, we took a tour of the living quarters for the soldiers, and we understood why Germany was able to withstand the enemy from the west for centuries. Nearby by is the Harburg, also on the right side of the Rhine—it has torture chambers and dungeons and was a gloomy experience for us.

Much later I would return to the Rhein with my four children and see yet two more Burgen, the Marksburg above Braubach and the Drachenfels near Königs-swinter. Those are very different relics, the first claims the honor of being the best kept Burg of the entire Rhein valley and the other of being the worst one. Only a few rocks and much rubble remain of that old castle. However, from the site of this ruin there is a wonderful view as far as the eye can see, provided it's a clear day. Below those old ruins a much younger Schloß has been erected just a few hundred years ago, which had to undergo renovations in 2005, when we were in Germany to celebrate my sister's ninetieth and my daughter's fiftieth birthday. We had traveled along the Rhine for two days before we arrived in Bremen. Now back to our trip in 1970.

When, still on the left side of the Rhein, we reached Das Deutsche Eck (German Corner), I had strange feelings looking across the Rhine from the tall cliff we were standing. About two hundred miles further south lies Strasbourg and I remembered standing on the west side of the bridge leading to Kehl, which is still German, from Strassburg, which would turn the same evening—November 23, 1944—into Strasbourg and would turn into a French city. Shortly after that I would become a prisoner of war.

After having seen the two castles near Koblenz, we left the Rhein and drove through the lovely Schwarzwald (Black Forest), past the falls of the Rhein by Schaffhausen, had our car ferried across the Bodensee (Lake Constance)—also evoking bittersweet memories from my time as a prisoner—and drove across the Swiss border to St. Gallen, where Peter Deuel's brother Herbert resided with his family.

Switzerland and the Deuels: The Deuels are Jewish and had to flee from Germany in order to survive. Peter's father and brother Hans had been brutally murdered by Nazi fanatics and the other sons did not want to suffer the same fate. The only daughter, Herma, fled to South Africa and some of her descendents are still living there. Another brother, Leo Deuel, writer of scientific books about geological history, immigrated to America and is still living in New York. Hans's name is living on in Peter Deuel's son, Hans Pascal Deuel who lives now in Mill Valley and has two sons of his own, Pascal and Jesse.

Herbert went to St. Gallen in Switzerland, where he established a successful medical practice. Peter decided to follow his brother Leo and embarked on a ship to the United States as kitchen helper. Soon he was promoted from dish washer to cook and arrived in New York in this capacity. Later he studied chemistry and became a professor at Sacramento State College, now Sacramento State University. Here he met Edith and married her, as already told. He had to suffer discrimination from her parents who were prejudiced against Jewish people in general. The elder Schmidts had had bad experiences when they where living in Poland during the war and did not trust anyone who was Jewish. Edith, who had given up so much in Germany to join her parents in America, was very unhappy about this. After many years of shunning Edith's husband the parents, first the mother, and later the father, observed that Edith's marriage was a happy one and had to admit that they had been wrong in their judgment. Now Peter is the patriarch of our family. He celebrated his ninetieth birthday in 2005 in Sacramento surrounded by family.

Not until the 1990's would Edith and Peter have a chance traveling to Switzerland and seeing Herbert and his family though they were warmly invited. When we told them of our intent to visit the Deuels in St. Gallen, they enthusiastically gave us Herbert's address and also wrote to him to prepare his family for our visit.

Therefore, in 1970, we were received like one of their family and enjoyed the red-carpet treatment. Herbert Deuel and his family were living in a beautiful house on Rorschachstraße. Everything in this four-story house was a work of art, beginning with the oak floors that are inlaid with multicolored wood. The furniture and doors are handmade by craftsmen who were born and raised in the area. Herbert told us that his house was not exceptional, and indeed we noticed on a tour around the city how many houses possessed intricately carved front doors. The Swiss and the Germans are famous for the *Fachwerkhäuser* (frame-wood style houses) in which the beams that carry the house are not covered by paint but stand out and are artistically carved and adorned.

Herbert himself gave us a tour of the ancient cloister of St.Gallen, where the first books ever written are found, carefully protected in glass shrines. Every visitor has to don felt shoes to save the beautiful inlaid floors. The highlight of that sidetrip into Switzerland was a tour to the Säntis—a mountain in the foothills of the Alps that is described in the book *Heidi* by Johanna Spyri. A gondola brought us up to the top of the Säntis, from where we had a spectacular view of the snow-covered Alps. We drove on to Austria and stayed one night in Innsbruck. From there we leisurely ambled back through the *Romantische* Straße (Romantic Road) with its medieval little towns like Rothenburg and Nordhausen (traveled before by me in wartimes, under different circumstances), saw a few more castles, and ended up again in Frankfurt where we spent a few days with the In der Schmittens. I would see this delightful family one more time in 1982 after my mother had passed away and I would come by myself to Germany.

When we came home to Castro Valley after five weeks, the children looked happy and well cared for, the house was spotless, and there was the new black kitten, which they had named Willi. Diana and John had done a good job!

Trips to England: In 1984 our daughter Doris and her husband Charlie Michaels lived still in Zurich, both slowly moving up in their chosen careers. Charlie's parents, Chuck and Christa Michaels, lived at that time in Beaconsfield close to London and they invited us to visit them. We always had a wonderful relationship with them and gladly accepted. We spent one week with the elder Michaels at their lovely home, played golf, visited Stratford on Avon, Shakespeare's town, and Blenheim, the home of Sir Winston Churchill together, and hiked in the green, lush hills of the area. During the second week of our stay my sister Julie joined us and all of us toured Salisbury Cathedral, Stonehenge, and Oxford. We missed seeing Doris and Charlie, but Switzerland was far too far away to visit each other.

Later, after the young Michaels had been transferred to London, we were again invited to England, this time to stay with our children who lived in a luxurious apartment in Hampstedt, close to Hampstedt Heath, where we attended several cultural events, sitting on the grassy hills, munching picnic food provided by Doris, and enjoying shows and concerts. My sister Dorothee was also invited and enjoyed the ambiance of Hampstedt. "I am in the city of Keats!" She started to recite, "*My heart aches, and a drowsy numbness pains…,*" but we were not in the mood to listen to the *Ode to a Nightingale,* and Charlie said cheerfully, "Lets have lunch, I'm starving." Dorothee stepped out of her poetic mood and confessed that she also was hungry. These two England trips took place after the children were married, so we were free to do what we wanted. Also another trip to Europe took place in 1988 that will be described later when two important family events occurred, Opa's death and Denali's birth.

One of the highlights of those trips to England was seeing Shakespeare's *The Merry Wives of Windsor* in Regents Park in the open air theater and afterwards strolling along the Thames River. Of course, we also visited the popular sights, the Tower with its crown jewels, and Windsor Castle. We even took a mini course in golfing. We had a great time with the Michaels.

Trips With Children

<u>The Trip to Yellowstone</u>: In 1971 we decided to go on a long family trip, this time to Yellowstone Park—not a backpack trip, but our first longer excursion by car. Our children were growing up rapidly. Leo Hermann was almost eighteen and would be graduating from high school soon, Doris and Barbara were sixteen and fourteen, and Marty was eleven. Leo prepared for the trip by buying a big new car, a Chevrolet Suburban, and mapping out the trip. I was in charge of the provisions and entertainment. Since this was our first non-backpacking trip, we had fewer restrictions on our choice of equipment, could even take larger tents, a little cook stove, books, games, and more clothing than we could before. We decided to make a huge loop, getting to Wyoming via Nevada, Utah and the southern tip of Idaho and coming back through Montana, northern Idaho, Washington, Oregon, and back to California on Highway 5.

That wonderful two week trip had a few highlights worth mentioning. We were driving through the Nevada basin and range desert and decided to spend our first night on top of Ruby Alps, one of the ranges. I had learned in Hamburg from Professor Kolb that the Nevada desert is not one big flat area, but it is interspersed by many mountain ranges, some of them rather high. We found a lovely campground by Angel Lake that fulfilled every promise of that heavenly name.

"This is the desert?" we asked, looking around from our lofty spot and beholding a lovely panorama of snowcapped mountains.

Angel Lake, a small round, clear blue water hole, lies right under a waterfall, fed by a snow field, and sends a little creek down to the desert. We fished, swam, and hiked around the lake. On a rock Marty even found an abandoned wallet that contained nine dollars and a camera with film still in it. We had the film developed later and had beautiful pictures of the little lake.

In Utah, near Wendover, the salt flats started. Our children were excited to see vast fields of a white substance and wanted Leo to stop and give them a chance to investigate closer. Leo not only stopped the car; he drove onto the salt flats to see if the surface could bear the weight of our vehicle (he had seen tracks on the salt). That was a mistake, because the salt just formed a thin layer over a deep bed of mud and did not support our truck. When Leo stopped the car, it instantly started sinking into the mud. We all ran and gathered sagebrush and wood to fill the hole under the tires, but in vain. A police car came by and stopped. Four tall men came out and helped us. A huge truck with two big cowboys also stopped. They whipped out an enormous jack, but nothing helped. The jack just sank in too, and the axle of our Suburban was almost in the mud. Finally the two cowboys connected our car to their truck with ropes and chains and pulled us out. That was close!

We drove on with mud still clinging to our tires and reached the shore of the Great Salt Lake. We had heard so much about the sensation of weightlessness one feels when swimming in concentrated salt water, so we had to try it. It *was* an experience, but not very pleasant. The lake was warm and sticky, swarming with insects—mostly tiny brine shrimp, and very salty. It felt strange to be held up by the water like a cork.

In Salt Lake City we saw the famous tabernacle and the Seagull Monument. Fortunately it was Sunday and there was no temptation to buy anything. We washed the salt off our bodies in Bear Lake on the border of Utah and Idaho and then entered Wyoming on scenic Route 89, which led us through beautiful Swiss-like valleys, passed the snow-covered Great Tetons and went into Yellowstone Park where we camped for several days. Just before we were ready to camp, the girls started wrinkling their noses. "Something stinks!"

We searched and found a coffee can with decaying earthworms that our fisherman, Marty, had stocked up on and forgotten. Poor Marty! Everybody was mad at him. After the coffee can was disposed of, we had peace again and enjoyed being at our destination. When we went to see Old Faithful, we were told that it had just erupted and we had to wait at least one hour. We sat down in the front row and waited patiently. Finally the performance began: a little eruption about three feet high, after five minutes another one even lower, and after a while just a burp. We had witnessed a dud. Leo had had enough and the rest of us called the geyser "Old Unfaithful."

We left Yellowstone on the north side, after visiting the colorful terraces created by the Mammoth Hot Springs and almost burning our fingers in the boiling hot waters. We drove back through Montana where two events were outstanding: one, a side trip to the Flathead Indian Reservoir where we saw a bison range, and the other in Butte, where a copper strip mine had created a huge hole in the earth. We drove through northern Idaho into Washington and saw the mighty Columbia River, where salmon and sturgeon climbed fish ladders to spawn upstream. In a fish hatchery we saw huge sturgeons, several feet long.

Near Walla Walla we crossed into Oregon, where we had planned to visit some friends near Portland and relatives in Salem. The friends were the Dosters, whom we knew from Lodi and whose farm we had often visited. They had invited us to drop in any time, and were very happy to see us, and showed us proudly what they had accomplished on their thirty-acre farm. We also took a nice trip together, the two couples and eight children, to Mt. Hood and the surrounding ranges of the Cascades.

The warm welcome we received from the Dosterts made us brave enough to travel to Salem and to drop in at the Roleders, Leo's sponsors in America, our pastor and uncle who had married Opa's sister, Aunt Selma. Uncle Roleder had retired from the ministry a few years before and they lived peacefully in a retirement home in Salem. What we did not know was that the day after we arrived, all six of us tired and dirty, there was a big family event planned, the fiftieth wedding anniversary of the Roleders! All four of their children, three of them pastors like their father, were gathering in Salem for this family festivity—they were very busy getting ready for the next day's happenings and had no time for us. We noticed at once the inappropriateness of our showing up *en masse* unannounced and wanted to leave. But somehow, the Roleders got over the shock, talked to each other, and invited us to stay at least for one night. We were lodged in trailers, on sofas, and on the floor and after all we had a wonderful evening together. We left early the next morning in order not to interfere with the ceremony.

On the long way home on Highway 5, Leo got carried away and got a speeding ticket, his first and last ticket ever.

Backpacking in Yosemite: I remember several backpacking trips after the one to Dog Lakes in 1971 after our Yellowstone excursion, each one with relatives or friends. In 1972, we had the granddaughter of my mother's sister Paula with us, Silke Rodewald, who had just finished school and decided to be a school teacher. She brightened our summer with her cheerful personality, taught us different crafts, and is still a very good friend of my daughter Doris. We took her with us backpacking and she was a wonderful companion for all of us. One time our Marty, the ever adventurous one, took off by himself to investigate Camp Merced, the goal for the following day, and did not return by dark. Leo and Silke went after him and, with the help of a ranger, found him looking for us by Camp Merced, not realizing what anguish he had caused us.

On that trip we also had a bear encounter. Leo always secured our backpacks, especially the food supplies, with ropes in trees around us so that bears could not get at them. One night we heard a noise. We scrambled out of our sleeping bags and there was a mother bear working on the ropes to hoist down our packs for her and her two cubs. She even taught the cubs how to hold the rope. Fortunately, we had a pot and lid handy and made loud banging noises which sent the mother and her cubs scrambling.

Silke later married a school teacher and now lives close to Bremen with her family; she still keeps in touch with my daughters and me. I visit her whenever I am in Bremen.

Barbara goes to Bremen Later that year we sent our daughter Barbara to Germany. Leo was against her traveling alone, but I persuaded him that she was old enough, in fact two years older than her sister had been, to venture out so far away. Again, the main objectives of this visit were for Barbara to see her grandmother and, of course, to get acquainted with the rest of the family. Barbara stayed at my mother's house all the time and even celebrated Christmas there. I am sorry that we were so concerned about Barbara not being a burden to the Kulenkampffs that we did not give her the permission to join them on a ski trip to Switzerland, so poor Barbara had to stay in Bremen with her grandmother while all the cousins had a good time skiing. Parents are not always right. But she looked happy and glad to see us all again when we picked her up at the airport at the end of Christmas vacation.

Grandparents' Golden Anniversary in Lodi: In May of 1973 a big family event took place: the fiftieth wedding anniversary of Leo's parents in Lodi. Edith and I had prepared a little play in honor of the couple. It involved all available grandchildren and a narrator. The play was performed in the garden behind the grandparents' house on Forrest Avenue in Lodi. The invited guests, the honored couple, the Roleders, the Schmidts—Alex and Anna, Dagobert and Leni, and the Deuels, were seated on benches placed on the lawn and we staged our play in front of them. The play consisted of seven scenes. The first was "Life in Russia", which showed how Waldemar made baskets to help his starving family and the second scene showed how he met Alice, who wanted to become a school teacher. Their first kiss, their wedding, their life in Poland where they had to flee from the communists, their life in Müden after fleeing from Poland in 1945 and finally their decision to move to America were the scenes that followed. The roles were played by the following actors: Waldemar by Doris, Alice by Barbara, Edith by Carol Ann, Leo by Marty, and Dagobert by little Hansi Deuel. I was the narrator and prompter. The entire script was in German and the children were wonderful. The play was a great success and the grandparents were overwhelmed. We would do more plays in the future.

Charlotte's Visit: In the following summer we had another young visitor from Bremen, this time the youngest daughter of my sister Julie, Charlotte, who, like Silke and her older sister Julie, had finished her *Abitur* and was planning to go to the university; however not to become a teacher like Silke and Julie, but a doctor. Her decision to visit us happened rather suddenly. We had planned to go on a week-long backpacking trip around July 4th, and Charlotte arrived on the last day of June, just a day before we were to leave. She must have been a little shocked when, instead of lolling leisurely in the nice California sun with her cousins, she was asked to don hiking gear and start on a strenuous hiking tour—even carry a heavy pack on her shoulders. But she took it all in stride, kept up with all of us veterans, and even earned the award for having the dirtiest clothes at the end of our trip. She had begun the hike in bright yellow pants that were black when we came home from our trip. She was such a determined person, achieving all of her ambitious plans, gaining admission to a prestigious university, and becoming a doctor, even marrying a doctor.

More trips and excursions were done by our family, but one of them was exceptional because Leo Hermann almost lost his legs.

The Midnight Hike of Leo Schmidt: One more backpacking trip to Yosemite happened in 1975, the year before we bought our cabin and it warrants special attention. This time we went with our good friends, Les and Shirley Kuller. There were five children in our group; three from our family since Doris was already studying abroad in Göttingen, and two of the Kuller's children, Loanne and Matthew. The trip, planned carefully by placing two cars at different locations in the vast park, ended abruptly with an almost fatal accident. Our son, Leo Hermann, already in college in San Luis Obispo for three years, had bought himself a pair of shining new hiking boots and wore them on the trip without having broken them in. He soon developed blisters and, in his quiet way, he suffered without telling us about his pains until he could not stand it any longer. We happened to be at a very remote spot in the middle of our trip, Benson Lake. Leo Hermann's legs had already begun to show signs of blood poisoning.

My husband made a quick decision. We left Leo Hermann at Benson Lake, in the care of his brother and sister. I was to go on with the Kullers and find a camp spot that night. (There was not enough room to put up tents at Benson Lake.) Then we were to hike out to Glen Allen above Tuolomne Meadows, where one of our cars was parked.

Leo himself was doing the seemingly impossible task of walking out as fast as he could to the authorities to get help for Leo Hermann. He did this hike of about twenty-two miles nonstop through the night in about ten hours—armed with only a flashlight, a compass, a map and a sandwich and, after he had arrived at Glen Allen, had a helicopter sent to Benson Lake to pick up our son and bring him to the nearest hospital on the Valley floor to receive the necessary care.

Marty and Barbara, who had faithfully stayed with their brother through the night and tried to make him as comfortable as they could, hailed the incoming helicopter and led it to their brother. After seeing Leo Hermann safely tucked away in the aircraft and watching its take-off, they started on their way to Glen Allen. The Kullers and I had spent the night at another lake, wondering how everything would work out.

How relieved we were when next morning we met Marty and Barbara on the way and heard that Leo Hermann was taken care of! So my husband must have reached his goal. Now we all had to hike the rest of the way out and meet Leo. When we finally reached Glen Allen, we saw a very tired Leo walking slowly toward us, unshaved and dirty, but happy to see us. He had reached the ranger station at five o'clock in the morning, had waited for the helicopter to get Leo Hermann, had taken him to the hospital where our son was treated, had brought him home to Castro Valley (a four-hour trip) and had just returned to meet us and bring the Kullers back to their car!

I still cannot comprehend how all this was accomplished, but Leo had saved our son's legs, if not his life. Father and son needed a few days of rest after this ordeal and Leo Hermann never took a hike in brand-new boots again.

Marty and I Visit Bremen: The trip to Yosemite with Charlotte in 1984 triggered yet another visit to Germany. This time I decided to go without Leo and visit Bremen together with our youngest son, Marty. He was then fourteen and wanted to see his grandmother too. Our family in Bremen invited us to come, so nothing stood in the way except the usual reluctance of my husband to let us go. But we prevailed, and toward summer's end, just in time to be back for school in September, my son and I went to Germany and enjoyed being so close together for two weeks. I had not been in Bremen for ten years and had the time of my life seeing the family again. Little did I know that this would be the last time I would see my mother. I stayed in my old room overlooking the garden. Marty alternated between living at the house of my mother and that of the Kulenkampffs. Christoph, who did not have sons, enjoyed having Marty as house guest very much. The two went together to soccer games and had "man-to-man talks".

My mother had aged considerably since my last visit. She was now ninety years old and had become rather frail. Quiet Barbara had been a comfort to her—but vivacious Marty was sometimes too much. She was very good to him, asked him what she could do to make him happy, and when he boldly asked for a pair of Lederhosen, she gave him enough money for two pairs, one for him and one for his best friend in Castro Valley. He often shuttled between the houses of the Kulenkampffs and my mother's, dribbling his basketball on the way.

At my sister's house, the two youngest girls were still living there and people were always coming and going, so our Marty fit right in. He and Uncle Christoph loved to watch television together, especially the then popular *Bonanza* sitcom, in German, of course.

Now all four of our children had seen their grandmother in Bremen and I could assure Leo that I would not bother him again with sending them over while they were so young. Later, of course, they traveled on their own or with their spouses.

Our visits to our married children in California should not be forgotten. Leo and Sharyn had settled in Arroyo Grande near San Luis Obispo toward southern California, and Barbara and Randy moved north, first to Santa Rosa and later to the rapidly developing city of Windsor. They had nice homes and each couple had two children. We visited both families frequently and had a chance to observe Blair and Donica, Jason and Brandon growing up.

My Scholastic Life, Learning and Teaching

This concludes our family trips because in 1976, we started a new chapter in our lives: we bought a cabin in the Sierras. Before I start writing about that consequential event, I would like to turn back to the year 1966, when I decided to go back to school. I had been teaching German to adults in the evening for a few years since 1964 and would be doing so until 1984. I loved doing it. But soon I felt that I could do more and wanted a full-time job. I could not get enough.

Obtaining Credentials: While our family was enjoying the long summer vacations together with friends, at the swimming pool, in the garden, and on trips and visits, the rest of the year was dedicated to school work. In 1966, when all my children were in school, I had more time on my hands than I used to have. After I had started teaching at the adult school, the principal, Dr. Marvin Smith, had asked me repeatedly to get a credential for this job, easy to obtain at the brand-new college at Hayward not far from Castro Valley. I enrolled in two required courses and liked going back to school so much that I did not stop at getting the adult school credential, but went on working for a full credential that would allow me to teach at any high school or junior high school, not just German, but math, biology, and geography as well. Because I had already done so much work in all those fields in Germany and had taken educational courses in Stockton, it only took about eighteen months, including student teaching in Newark, not far from us, to finish up and receive life credentials for teaching German and math as major fields, biology and geography as minors. In 1968 I had accomplished my goal and was ready to look for a job.

In retrospect I am not so sure that it was wise to put my aspirations so high at my age. I was forty-two years old when I started to work for my high school credentials and really should have stayed with my adult school job, which was so satisfying. But I got greedy and also addicted to going to college.

Let me describe what went on at home while I was starting to live my own life. In 1966 our children ranged in age from thirteen to six years old and still needed their mother very much. So I planned my classes whenever possible around school hours. Should a class fall into the late afternoon or evening, I cooked a casserole early in the morning, put it in the oven, and had the girls turn it on and heat it in time for dinner. Every one of the children had chores to do: setting the table, serving the meal, and cleaning up. Poor Leo had a lot of casseroles to eat during this time. He was not quite sure if he liked to have a wife who went to college, but he did not know what was yet in store for him. Actually, I still had enough spare time between classes to do my other household work, to tend my beloved garden, to supervise the children's school work and practicing their instruments, and to enjoy life.

Getting a Job: Things became hectic, though, when I started a teaching job that was offered to me at the junior high school in Castro Valley, A. B. Morris, the same school Leo Hermann had already gone through, Doris was attending now, and Barbara would enter the following year. I was offered a half-time position as a German teacher and thought that this was ideal and would fit well into my busy life. I would, for the first time, make a regular salary. The adult school teaching was only scheduled once or twice a week for two hours, while now I would teach every day for four hours. What I did not realize was that teaching children was entirely different from teaching adults, especially junior high school-aged children. Innocently thinking that I could handle children well, as my own children had proven, I discovered to my dismay that standing in front of an entire class of young teenagers was a completely new experience. The children were noisy, rude, obstinate, and did not mind me at all. They must have noticed at once that I was new and inexperienced at being a teacher and they took full advantage of it. I was told by the other teachers to be firm and calm, and to concentrate on the lessons. "Just don't let them get to you" or "Today must not be your day," they would say nonchalantly when I mentioned my troubles to them in the teachers' lounge.

I had learned in college that it was most important to be prepared for each lesson. I was not only prepared; I was over prepared. So many lesson plans, so many dittos, so much homework for the students—no wonder they revolted! It was so hard to calm them down that I gave quizzes almost daily, just to have some moments of peace. As in any normal classroom, the bulk of my three classes consisted of good students who were willing to learn, but there were a few troublemakers who stirred up unrest. With all my years of learning, I had not mastered the art of controlling those instigators and therefore lost control of the entire class. I was glad that my own children were not in any of my classes to watch their mother's dismay. Doris was a busy eighth grader and had chosen Spanish for her language requirement and Barbara was still in sixth grade at the elementary school.

Things got a little better toward the end of the school year. I was less tense, the troublemakers got tired of taunting me; everyone wanted a good grade, and I thought that now the worst was behind me. During the spring quarter of 1969, Mr. Kerr, our principal, came into my classroom several times for evaluation, sat quietly in the back, and took notes. Of course, the children behaved wonderfully when he came in, no discipline problems, just rows and rows of little angels. His comments of my teaching methods were satisfactory, little things had to be improved: "Don't raise your voice, that irritates the students," and "Don't teach with your back toward the class, so you're always watching the students," and other golden rules, easy to understand but oh, so hard to follow!

I was looking forward to another year of teaching after a long relaxing summer vacation. But then the blow struck—my German position was not available anymore. The economy had worsened, teachers were dismissed all over, others had to double their load, and classes were enlarged. In the foreign language department, high school teachers had to take over the half-time positions at the junior high schools and my position was taken by Mrs. Wheeler, the long-time German teacher at Castro Valley High School. My principal, Mr. Kerr, told me the sad news on the last day of school and also offered me another job, teaching math full-time. That meant six periods of teaching and two preparation periods. Since the job was open and math was my other major field, the job was there to be offered, and, as I had lost my German teaching position due to unforeseen circumstances, he wanted at least to give me a chance to continue working at his school.

Teaching Fiasco: Mr. Kerr did not do me a favor with this offer. I could not resist the temptation of accepting the job, though I should have known better. In my German classes, at least the majority of the students had liked the subject matter. They had done their homework diligently and had been supported by their parents, most of whom had a vital interest in the language; but math was a highly unpopular subject, even hated by many, seldom liked by parents. It was a great challenge to transfer my love for this field to the children and I lacked the skills and confidence to change such unwillingness to learn. Instead of me leading them, they had the upper hand. As I had done the year before, I made the mistake of overloading my students with quizzes, tests, and homework. No wonder they hated me. Also, I had to correct all their papers and that meant going home with stacks of work to be done because the two preparation periods were not nearly long enough to do all of it. Classes were full to the brim. I had close to two hundred students on the roster. Roll call alone was a chore. It had to be done very carefully and had financial consequences for the district if done incorrectly. The only good part of teaching full-time was receiving a full pay check every month, money we could well use in our household with six people.

But man—or woman—does not live on salary alone. Soon my home life began to be affected by me constantly being overworked and unhappy. There was no more time to work and play with the children, I had hardly enough time to do the household chores and the cooking, and the garden was neglected. I became cranky and my husband was more and more irritated with the whole situation. The sign on the wall was there. By Christmas I started to get run-down and sick and found it harder and harder to face the mob every morning. By the end of the winter quarter I had made up my mind. It was living hell and nothing could persuade me to go on—I went to Mr. Kerr and announced my resignation. He did not seem too surprised and told me that I had a very tough assignment, that I should try to get a position with older students, and that he could understand my decision. A substitute teacher, who had taken the classes when I was sick, was asked to finish the school year for me, and my upcoming salary for the three spring months was just enough to compensate the district for my breach of contract.

So I said farewell to my high aspirations of being a math teacher at the junior high school and went home that day with a great feeling of relief. What I had lost in prestige and revenue I had gained in happiness and joy of being a good mother and wife again and easily recovered from the ordeal of the last six months. This happened in the spring of 1970 and triggered my decision to go to Germany with my husband for the five weeks I described above.

Substituting and Home Teaching: When we returned in July of 1970, I started looking for a high school position, but I found that the job market had tightened so much that only teachers with tenure (at least three years of successful teaching) were accepted—if there was an opening. I realized that I would never find a regular job with my spotty background, at least not that year, and signed up as a substitute teacher. Since I had credentials in many different fields, I was qualified to fill in for almost any job that was needed, and I was soon a favorite candidate on the list of four surrounding districts: Castro Valley, San Lorenzo, San Leandro, and Hayward. By nature, substituting was an irregular job, paid as piecework, with no benefits, but also without the stress of responsibilities. I avoided being called for teaching at junior high schools and discovered that I was a good substitute for high school, even liked by the older students and often asked for by the same teachers who (like myself before) were habitually sick, unhappy with their jobs and in need of a break. In a few instances I had to take over a class for an extended period, sometimes weeks, even months. I remember an English class whose teacher had been taunted by her students and had resigned. I gained the confidence of the students by teaching them Greek mythology among other subjects dear to me. For the first time (if I do not count my wonderful experiences with adults), I appreciated the joy of teaching and sharing my knowledge with younger people.

I liked substituting so much that I signed up for the job year after year, and even added home teaching to it. Eventually this one-on-one type of teaching proved to be my real forte, and in time I became the sole home teacher in Castro Valley which was almost as demanding as a full-time job without the horrors of having to confront an unwilling crowd of students daily.

This was the state of my career in 1976. I was in full command of my home life again, had a fulfilling job, and even made some money to buy extras—like nice crystal and silver—or help Leo pay for utilities. Christmas and birthdays were provided for by my income, and we could afford to have summer guests and take our wonderful trips.

Back to College Once More and Obtaining the Masters Degree: In 1978 Leo and I were mostly by ourselves; the house in Castro Valley, which had been so crowded when the four children had lived with us, was all ours and we felt like royalty in a palace. Leo was happy in his job at Manor Research. I was satisfied with substituting and home teaching. Everything was almost too perfect. Leo Hermann was working in San Luis Obispo, Doris lived in Berkeley and was finishing up her studies, Barbara and Marty were occupied with their lives, and on holidays we met at the cabin. The avalanche of marriages had not started yet when I felt that I wanted to go back to college once more. I felt that now was the time to really concentrate on studying and maybe find a good and well-paying job after all my failures in the career world. The demand in the late seventies in the field of teaching was for teachers of the handicapped, who had won great victories for themselves at Capitol Hill in 1973. The handicapped were entitled to an adequate education now by law and teachers were needed for them. I had no difficulty finding a place at California State Hayward in a newly created course for the training of teachers of the handicapped and in less than two years, I was not only the proud recipient of two credentials qualified to teach learning handicapped and severely handicapped persons, but also of the Masters degree in Special Education. I had chosen for my thesis the role of the home teacher with the title *The Broken Leg Syndrome*. This title because many of my home students were ski accident victims with broken legs.

In 1980 three members of our family graduated from college, our two daughters at Berkeley and San Jose and I at Hayward. This month of June in sunny California with the family around us was one of the highlights of my life. This time, I swore to myself, I am going to *use* what I have learned and make a success of my career after all. Why was I so bent on a successful career? And why in teaching?

Teaching the Mentally Handicapped: The next year saw me as the teacher of severely handicapped students in an elementary school in Pleasanton. I had one assistant named Jewel, and what a jewel she was. She practically ran our class of twelve more-or-less severely handicapped students between the ages of twelve and twenty-two. Another class of students *under* the age of twelve was taught by a male teacher who had his wife as an assistant. These two "special" classes were housed in a regular elementary school consisting of students from the first to sixth grade. The purpose of this arrangement was the implementation of the concept "mainstreaming." Though the students in our classes did not participate in regular classrooms, as other handicapped children were doing if they had normal intelligence, they were supposed to mingle during recess and thus were not completely isolated as had been the case before. The "normal" children were thus encouraged to play side by side with our students, and in many cases this arrangement enriched the lives of all students.

My class consisted mainly of children afflicted with Down syndrome. Only a few of them had an IQ of above fifty. We used a system consisting of pictorial codes to give them a feeling of learning to read. Number concepts were practiced with a variety of objects, as were colors and shapes. Money and traffic signs were studied and applied. We played games, did simple crafts, basic cooking, and arts and music appreciation. Hardly any of our students reached a mental capacity of above four years, but most of them developed physically. Some were multi-handicapped; in addition to being mentally retarded they were blind, deaf, or emotionally handicapped. Jewel had been with these young people for several years and knew all their personalities and characteristics well. The students loved and trusted her, whereas I was new to them and they were new to me. We encouraged the parents to come in as often as possible, and often I stayed after school to confer and visit with parents or relatives and got acquainted with the background of each student, the home life, the relationships with brothers and sisters and the neighborhood. Each child was different and represented a whole group of caring people around him or her. I not only touched the lives of my students, but that of their families as well. I also reached out to the other teachers at that school, visited their classrooms, shared parties and activities with them, and had interested students, mostly six graders, visiting our classroom. Our students loved sports; and during recesses we organized basketball and baseball games. Those were two good years and we all were sad to hear that the entire program was discontinued due to lack of funds.

My Accident: Toward the end of those years of teaching the handicapped, I had an accident that totaled my little Volkswagen but left me almost untouched and I was wondering again if I had an angel in heaven watching over me. I was on my way to school, already in Pleasanton, on a ramp leading to an overpass, when my car went off the curb of the road, slammed against a stone lamppost, and tumbled down the shoulder of the ramp, turning completely over. When it came to a stop, I found myself at the bottom of the shoulder, about five feet below the road, and assessed my situation. My body seemed to be in one piece, my satchel was next to me, but the car looked different. I tried to get out, but the driver's side door was stuck. I reached over to the passenger side door and it seemed to work, so I opened it with a push.

After I had climbed out of the car, I saw that this vehicle was not fit to be driven anymore—it was totaled! Not a soul was around. It seemed that nobody had seen my rendezvous with the lamppost. *He*, the lamppost, was my only witness. I scrambled up the hill and observed the cars flitting by. Those drivers probably wondered where I came from. One of them, a teacher at our school, stopped and asked me if I needed a ride to school. It was late, so I agreed and climbed into his car, acting rather dazed. If he was wondering what I was doing with my satchel without car at the side of the road five minutes before classes started, he did not show it and I did not volunteer to tell him.

I went to class as usual, got involved in the usual daily activities and even had a parent conference at the end of the day. However, I had taken a few minutes out of the class time in the morning to phone Leo at work and ask him to pick me up from school. He was horrified when I told him what had happened and asked me if I wanted him to come right away. "No, just be there after work and look for the car if you can."

I hoped that by the same miracle that had saved me, maybe the car might stand there by the road in one piece and the whole thing was a bad dream. Leo was there after work, but hadn't seen a trace of the car. The lamppost stood silently, showing a slight scratch; so Leo could see that I was telling the truth. Together we phoned the Highway Patrol and were told, "Yes, we towed a totaled Carmenghia from the side of the road this morning at 10:16 a.m. If you are the owner of this vehicle, you have to come down to the wrecking yard in Pleasanton and pay your fine for our towing services." When we got to the wrecking yard and saw my poor little vehicle that had served me faithfully for fifteen years, I finally realized that this was reality, that the car was dead, I alive, and somehow life must go on. Again, my Guardian Angel had been involved.

That same day Leo and I went to the nearest car dealer, which happened to be Crown Chevrolet in Pleasanton, and bought a brand-new Chevette which I learned to drive that very evening. Leo also insisted that I see a doctor the next day after work just to make sure everything was all right. The doctor could not detect anything abnormal except a few bruises on my ribcage from bumping against the steering wheel when the car had turned over. Whenever I drove past that spot on the road, I nodded to the lamppost like to an old accomplice—he and I were the only ones who knew!

This would be the second and last year of my career as a handicapped teacher since the Pleasanton School District revamped the handling of their Exceptional Student program, as it was pompously called and they put someone from their own district in my place. I had been hired by the Hayward district and so I was "bumped."

Toastmasters: So, in 1981 I was without a job again and tried other activities. My daughter Doris, happily married now to Charlie, had joined a Toastmaster's group that met in Oakland at a small restaurant close to Lake Merritt, and she invited me to do the same. The location was good for both of us. It was between Berkeley, where she and her husband lived, and my home in Castro Valley. Once a week we met at seven o'clock in the morning in the little café on Grand Avenue and I fulfilled one of the numerous offices every member of the group had to hold such as "speaker," "evaluator," "timekeeper," and so forth. Since everyone was involved at all times, these meetings were never boring and all of us learned to make speeches, present them, capture the attention of the audience, and have impressive beginnings and endings to our speeches. Time was strictly limited—the timekeeper had a flashing device in case of overtime. If you had planned a dramatic finish and ran out of time just before delivery, you had to bite your tongue and stop when the red light flashed. Too bad! Business people, teachers, politicians and anyone who needed to improve his or her speech-making skills took part in this great opportunity. At this time I composed my "Icebreaker," *Life begins at Sixty.*

The rest of my days were spent in catching up with my sorely neglected housework, writing letters to my mother and my children, and just enjoying life. Our garden was so beautiful, working in it so invigorating, and lying on a chaise reading a book so relaxing that we did not need to travel much during this time.

Volunteering at Family Tutorial: Before telling about our cleaning business, which started four years later in 1984, I have to talk first about one more period in my life related to teaching. In 1981, when I had given up on teaching at the public schools and when I had all my time available for a new adventure, I discovered that volunteers were needed at a nonprofit organization called "Family Tutorial." This agency was founded by a remarkable woman, Sotera Brown, whose only goal was to help other people. From her wealthy family she had inherited silver mines in her native Mexico and used the income from these mines toward the fulfillment of her dreams to create an organization that helped poor people of all backgrounds to lead a meaningful life.

When I talked to her about my willingness to help, she happily gave me an assignment as an English teacher to refugees who had just arrived from Afghanistan, having fled the massacres by the Russians in their country. I was supposed to go to the homes of these Afghan families and teach everyone there the rudiments of English. This was a very fulfilling job and the Afghans proved to be willing and bright pupils. I served several families, all housed in cramped little apartments around Hayward. The older children were enrolled in the local schools and learned English there. The little ones learned together with their parents. It was an exhilarating experience to be part of an Afghan family. All family members treated their "teacher" like royalty and listened to every word I uttered. I taught them the basic rudiments of our language that were necessary to be able to survive in our culture, even took the whole family shopping at the nearby supermarket. One thing I did not like was the excessive smoking that most of the fathers did right in front of their children. I told them that I was getting sick from the smoke and they obediently put out their cigarettes or pipes, probably shaking their heads inwardly. The wives, who apparently were not allowed to smoke, seemed astonished about the fact that another woman could tell their husbands what to do.

The fathers of these families needed jobs more than anything else because the benefits they were given due to their refugee status would run out after eighteen months. They would be potential workers for our cleaning business that we started in 1984.

Business

Amway: In 1982, Leo and I had started a business venture. Leo, who had always worked for others, felt like trying something on his own during his spare time, and I was willing to help him. I was still hanging on to my adult school teaching in the evenings, now in the eighteenth year. But I would not mind doing something together with my husband during my spare time, since I had just lost my job teaching the handicapped class in Pleasanton. Old friends of ours from the swim club times, the Fosters, had been building up a successful Amway business (probably an acronym meaning: *The American Way*) and by chance, our daughter Doris and their daughter Laura, a classmate of hers, had visited each other and talked about this occupation of Laura's parents. At the dinner table, Doris and Charlie—they were just married for a few months—asked us, "Dad and Mom, how would you like to make a million dollars?"

We had not heard this common Amway approach and perked up our ears. The next day I gave Phyllis Foster a call and asked her about their business. "Oh, you mean Amway," she said. "Come on over, we are having a meeting tonight."

That's how our unsatisfactory career in the business world started. We got involved and intended to make that million that Doris and Charlie had talked about. They had not meant to be taken seriously but only wanted to make a joke of it—they were almost shocked when they realized that we were becoming extremely involved.

Leo and I had many happy hours together, sitting in sales meetings, going to conventions, even taking wonderful trips to Acapulco, Hong Kong, Jamaica, and Missouri with the Amway people and also putting up the whole line of products in our home, but we never made any money. We had numerous customers. Some stayed good friends, some became enemies, some became "down lines" fizzling out later, some left town and became successful with other "up lines"—we did not gain; we did not lose; we did not make a million dollars. But we did something together, met people and widened our horizons.

During that time I also tried my hand at selling Avon. Whereas the Amway business is built by making phone calls and just talking to people, Avon representatives actually go from house to house in a certain limited area of the town. I had chosen my immediate neighborhood as my territory; obediently walked from one house to the next, presenting myself as the new Avon lady, showing off my brochure, and giving little gifts of appreciation for just listening to me. When people seemed interested—mostly they just slammed the door in my face—I subtly introduced Amway to them and found some lasting customers and even friends.

Pascarellas: One of these new friends was Ingrid Pascarella. I knocked on her door one sunny morning in July and her husband Don opened it.

"I am your new Avon lady," I said brightly. "Would your wife be interested?"

Don turned around. "Ingrid," he shouted. "Here is someone from Germany who wants to talk to you."

He had gathered from my accent that I was German and thus aroused Ingrid's interest. She came, clad in her robe, with little Ina by the hand who had a runny nose and evidently just learned to walk. The two of us hit it off instantly. She asked me to come in. We had a cup of coffee; she ordered several things from my Avon catalogue and seemed also interested in Amway soap. This new friendship proved to be very consequential for our life because not only had we gained a good customer and friend but also we were introduced to a new dimension in life, at least for me—the life of a blue collar worker.

Ingrid had come from Germany in 1964 as a young married woman. She had met her first husband Jim in her hometown, Frankfurt, where he was stationed with the American Air Force. When Jim was transferred back to California, his home state, Ingrid came with him as his wife. After a while the two got divorced and Ingrid did office work to take care of herself and her small son. She must have been a chic young lady, dressed in a miniskirt, when one day around 1970 she stepped into a 7-Eleven store near her office to buy a pair of pantyhose. Don Pascarella, the owner of the store, was talking to a young lady who happened to be a friend of Ingrid. The lady recognized Ingrid and introduced her to Don. He had just lost his wife and was living with his three children in a big house on Lamson Road in Castro Valley, just behind our street. It must have been "love at first sight"; they started to go out and were married within a year. Ingrid helped

Don with the store and took over the first one when Don bought a second 7-Eleven store.

The couple did well and at one time even considered buying a third store. However, the wear and tear of operating a twenty-four hour business made them consider other options. In 1994 the Pascarellas acquired a friendly neighborhood store at the bottom of our street and eventually they sold all their 7-Eleven stores.

The Seven-Eleven chain of convenience stores is one of the businesses that operate under the Southland Corporation, a mega-conglomerate that has franchises all over the world. The Seven-Eleven stores were initiated in the early 1960s, and at first they were open from seven a.m. until eleven p.m., as the name indicates. About ten years later they were the first chain to introduce the "all night open" concept, which was followed by many other businesses.

Our Cleaning Business: We liked Amway products and I had thought of a last ditch effort to increase our dwindling sales by starting a cleaning business where we would use Amway products exclusively and be reimbursed by the fees our customers would pay. Amway had just come out with a whole line of floor-cleaning products and we wanted to give it a try. I started my plan by asking our friends, the Pascarellas, to let me use one of their stores to try out our products as guinea pigs. I would use my pupils from Family Tutorial as workers.

"Let me do one of your stores and try out our products," I approached the subject, and was met by unexpected enthusiasm on Don's side.

"I want you to do the floor in Ingrid's store. It needs stripping badly and there is no cleaning company around at the moment," he told me.

I had to confess that I didn't even know what "stripping" meant—besides taking off your clothes in a night club.

"I'll help you," said Don, "just bring some helpers and your stuff and I'll be there with someone who knows about stripping and has a machine."

So the following night I reported to Ingrid's store at eleven o'clock p.m. with two sleepy Afghans, a basket full of Amway products, and lots of enthusiasm. I met Don and his "expert," who took himself very seriously, introducing us to the art of stripping a floor. Ingrid had prepared the store by storing away any boxes and packages that might hinder our efforts. At one o'clock that night the entire floor was swimming with a greenish slime, dissolving the embedded dirt of at least a year of use. I stood at the entrance, helping potential customers who wanted to buy cigarettes or beer, and who were insisting on their rights to use the store all night to have Don and Ingrid serve them. My workers were busy mopping up the mess and rinsing the bare floors with clear water. After all was dry, we applied the wax, as thin as possible, had it dried with the help of fans, and buffed it up with the electric buffer our expert had provided. At about four o'clock in the morning the floors were done, shining new and inviting. I came home exhausted but excited just when Leo was leaving for work, and went to sleep instantly.

That was our first strip night and many others followed. We learned to do the work more efficiently by buying our own machines, switching to better and more efficient products than Amway, and hiring more people. We were in business. We called our business LMS (Leo & Mathilde Schmidt). Don introduced us to other 7-Eleven store owners. We were hired to care for the floors on a regular basis after the initial stripping and soon had to employ more workers. By 1985, just one year after our first job in Ingrid's store, we had about one hundred accounts, mostly 7-Elevens but also a wide variety of other stores, all commercial businesses; had a full schedule of six nights and a few days; and had five full-time employees working for us. We had bought more equipment, owned two propane buffers, had invested in four vehicles, and were growing steadily. I did all the outside work and Leo took care of the book work, reports to the employment office, insurance payments, and ordering of supplies.

My life had turned into a nocturnal routine. Since we had up to five repeat cleaning jobs per night, which took at least five hours, and since I was supervising every one of them, I left home usually by ten o'clock every evening and returned home in the early morning hours when the sun came up. Stores that did not have to be open all night—like hardware stores, beauty shops, car dealerships, and others, could be done earlier, as soon as the stores closed. The maintenance of the average store took about one hour, so we could easily fit four to six stores into one night, starting with early jobs and ending about four o'clock in the morning with 7-Elevens, Quick Stops, or AM/PM stores. Then there were the strip jobs, which took several hours.

Nightly customers always presented a problem since, by law, the owner of such stores were not allowed to close up completely, even when it was very dangerous to walk on the slippery floors. At one time I was confronted at knife point by an angry customer and had to be rescued by the alert clerk, who had a baseball bat handy.

It was a very strange, exhilarating life, a life my mother had never told me about, a life I had never imagined. I heard many new sounds when I was crouching on the floor, doing "edges" by hand, a trademark of our business; loud soul music of the latest raps, much swearing and four letter words, angry shouting of drunk fellows, crude talk by made-up girls looking for company, and the droning and clicking of cash registers and video-game machines. When I was present, my workers tried to converse in English, but as soon as I turned my back, they fell into their native Farsi, Spanish or downright street talk. I had employed many different workers over time. The turnover was large and we were flexible.

Store owners were seldom present when we worked. I met them in the daytime while collecting the fees for our "slavery." This collecting was a job in itself. It had to be like piecework, or the money would not come in. I personally had to go to every one of my customers and present my bill. Most owners paid willingly when I showed up, but some were tough customers and managed to disappear when I came. One extremely evasive customer was Mr. Lalani, as he called himself. Most of my customers were informal, and we conversed at first-name basis. Mr. Lalani was a Shiite Muslin from India, looking weird and forbidding with his turban, and trying to wheedle me into doing his faraway shop (on the opposite side of San Jose) without pay. He did not reckon on my stubbornness and had to finally pay all his debts, hundreds of dollars, before I stopped serving him. I had Leo talk to him on the phone when he tried once more to sweet talk me into coming to strip his floor.

We also had legal cases where customers of the stores feigned a fall on the slippery floors and sued the store and us. The suits involved costly litigation and in time caused our insurance company to increase our premiums.

By 1986 the insurance costs had risen so high that they wiped out our profits, so it was time to quit. In December we closed the business, paid all our workers one more time, and then collected in the beginning of the following year all outstanding debts, making still close to twenty thousand dollars in profits, because there were no more insurance bills to pay. Little by little, we sold our machines, gave some away, lent some of our vehicles out, and relaxed. It was wonderful to be able to go to bed again like a normal person and to sleep all night!

Important Family Events

Our Cabin: In 1975 Leo, who was making good money and had paid off the debt on our house in Castro Valley, started looking for a cabin in the mountains. I was skeptical at first because I had just regained my self-respect after my teaching fiasco at the junior high school and enjoyed taking care of the house and garden again. How would it be when there was a cabin to take care of too? And moreover, did we want to spend at least six hours of driving on weekends when we went there? But gradually I got accustomed to the idea and became as enthusiastic with the idea as Leo.

We searched for half a year on highways 80, 50, 108, and 4 and finally found exactly what we were looking for in Arnold, about thirty miles above Angels Camp on Highway 4, on the way to Bear Valley Ski Resort and Lake Alpine. We agreed to buy a small cabin, preferably an A-frame, which we could build out later.

In June of 1976, our son Marty, the avid hiker and mountain climber, had decided to do part of the Pacific Crest Trail from Lake Tahoe to Mt. Whitney by himself and needed us to bring him food. We decided to meet him at Lake Alpine, above Bear Valley, and spend the night with him under the stars. Marty was overjoyed at seeing us and encouraged us to keep on looking for a cabin in that area. Although we were both very tired next morning—neither of us had slept very well—we stopped in Arnold to confer with a Realtor. We described our preferences and he told us that he would show us some properties. There were eight cabins, one always a little less desirable than the previous one. Finally, when we had almost decided to discontinue he said, "There is just one more place that I want to show you."

We agreed to see just one more cabin and knew instantly when we saw it that this was *it*, a small inviting A-frame, surrounded by pretty trees, close to a murmuring brook, with enough sunshine to take sunbaths. It was within walking distance of a small, clear lake dotted with sailboats, and featured a sandy beach. Leo looked at me sternly to warn me to conceal my enthusiasm and started to bargain about the price, which was soon agreed upon. We could afford it and the cabin became ours. Later, at our golden wedding anniversary party, our grandchildren would enact the purchase of the cabin in their play.

From then on, our lives took on another new dimension. We had two homes now, and instead of being an added burden, as I had feared, the cabin became a source of renewed energy and joy for the entire family. We now have owned the cabin for thirty years and cannot imagine life without it. From the beginning we decided never to install a television in the cabin in order to keep life pure and natural. Instead of television, we invested in a good sound system to listen to music, we play games, talk, hike, swim during the summer, and in winter we enjoy the snow and ski, and sit around the fire together.

In time we added on—the once two-bedroom, one-bathroom building now has four bedrooms and two bathrooms and the living room has been slightly enlarged. We can easily sleep and entertain up to fifteen people. Most of the furniture was made by Leo, while most of the blankets, pillows, and curtains were made by me. Since we have the cabin, the family gathers there on holidays, during vacations, and whenever possible. Both of the girls spent parts of their honeymoons at the cabin, which was then dubbed "the love cabin", and the sons also brought their wives and later their children here to be with the family. The distance between Castro Valley and Arnold seemed to become shorter and shorter every time we went. Later, we bought the two adjoining properties that had not been built on, so our cabin now stands on one full acre. As the family grew, some of the younger generation followed our lead. In 1990 the Michaels bought a cabin in Arnold and a few years later the Tussys did also. The Kreiders are toying with the idea too. So we have a nice little colony of our family up in the Sierra foothills and will never be lonesome.

Deaths, Weddings and Births: My father died in 1960, as has already been described. He was still able to appreciate the birth of Marty, and was very proud of his new grandson. He left a void in our family as well as in the community of Bremen.

My mother had always run the household with an iron fist and she kept on living in our house on Richard Strauss Platz. When she was younger and the children were still at home, she always had two helpers, and later, when we were all gone, one maid was enough. In time my sister hired a nurse to take care of my mother. She lived, surprisingly, for twenty-two more years and was able to pay off the debt to Christoph Kulenkampff fair and square. I visited her three times, in 1964 to celebrate her eightieth birthday, in 1970 with my husband, and in 1974 with my younger son Marty, when she turned ninety. That big event, though, had already taken place earlier in the year, so we had missed it by over half a year. I always exchanged letters with her, at least every week. During the last two years her handwriting became shaky and the content of her letters almost incoherent. She died in May of 1982 from heart failure. I decided not to go to her funeral, but came a few months later to help my two sisters, Dorothee and Julie, to dissolve the household. Our oldest sister had to cope with her husband's health problems and did not go. That certainly was *not* a fun vacation—I returned to California as soon as everything about the house and the inheritance was settled. I had my own problems at home and hurried back.

Leo's parents were younger than mine. Neither one of them reached the age of ninety—Omi passed away at age eighty-three, and Opa at age eighty-six. My father was eighty-four and my mother reached the ripe old age of almost ninety-nine. Leo's father lived a quiet independent life in his little house on Forrest Avenue in Lodi after the death of his wife. He was visited by his family almost daily and kept busy taking care of house and garden and enjoying the development of his grandchildren. The situation with Edith had slowly improved since it was

Omi's fervent wish to forgive their daughter and accept her choice of husband. He must have felt that his general hatred for Jewry was unfounded since Edith's married life was a happy one. When a few years later also Uncle Alex (Opa's brother) and then his wife Anna left this earth, we found ourselves left without any family of the old generation.

The first one of us, now the *old* generation—to pass away because of ovarian cancer—was seventy-five-year-old Edith, leaving her nine years older husband Peter to fend for himself. Unfortunately his daughter, Carol Ann, also died later in 2005, leaving her twin girls with her widowed husband. The son Hans Pascal, born in 1965, is raising a happy family. These grandchildren are the joy of Peter; now a frail ninety-year-old. He is still managing his estate, consisting of a four-plex in the heart of Sacramento and the house where he is living in the suburbs. He is now the patriarch of our generation.

In 1976 our son Leo Hermann was in his last year of studying engineering in San Luis Obispo. He met his future wife, Sharyn, at a college dance and intro-duced her to the family at the sad occasion of the funeral of Leo's mother in Lodi in December of 1977. Omi had suffered a stroke at the house in Lodi and had been kept alive in the hospital by artificial means for two weeks—until our Opa ordered the doctor to put an end to it. It was the first tragic event after so many happy years and we all missed her very much. Just before she passed away, Opa had been invited by us to the cabin, and Omi had decided to stay home because she did not feel well enough to undertake such a trip.

Due to the coincidence of fate there was a connection between generations: in 1960 my father died and our youngest son was born and in 1882 my mother passed away and our first grandson was born. In 1977 Leo's mother died and Leo Hermann met his future wife, Sharyn.

After Omi's funeral we all went to the customary banquet at the church and then we all went to our mountain cabin and got acquainted with Sharyn. We went skiing at Lake Alpine. Sharyn referred to herself as "Leo's girl friend" and soon became one of the family. They revealed to us their plans to marry the next summer, in 1978. This was the first wedding in our family, and all of us were excited by the big event. The wedding was held in Arroyo Grande, at their home near San Luis Obispo, and only the immediate family members were invited. We felt sad that our mother in Germany, then ninety-four years old, was not able to enjoy with us the first wedding of her grandchildren in America.

Shortly after this, Randy and Barbara married in August of 1979. The two had met in 1974 when both girls were working with handicapped people in summer camps. Randy Cruz was then an assistant teacher; Barbara was just a volunteer. In fact, their dedication to the care of the handicapped people had triggered my decision to start studying in this field in 1978. On August 25, 1974, Barbara and Randy got engaged and promised each other that they would get married in exactly five years, on Saturday, August 25, 1979. They really did get married that very day in our backyard in Castro Valley, where we had about eighty guests, who enjoyed the beautiful weather of late summer with all the flowers still in full bloom. Now the second child left our home, but just like Leo and Sharyn, Barb and Randy came to the cabin often and thus helped us to overcome our loss.

To make the marriage trend of our three older children complete, Doris had invited to the cabin a young man whom she had met at the university in Berkeley, where she was studying during the year of 1977/78. Our good friend Ethel Slaggie, who happened to be spending Thanksgiving with us also that year, felt that the young man, Charles Michaels, would probably be Doris's future husband.

Wise old Ethel was correct, because in January 1979 the two announced to us their engagement and on January 5, 1980, we had another wedding. Doris had chosen this date because her grandmother, my mother, was having her birthday on that day. She was ninety-six years old on the Michaels' wedding day.

The church ceremony took place at a nearby little chapel and the reception was held on the Berkeley campus at the Women's Faculty Club. This time, we had a more formal affair. The other two weddings had been more or less informal, with pastor friends performing the marriage rites on private properties. To this wedding in Berkeley over one hundred guests were invited, mostly college friends and relatives from both sides. Leo's relatives from California all came, but my relatives, though invited, could not make it. Leo and I did not have to worry about anything concerning the wedding. Everything from choosing music and flowers to exact planning of events was done by Doris and Charlie. Charlie's father, Charles Michaels, held a wonderful speech in honor of bride and groom.

One unfortunate event is worth mentioning because it highlights the great attitude of Charlie's grandparents. They were coming from New York and had all their finery and wedding presents in their suitcases. Unfortunately, there was thick fog on the day of their arrival, January 4, and somehow the poor couple, getting on in age, lost all their baggage. They had to stay in their traveling clothes all during the wedding and had no presents to give. But they seemed to take the loss so cheerfully that hardly anyone knew what had happened and no trace of a shadow fell upon the happy affair. With Charlie as a husband, Doris gained a wonderful second family, and we all have continued to nurture this relationship over the years.

Our grandchildren started to arrive in 1982 (when my mother died) and the youngest one, Sequoia, was born in Napier, New Zealand on a dual date. She was born officially on New Years Day in 1991 when it was still New Years Eve of 1990 in California.

But before I go further into describing Denali and Sequoia, I shall first sketch Marty's life.

Go West, Young Man

<u>**Marty, the Different One**</u>: In 1980 only our youngest, Marty, remained single and unattached. He would marry much later, in 1988, but was now in the middle of a Sturm und Drang period. He had finished high school early and thus avoided the big graduation ceremony that the two older children had gone through in previous Junes, capped and gowned; with us parents sitting in the bleachers and wondering what would happen next. Barbara had already started the trend of graduating early without "pomp and circumstances," and Marty followed her. However, he was more extreme and had proposed to us at the end of junior year that he was going to quit school altogether and take a job. We had to coax him back to school and were glad that he finished his senior requirements somehow to earn the high school diploma.

One thing was sure; Marty did not want to go to college. He had visions of living by himself in the mountains and somehow "making it." For two years, he tried to make money by manufacturing wooden animal planters that were trendy in the late 70s when anything that could hold a plant was "in." Marty was very creative and had gained experience in making these planters by working for a man who mass-produced them, struck it rich, and then disappeared. So our son intended to take over the abandoned market, persuading his father to help him build a little factory in Arnold, and soon he was in business. His factory was in an old Nissen hut, similar to the contraptions made of corrugated steel that were used at the Hamburg campus after the war, which also served as his living quarters. In order to get to his bed, which was placed on a floor above his workspace, he had to swing himself up on a rope. Marty soon had a large supply of planters with different shapes, in fact, a great zoo with reindeer, lions, elephants, llamas, pigs, and even grasshoppers. His imagination ran wild. He did not stop at making planters of all sizes. Soon the planters were followed by cutting boards, coat hangers, toy chests, and rocking horses.

The problem was to sell all of this and make money in the process. Marty did not know enough about marketing and soon found out that mass production was not always followed by mass sales. He took his wares to local fairs where fellow craftsmen were selling their products by moving from city to city. This led to some orders that had to be filled and shipped out. Marty's one-man operation became a multifaceted activity—either he was in his factory producing stock, or sitting behind his displays at fairs, or packing goods and shipping them off. When he looked over his finances after two years, he discovered that his expenses had exceeded income and that there did not seem to be any gold at the end of the rainbow. Also, the crest of demand on which his predecessor had ridden was beginning to subside and it was time to go on to other ventures.

We had hoped to persuade Marty to go at least to Laney College then. He even enrolled in a sheet metal class, but not for long. He found another route for his life. He joined the Air Force. This was a great surprise to us. In July 1980, Leo and I had gone on a little trip by ourselves and when we came back, we found a note on our kitchen table: "I am in Texas with the Air Force. Love, Marty." We thought then that this decision was a wonderful solution and we could stop worrying about Marty. When, at our next visit to the cabin, we stopped by his factory, we found a little note on his door saying: "Be right back..." Evidently he had just dropped everything and left. He dissolved his business during his first furlough during the fall. We helped him by taking over his supply stock, and still have our attic full of strange looking creatures. So our adventurer had found his own way to get an education. Marty sailed through boot camp splendidly and chose becoming a Para-Rescuer as his career. Para-Rescue is a specialized group of the Air Force, whose most important role is jumping from helicopters with parachutes and rescuing people in distress.

Two years later we were invited to Albuquerque to attend his graduation. He had excelled in all the subjects of his chosen field. Since he had graduated with honors, he could choose where he would serve his active-duty years. His first choice was Alaska and there, at Elmendorf Airfield in Anchorage, he spent two more fulfilled years, working on different life-saving missions, and building his character. His old love for mountain climbing was kindled again by the closeness of the towering Mt. McKinley in Denali Park.

What was the reason for this persistent drive to climb in our youngest child? Two encounters might have triggered and enforced this ambition. When the children were small, we used to put scrapbooks together, and among other things, a picture of Sir Edmund Hillary was in one of those books. He had conquered the first ascent onto Mt. Everest, the highest peak on Earth. That great accomplishment had just happened soon after my marriage in 1953, and the entire world was fascinated by it. Little Marty's first consequential impression was that picture.

Another event took place in 1974, when Marty was fourteen, during a visit to our friend Ethel Slaggie. I had taken Marty with me there, at her little house in Albany, and we met Ethel's son, who was an accomplished mountain climber and had all his gear laid out on the floor of Ethel's living room. Marty was mesmerized and soon had invested his spending money in similar equipment. From then on he devoted himself mostly to climbing mountains.

As soon as the Air Force released him, Marty started to climb mountains exclusively, and he joined a company as an official guide to lead their customers to the top of Mt. McKinley. After he found out that this company used his skills to their advantage by not risking anything themselves and underpaying him, Marty founded his own guiding service and built it up into a well-established business, Marty Schmidt International Guiding, in short MSIG. Marty's clients started coming back to him, and brought him more business by telling others. The interest in mountain climbing was rising, especially among professional people who had stressful jobs and made enough money to afford the expensive pastime of conquering mountains. Soon it was not only Alaska. Marty also climbed in California and his clientele grew. He extended his business to South America, to France, and even to Russia. K2 and Mt. Everest in the Himalayas were planned for the future. Eventually, he chose New Zealand as his headquarters.

He met his future wife, Joanna Munisteri, in 1986 when she was working at the theater in San José and he was painting houses to make some extra money. They fell in love and decided to have a baby. Before this baby was born, Joanna decided she did not want to be an actress any longer, but signed a contract with a museum that needed dolphin trainers. Joanna, no less adventurous than Marty, signed the contract and the two lovers went to Australia. They settled in a small town, Nambucco Heads, not far from Coff's Harbour on the coast between Sydney and Brisbane. They decided to get married one month before the birth of their child. They had a simple wedding in the backyard of their rented home. No family members attended the wedding because no invitations had been sent. The guests were friends and neighbors.

The baby, named Denali, which means "The High One," after the tall peaks of Denali Park in Alaska, was born one week after Opa's death. The couple had another child, a daughter, who was named Sequoia, after the giant trees in California. They were living in New Zealand at that time. The marriage started to deteriorate when Joanna was overburdened with a teaching job and care of her two children, and Marty was away for long periods of time to climb tall mountains. Their promising marriage turned out to be a disaster.

In 1999 they got divorced. After moving from one place to another many times they finally ended up in New Zealand again. Now a battle over custody of the children ensued. They became estranged and even hateful to each other. The poor children were suffering but still kept thriving. Both are very talented, Denali for fine arts, drawing and painting, Sequoia for performing arts, dancing and acting. At first Joanna still had custody of the children, but gradually this shifted in Marty's favor, mostly because the children preferred to be with him. Both mother and ex-mother-in-law are grieving for her and cannot do anything to help her. She is roaming the world and from time to time we receive unflattering emails from her, which we ignore. Since then Marty has found someone else, a wonderful woman from the Old Country. They will get married in 2007.

Opa Schmidt had just passed away the week before Denali's birth. Again the flow of the generations had moved on and the oldest member of the family was now replaced by the youngest.

Grandchildren: Our last grandchild, Sequoia, was born in Napier, New Zealand, where the young family had moved. Joanna had changed jobs again and was now preparing to teach at a Steiner school, a private organization. That event brought the number of our grandchildren to six.

In 1982 our first grandchild was born, Blair Martin Schmidt, in Arroyo Grande. From now until 1991, we would have five more grandchildren: Jason Michael Cruz in 1983, Donica Marie Schmidt in 1985, Brandon David Cruz in 1987, and in 1988 and 1991, the two children of Marty and Joanna far away in Australia and New Zealand by the exotic names of Denali Martin Waldemar and Sequoia Patti Karanema Schmidt. It is an indescribable experience to become grandparents and to observe one's offspring growing up. The original "Omi and Opa" were gone and we took their place and their endearments in the ever flowing chain of family hierarchy. Denali and Sequoia will most likely settle down under and our family is spreading around the world.

My Retirement

I was free now of any obligations and could do whatever I wanted. I looked for new activities and soon was as busy as ever.

Hiking Group: In 1986, when my life had turned to normal again after dissolving our cleaning business, I joined a group of ladies who, like me, were getting on in age but had kept young in spirit and were walking every morning on the shore of Lake Chabot. It takes a good hour to walk to and back from the dam that created the lake more than a century ago from a small creek that sprang from the foothills surrounding Castro Valley, and we have been hiking on the delightful trail ever since. Some of the ladies I knew from the times at Chabot Swim Club when our children were acquainted with each other. Others I knew from Scouting, and I also made new friends. My old friend Shirley Kuller had been one of the first ladies in this walking group.

The little hike from six to seven o'clock every morning has been part of my daily routine now for close to twenty years and will be hopefully for many more years. It is a great part of my social life since we share joys and sorrows, births of grandchildren, and deaths of relatives and old friends, and even political events. Talking while walking we take part in each other's family happenings and enjoy the trips and parties of our fellow walkers. We even celebrate our birthdays by giving little parties either in our homes or at the lake or in restaurants in or out of town.

Every morning we marvel again at the beauty of the lake, it always looks different, sometimes still and serene, sometimes wavy, and during the winter months sometimes choppy. Because we walk all through the year, rain or shine, we experience the entire spectrum of our weather and learn to appreciate any variation of it. Since in our wonderful climate the weather is almost never extremely hot or cold and since there are hardly ever severe storms, we only miss this great routine when we are sick or detained by family events or trips. The only other people we meet are hikers or fishermen who sit at the bank of the lake and converse with the ducks, geese, and coots that populate the lake. The park administration takes care of stocking the lake with various kinds of fish, so there is the opportunity to catch a good dinner for everyone with a fishing license.

Apelt Girls' Reunions: In the middle of the 1990s, when my sister Cornelie was still in good health and liked to visit with her children, the Kreiders, we started meeting with other descendents of Hermann Apelt in California. To boost these events we also invited the sister of Charlie, Susan Tussy, because she was one of our family by then and we saw her often. Phyllis, Doris or Barbara organized these reunions and we held them at different places. We met in San Francisco, at the coast, in San Rafael, and also near Leo Hermann's home at the Madonna Inn in San Luis Obispo. Of course, that gathering included Sharyn, Leo Hermann's wife and, since Barbara Allen and daughter Kathy just "happened" to be in Los Angeles, they also were invited.

One of those reunions was held in New Orleans. The memory of this four-day event is very precious now since the terrible hurricane Katrina in September 2005 has destroyed so much of the beauty of this unique city. My two sisters, Cornelie and Julie, joined Doris, Phyllis, and me and Walt, Cornelie's son and Phyllis's brother was our guide. He had lived in New Orleans for much of his life and loved showing us the sights of his home town. He was a prestigious architect and had designed many buildings, which he proudly pointed out to us while we were enjoying the view of the city having a drink at a revolving restaurant. For me this trip stirred up memories of my previous visit to Louisiana in 1952. Walt died in 1999 of a heart attack, shocking for all of us, especially his grieving mother who passed away just seven months later on February 28, 2000.

Even after Cornelie's death we held up the tradition. Later we ventured further to New York in 2003 and one unforgettable event was held in Germany when our Doris was fifty on May 4, and my sister Julie ninety years old on May 5 in the year 2005. Another get-together is planned for 2006 in Chicago where most of the descendents of Cornelie are living.

Our Second Trip to Europe in 1988: Doris and Charlie were in Switzerland at that time and tried hard to invite us to see their new home in Zurich. At the yearly family gathering at the cabin during Thanksgiving in 1987, Leo surprised us all by declaring he wanted to take a trip with me the following summer to visit Switzerland, France, Germany, and Austria. I was delighted and started getting prepared right away by taking French lessons to be able to talk with the people in France. I was always ready to go to college if there was only a reason. This time I chose the Livermore campus of Chabot Junior College, which offered beginning French at a convenient time around noon twice a week. Again, I was a student. The fellow students around me were mostly young, but some were older adults like me.

I had studied the French language several times in my life. When my father had found out that I would not learn French in school—it was offered only during the last three years, which I had missed—he bought a beginner's book and taught me the rudiments of that beautiful language. I still have that book. Later I tried teaching myself on my own. Much later Leo and I took a night-school class together, which was taught by Regina Keown, who became a good friend of the whole family.

We also contacted our friends and relatives in Germany to inform them of our visit. Our trip was planned to last five weeks, from the end of April to the beginning of June, and was coinciding with a series of unexpected events.

Leo's father had been feeling poorly all winter but had refused vehemently to go to the hospital in Lodi for observation. We were very concerned about his health when he told us he could not open the garden scissors anymore for cutting his roses and could not work the buttons on his clothes. We saw him always when we were on the way to the cabin, almost every other week. His doctor had told him to "take it easy", a hard thing to do for the eighty-six year old gentleman who had been busy all his life. Just a few weeks before his death all of the family, including our Doris, had gathered at his house to celebrate his eighty-sixth birthday and he had been a most charming host.

On April 19 we got a phone call from Leo's brother Dagobert that Opa had had a stroke and that his brother Alex had brought him to the hospital. Opa had phoned Alex and told him, "I don't feel so good," an admittance that he finally understood that the end was near. We went to Lodi at once and waited with the rest of the concerned family outside Opa's room. We were later allowed to go in and visit him, just two visitors at a time. He sat in his bed, with his dinner tray still before him, having needles injected into his body, and looking calm and composed. "They finally got me here," he said. "I will not go home again."

He knew and he was at peace with himself. He and his wife had been good Christians all their lives and he was looking forward to being with Jesus soon. We said good-bye to him and told him we would be back the next evening, but during the next morning he had passed away; another stroke had stopped his already damaged heart.

The funeral was slated for April 22, and the entire family, including his four grandchildren from California, came together and we accompanied our father to his last resting place at the cemetery close to Lodi. There he lies next to his wife and is visited often by his family. We all miss him terribly. The house on Forrest Avenue was sold soon after his death and we had to adjust to life going on without our patriarch.

France: On April 27, just hours before we had to be at the airport, our grandson Denali was born in Australia. It had been a painful birth for Marty's wife, Joanna, and it did not help that the two had chosen to have the baby by the method of water birth. Joanna had read about this procedure and she and Marty had agreed that this was a wonderful way to bring a new human being to enter this world. They had prepared for this by hiring midwives, renting a large tank for the water, and following the instructions for the water birth minutely. But it turned out that Joanna was not built to have a normal birth, and what was supposed to be a pleasurable event, turned into a nightmare. Finally, after more than forty-five hours, they had to give it up, load the poor mother onto a truck, and bring her to the nearest hospital where a completely normal, strapping son was delivered by cesarean. Just a few hours before our departure to San Francisco Airport, Marty called us that the baby was born. His voice was shaky and he was afraid for his wife's life. We had already made up our mind not to go on our trip if the baby was not born by that very night, when the call came. We were relieved then, and we told Marty so and hoped for the best for Joanna. We were able to catch our plane and were on our way. When we called Marty after having landed in Paris, we heard that Joanna was recuperating slowly, but that they now needed money to pay for the unplanned expenses at the hospital. We assured them that we would send a few thousand dollars as soon as we arrived in Zurich.

So we started our trip on April 27 in 1988 after all these turbulent events and were soon immersed in a different culture. Our plane landed in Paris, where we intended to do some sightseeing and also to visit our nephew Wulf Rohland in Burgundy. We managed to see the most outstanding sights in Paris, to visit ancient Mont-Saint-Michel on the coast of Normandy, to tour four castles on the Loire, and to have a delightful visit with Wulf, his wife Florence, and their two young children, Alice and Thilo—all in the span of three days. Wulf, though he has a doctor degree in economics, earns his living as an artist; he makes pottery and has built up a well-designed factory in Beaune. These much-too-short three days whetted my appetite for visiting France again, and I did indeed go back to Paris two years later for several weeks.

Switzerland: After our stay in France, we arrived in Zurich where Doris and Charlie hosted us splendidly in their spacious apartment on the fourth floor of a large house in town, from where we could overlook the city and even see the snow-capped Alps. Since Doris and Charlie both worked, Leo and I had ample time to get acquainted with Zurich during the day, and when they came home, they drove us to remarkable sights outside the town. My sister Dorothee, who attended a yearly medical convention at the same time we were there, visited us and brought a big bouquet of flowers in honor of Denali's birth. Over the weekend we took a trip to Lake Lucerne and followed the footsteps of the hero in Schiller's *William Tell*. I actually sat on the "bench of stone" that had given me so much trouble when I was a teenager at school in Germany. Another weekend we spent in Grindelwald, high in the Alps, where we took wonderful hikes together.

Kleve: After several days we left Switzerland and took the train to Germany, where we visited my sister Dorothee, home again by now, and her husband Wulf in their charming house in Kleve, close to Düsseldorf on the Rhine River. They treated us with a trip to an art gallery in nearby Holland.

It was ominous foreboding that Wulf and Dorothee showed us a little church near Kleve where they wished to be laid to rest, should this be necessary. Only one year later, in February of 1989, Wulf would die in South America, while the couple was visiting their daughter Regula in Argentina. Dorothee had to fly home to Germany, holding the container holding the ashes of her late husband on her lap. Though his ashes were buried in the family plot in Bremen, the memorial service was held in this charming little church in Kleve.

We met Wulf in the United States, shortly after we had visited the Rohlands in 1988. He and Dorothee had been invited to attend the wedding of Cornelie's oldest granddaughter, Kathy, in Dayton, Ohio, This wedding was an opportunity to gather Cornelie's clan around her and the Rohlands were happy to accept the invitation. My other sister, Julie, could not come because she had to take care of her ailing husband. After the wedding in Dayton the Rohlands visited us in California and we noticed that Wulf was a little disoriented and prone to falling down. This imbalance should have been a forewarning for us, and should have been taken seriously. Only half a year later, he collapsed while walking with his wife in Patagonia, where their daughter Regula and her husband Wolfgang Langbehn have a vacation house on a beautiful lake. They were hours away from the Langbehn's estate, and when Wulf was finally picked up by an ambulance and brought to a nearby hospital, he was pronounced dead.

Bremen: Our next destination was Bremen, where Julie and Christoph expected us and arranged to meet most of the relatives whom we had not seen in eighteen years, when Leo and I visited Germany in 1970. Especially interesting for Leo and me was a visit to my old home on Richard Strauss Platz, where Julie and Rainer Kohlrausch now lived with their three growing sons. The house was renovated after my mother's death, but it was still the house where I was born and grew up—at least the foundation! The Platz was still the same with its oval lawn surrounded by the horseshoe-shaped street, on which young children played—not my playmates, but new generations. The Ulrichs were still living in the same house, but now it was their grandson, Uli Bock, who owned it. Uli had become a good friend of Rainer and Julie, the grandchildren of my parents. No more cobblestones, no more blue and white carriages with Bölken milk, no more Rolls Royce waiting for my father to take him to work.

Austria, St. Georgen and the Ernsts: After this little bout of nostalgia, the four of us, Julie, Christoph, Leo and I, set off for a two week trip to Austria and Italy. In Austria, we visited Salzburg, the Mozart town, which neither Leo nor I had ever seen. Then we headed for Graz and St. Georgen where Walter Ernst's father had lived in an old castle, which he had bought at a bargain price when it was in a ruined state. He renovated it over the years and it became the charming center of a small Austrian town. The castle stayed in my sister's family for a long time. Paul Ernst, the writer and poet, had lived there with his third wife, Else, my father's sister, until his death in 1933. He was buried on the property and was fondly remembered by many of his readers.

On this occasion in 1988, when we visited St. Georgen, a great conference was held at the castle hosted by the head of the Paul Ernst Gesellschaft (society managing the writings of Paul Ernst)) and the new owner of the castle, a young doctor and his wife. As in the fairy story, *The Seven Swans*, the couple had seven sons and one little daughter, and it was charming to see this big family lined up in the ancient square of the castle next to an old well. The doctor's wife had been busy with preparing the castle for the many visitors who were expected for this festival, and even the old *Rittersaal*, (knights' hall) gleaming in its tastefully renovated state, ready to entertain the crowd of Paul Ernst lovers. The whole village participated in the entertainment, which included reading, live drama, and even a film made after a short story by him.

Long ago, my three sisters had all been at the castle except me. I was too young and when I became old enough, the war broke out. Julie had even spent one year with the elder Ernsts and had learned to run a large household under Tante Else, who used to be a strict, if not bossy, teacher. Dorothee had studied medicine in nearby Graz and had visited the castle occasionally. Cornelie and Walter, who had met at the castle, were frequent visitors, and, until the castle was sold, the children visited the castle too.

Paul Ernst was born in the *Harz* (Hartz Mountains), the son of a miner. He had to work diligently to become a writer. Else was my father's older sister and had met Paul Ernst through my parents during a convention in Weimar, I believe, when he was still married to Lilli von Benda. Walter, my brother-in-law, and his sister, Emma, were children of that marriage. There had been an earlier marriage with a Russian woman, but she had died without leaving children. Else, too, had been married before to Ludwig von Schorn. As I mentioned before, Lilli von Benda came from a highly gifted musical family; one of her forefathers had been first violinist in Frederick the Great's ensemble, which he subsidized in his own castle and which had to be kept secret from his stern, military Prussian father, William I. There is a blood relationship between my sister Cornelie and Aunt Else, but not between Walter and either one of them. Else would become Walter's and Emma's stepmother after she married Paul in 1916. Lilli had divorced Paul before Else and Paul got married. She died in 1918, presumably of grief.

When Paul met Else in 1911, they fell in love instantly. A son was born to them during the same year. This boy, Karl, dubbed "the Lovechild", was our cousin; his age was roughly between that of my two older sisters. Karl was very bright and smart-looking. He visited us once as a young man when I was about ten and he impressed me as extremely dashing. He became an attaché; a political post, which was mentioned in our family with awe. He married a woman who was fourteen years older than he when he was twenty-eight. Karl was killed in the war soon after his marriage. His widow, a former Countess von Saurma-Jeltsch, yet another Barbara, referred to by us as "crazy Barbara," took over the castle in St. Georgen after Paul's and Else's deaths and was hated by everyone around. I remember her, when she visited us in Bremen once, as a spindly creature with copper-colored curly hair sticking out in all directions, my perfect model for a witch. Fortunately, there were no children in this misalliance. It seemed fairly obvious why she had married Karl, but it was harder to understand why he had married her.

Paul and Else also had visited us in Bremen, quite often in fact. I remember Paul's long white beard, which made it hard for him to eat. Else was always bub-bly and seemed to have a figure made of balls, like a snowman. Everything about her was round—her head, her body, and her extremities. Both wore strange clothes, he a dark, baggy cotton suit, she a long, flowing gown that swept up the dust.

Phyllis Kreider had told me the following story about her father's parents. The affair between Paul and Else, which started when Walter was about ten years old and Emma a few years younger, left an everlasting horrible impression on the young children. Their mother was booted out of their parents' bedroom and cried herself to sleep while the new woman in Paul's life took her place in the nuptial bed. I did not know these facts when I was a little girl; they were revealed to me just recently. I only had heard Paul Ernst praised in reverent tones by my mother, who worshipped him. My father did not say much about anything con-cerning his own sister, which is understandable. That revelation explains why Walter often seemed depressed and why Emma, who died at about thirty-five of multiple sclerosis, often seemed unhappy. It must have been hard for my sister to dispel these gloomy feelings in her own home and create the happy, sunny atmo-sphere that I had experienced.

I have several books by Paul Ernst in my possession and read most of them with pleasure. He was an excellent writer, but he had treated the mother of his older children badly. As mentioned before, one of his staunch admirers was my mother who is quoted to have coined the words: "A famous person is above the law." Wouldn't O.J. Simpson have liked to hear this?

Paul Ernst's writings and poetry were strictly for a special circle of German readers—I don't think any of his works were ever translated into other languages. His most remarkable contributions to German literature are his short stories, some of which are of classical beauty. Else also was an accomplished writer. She liked to creat ghost stories. Her talent for artistic design came to good use when she illustrated some of her works and her books, if they had appeared on the market, would have been priceless. For a while she thought she could earn good money, especially during the stringent war years.

The castle stayed in the possession of the Ernsts until recently; it still belonged to them when we visited it in 1988.

Italy: After the stay in St. Georgen, we followed the River Drau, a secondary tributary of the Danube, into Southern Tyrol, which is now part of Italy. I had spent one summer with my mother in Seefeld, then German, and felt strangely reminded of my youth in this little town that now was completely Italian. After driving through Seefeld we rode on to the most picturesque part of the eastern Alps alongside the Dolomites, went over the Cortina Pass, and stayed the night in an ancient cloister that had been turned into a fashionable hotel near Brixen, the Sonnenburg.

We visited some of the old Tyrolean cities and stayed over night in Clausen where we climbed a steep mountain to see an ancient cloister. It was interesting to shop in Italy; the lire were such small valued coins that we needed thousands of them just to buy a loaf of bread. (Now the Euro is used in most of Europe.) Our trip ended in mountain-walled Innsbruck, where the Kulenkampffs left us to go north again and we went west to Switzerland to see Doris and Charlie once more before heading home.

Natural Disasters.

Living in California means that earthquakes might happen at any time. Strange to say, after having lived more than forty years in the state, I have yet to feel what a real earthquake is like. It is an ironical fact that our daughter Doris experienced an earthquake of considerable magnitude while abroad in Tübingen. She was spending the summer of 1976 there in connection with her studies at Santa Cruz University.

Doris was literally thrown out of her bed by the quake, whose epicenter was in Tübingen. She described the frightening event in drastic words in her letters to us and to my mother. Nobody around her could believe that she was not accustomed to earthquakes in California.

Of course, we all are aware of the fact that some day a "big one" will strike, but that day hasn't come yet. The famous Loma Prietta Quake of 1989 did not interfere with our lives; we are too far away from the San Andreas Fault. Being completely unaware that something was extremely wrong, I noticed the hanging flowerpots on my patio swinging and asked Leo, "Why do the baskets move when there is no wind?" Leo informed me that it could be an earthquake. Indirectly we all suffered from the impact of that disaster by experiencing enormous traffic interruptions for several years, and baseball fans will never forget the moment at five o'clock on October 19, 1989. Neither did we suffer directly from the firestorm in the Oakland Hills that happened a year later, nor did our cabin get burned when a huge fire roared near Arnold in 1992. We were so lucky, and hope it stays that way.

An annoying phenomenon for those living on the West Coast is the alternation of long periods of drought with periods of too much rain. We were in the middle of a dry spell when we bought the cabin in 1976 and found it very convenient to have two places to use water since the allotted water ration for one household was very limited. I used to bring part of my laundry up to the mountains for washing and managed that way to stay with my quota for water.

While I was first writing my memoirs in 1995, we were experiencing the break of one of the longest droughts, the flood of 1995, with such deluges of rain that our state was declared a natural disaster area. Fortunately our house has its foundation solidly built into rocks, and our garden is fortified by Leo's expertly built retaining walls. Until now nothing serious has happened.

Other states—in fact, countries throughout the world have to cope with natural disasters. In California at least we have great weather most of the time, which makes living here so enjoyable. Our pleasant climate was a major factor in the decision of the Kreiders, our niece Phyllis and her husband Don, to move to California permanently. They never regretted their decision and are now living in fabulous San Rafael in Marin County. Their only complaint is that the people of Marin never wanted to build an extension of the Bay Area Rapid Transit system across the Bay into San Rafael. It would have been so much easier to visit back and forth.

One more "Act of God" happened in 2004 after a very rainy period all through December followed by a severe winter storm with ice and snow. The roots of trees around our cabin, one tall cedar in particular, were soaked to capacity and were not able to support the heavy tree on top of them. After one very lovely Christmas and New Year's at the cabin our guests had just left us and we were packed and ready to go. I was just coming down the driveway to get one more thing, when I noticed to my horror that our big cedar was tilting its crown toward the cabin. Leo was at this moment in the process of shutting down the electricity and moving toward the front door to lock it when he looked up, and quickly jumped underneath the eaves of the house before the huge tree came crashing down, splitting into two parts on our roof and filling the entire driveway with its icy branches. All I could think of was Leo being flattened under that heavy weight because all I could see was a big green and white mess. It was time again to pray to my Guardian Angel!

How relieved was I when, after a few minutes, a completely whole Leo emerged from that heap and joined me on the driveway. (The cabin stands in a canyon and the driveway goes up to the road.)

"That was a close one!" was all he could say.

Together we looked at the big trunk and the ocean of branches.

"We are lucky that the roof is so sturdy". He seemed relieved that the main structure was still standing.

Later that summer, when we finally finished cleaning up all the debris, we had our insurance agent assess the damage and, lo and behold, we got a brand-new roof out of the disaster.

There is a silver lining to everything.

7

The Rest of My Life

It was wonderful having my niece, Phyllis Kreider, move so close. All these years I had none of my own relatives living in California. Leo's family has been around and that has been wonderful, but it hasn't been quite enough for me. Now not only have I two of my children, Leo Hermann and Barbara, nearby, and also Doris part-time, whenever the Michaels visit their cabin in California. Marty comes in now and then for climbing expeditions, and now we also have the Kreiders about half an hour's drive away.

Part of My Sister's Family Moves West: In 1990 the Kreiders moved to California from Minnesota, where they had a big house and many friends. Don was transferred by the insurance company he worked for to a branch in San Rafael. Phyllis, who is an extremely outgoing person—making friends wherever she lives—liked California mostly because the weather is so much nicer than in Minnesota; but she regretted leaving all her friends behind. However, as soon as they had found a house (smaller than the one back in Minnesota and more expensive), she met new people. Their favorite activity is tennis, and by joining a club and participating actively they built up a large circle of wonderful, vivacious friends. They also like to travel and take several great trips each year. We see them often at our respective homes or at the cabin and even travel together. My two sisters in Germany visited when Cornelie's daughter Barbara got married in Dayton and Dorothee and Julie came to the wedding of Phyllis's daughter Johanna, which was celebrated under tall redwood trees at a park near Napa. We were getting older now and I was looking forward for my husband to retire.

When Will Leo Retire? My husband loves his work and tells everyone, "My wife has too much to do for me at home, I rather go to work." Leo's work is very interesting and, though his original boss at Manor Research was replaced by the son and then the company was bought by a larger firm, Ilmberger Tool & Die, Leo is still employed and they love to have him. I wish I could write more about his work, but he does not talk much about it. Only, when we have company and all of us had a little wine, he thaws and shares his work experiences with us. The company is located in Hayward, not far from Castro Valley and his faithful Ford Falcon transports him there and back. All I know is that Leo's firm works for large private companies like General Electrics and that part of their contracts have to do with the airline industry.

Our son Leo Hermann works in Fremont at LAM Research as a senior technician, a hands-on position, which he prefers. His hearing loss has not improved, but he has a very good hearing-aid that helps him leading a normal life. He lives with us now and every few weeks he commutes home to his self-built house in Arroyo Grande near San Luis Obispo. Sharyn refuses to be relocated and I do not blame her. She lives close to her parents and both children are studying at nearby universities, Blair in San Diego and Donica in Long Beach. It is very nice and rewarding to have one of our children now living with us.

I am occupying myself with numerous adult school classes and Leo and I see shows and movies together whenever something worthwhile is offered. I belong to book clubs, writers' groups and the AAUW (*American Association for University Women*). Also, I do translating from German to English; something I started after my German classes ended. It is very rewarding to stay in contact with my mother tongue. It is so revealing to read the century-old letters that I am asked to translate. People were very much the same then; they gossiped, struggled through life, begged for money, and bragged about their children.

We are traveling about once a year, sometimes Leo and I together, and sometimes I go by myself. A few of these trips are worth mentioning.

When Leo and I went to Europe for the second time in 1988, we spent some time in France. I had taken a college course in French at the junior college in Livermore to prepare for the occasion and was motivated to take a more advanced class after we came back. In 1990 I started to study French at California State University, Hayward, now California State University of the East Bay.

My Trip to France: We had an energetic teacher who not only had us stage a play about *Dennis the Menace* in French (where I played the dog, Rex), but also she arranged a six-week trip to Paris, which seemed very attractive to me. I decided to go and had a wonderful time. About sixty students from Cal State, Hayward participated. We were housed on a Campus on the outskirts of Paris and had to take the RER Metro to get into the center of the city. In the mornings we had classes like Survival French and Global Economy where we studied the growing movement to break down the monetary barriers between countries in Europe and creating the Euro. The afternoons were ours to roam and explore

Paris on our own. Not only did I learn to speak French by "total immersion"; I had enough opportunities to visit most of the sights that this world city has to offer. The weekends were filled with field trips to more distant spectacles.

On one of these outings we visited Rouen, where we saw the place where Jeanne d'Arc had been burned, and then ventured to Giverny to view the pink and green house of Monet. Standing on the famous bridge over the water-lily pond and strolling through his gardens heightened our admiration for this famous impressionist. On another excursion we saw Fontainebleau and scrambled up the renowned staircase were Napoleon had given his farewell speech. Another weekend was dedicated to visiting the Chartres Cathedral, the great monument I had missed seeing more than forty years ago when I was caged up in a truck as a prisoner of war. We also made a trip to the wine country around Reims and Champagne and drank those authentic wines. One weekend I spent in Beaune with my nephew Wulf Rohland and another in Bremen with my sister Julie and her family. Doris and Charlie came over from Zurich and I was able to guide these world travelers around *my* city. We spent an entire morning at the Picasso Museum in the Marais. Did I mention the Eiffel Tower, that mountain of steel and girders, overlooking Paris and never overlooked by visitors? It was fun scrambling up those umpteen stairs—instead of using the elevator—and having a cup of coffee at the café on top.

Our Trip to Alaska: My husband and I took a cruise to Alaska in 1994. This was the easy way to travel; everything was planned for us. Our son Leo Hermann, then looking for a job at the Bay Area, took us to the airport. We flew to Seattle and from there to Fairbanks in a small commuter plane. We could see the top of mighty Mount McKinley in Denali Park sticking its white head out of the clouds and thought of our son Marty who has climbed up to this top many times. From there we took a land tour by bus and train to tour the beautiful state. We saw an old gold mine, panned our own few morsels of gold, and visited the famous pipeline from Purdue to Valdez. We also ventured to Denali Park, named after the other high peak near Mt McKinley, and after which our grandson is named, meaning "the Great One." We were discovering bears, moose, and Dall sheep, and admiring the majestic high, snow-capped range, Marty's climbing ground, this time from below. We took the Midnight Sun train to Anchorage, again thinking of Marty when we visited the Elmendorf Army base, marveled at the telltale signs of the great earthquake in 1964—one part of Anchorage actually dropped down thirty feet and people had to live beneath the earth with the chimneys of their houses sticking out of the ground like submarines—and then spent two nights on the Kenai Peninsula, where we took part in an all-day white-water raft tour. The land tour was followed by a week on a cruise ship that took us alongside glaciers and quaint cities through the Inside Passage. We had a grand time, not to mention fabulous food, and royal treatment on the ship. During the voyage through the Inside Passage we had several intermediate stops at historical places like Skagway (an old gold town), Juneau (the capital of Alaska) and Ketch-ikan, where we visited the house of Dolly, a famous Madame. This house, in fact all houses on this street is built on stilts, so it is above the water level.

As soon as our ship left the dock of our last Port of Call, gambling was allowed. I had never used slot machines before and how amazed I was when, after inserting a few tokens into the slots and activating the machine, an avalanche of little tinny coins came flowing out of the dispenser and filled the container underneath. I turned around in dismay, fearing that I had broken the gadget, but people had gathered around me and assured me that nothing was wrong—I had hit the jackpot! The person before me must have given up just before the big one struck. "Beginner's luck" was what I had, and when I gambled again the next morning, hoping to continue winning, I lost most of what I had won the day before. But I had enough money left to buy myself a nice wrist watch, which is still with me.

Leo did not join me while I was roaming the ship—he had developed a nasty cold and slept most of the time. But we saw a movie together, *Philadelphia*, starring Tom Hanks and learned how serious a disease AIDS is and what true friendship means. On the first evening, before Leo got sick, we danced together on the elevated stage and almost fell off when the ship started to roll. After fourteen days of cruising we had enough and were happy to get back home.

The Four Sisters Meet in Germany: Another trip to Germany took place in 1995 in order to celebrate the eightieth birthday of my sister Julie. Cornelie decided to join us and so did Dorothee, and the four of us enjoyed being together. We took a trip to Weimar to visit the birthplace of our father and Leo chauffeured us in our large rented car. We loved Weimar and its culture. The spirits of Goethe and Schiller are everywhere. At a little castle nearby, Belvedere, Leo detected a portrait of Catharine II, about whom he had heard so much from his parents, and he was quite excited. After a visit to Charlotte, who lives in Frankfurt with her family, we drove to the airport, dropped our rental car off and flew home.

We Study American History at its Source: This time we took two weeks to visit the East Coast. First we flew to New York and stayed three fun-filled days with Doris and Charlie in their plush apartment, then drove leisurely up the coast to Newport, saw the entire sickle-shaped peninsula of Cape Cod, and ended up in Concord, Massachusetts. Here we stayed over night, went to Walden's Pond the next day, looked at the replica of his small house, and visualized his bean fields. I had brought a pocket edition of Henry David Thoreau's *Walden* and per-suaded Leo that we *had* to see this little lake. Nearby is the famous North Bridge with the statue symbolizing the Minute Men. That reminded me of my coura-geous husband who, by walking all through the night, had rescued my son's legs, if not his life. It happened in 1975, more than twenty years ago. We drove on, through Lexington, where the battle against the British had been fought, and to Boston. Here we walked the Freedom Trail, climbed Beacon Hill, visited the har-bor, where the Boston Tea Party had taken place, and wound up at the airport, where we had a delicious meal at the restaurant with authentic New England cream chowder and Boston cream pie.

From Boston we flew directly to Washington D.C., where we joined a bus tour with forty other travelers. We toured Washington's sights, had dinner in Alexandria and visited the historic places of the area. This tour included visits to Mount Vernon, Youngstown, Jamestown, Richmond, the Shanandoah Valley, the battle field at Gettysburg, the Amish town of Intercourse (what a name!), Philadelphia, (which stirred up my memories of more than forty years ago), and finally back to Washingon D.C.

Y2K and 9/11: Much was made of bridging into the new millennium. Our daughter Barbara had to work day and night during the year 1999 because her company was in charge of averting great computer catastrophes. Everyone thought that Y2K might be a sort of Armageddon. However, Barb's company must have done their job well; we sailed into the year 2000 without a hitch.

The hitch came later when on the morning of 2001 disaster struck. I had been walking with my friends at our lake and was in the process of turning off my motor, when I heard the announcer cutting into the morning news.

"Special report! Just now one of the World Trade Center towers has been hit by a passenger plane and is erupting in flames. It is crumbling…!"

I jumped out of my car and ran into the house to turn on the television. There it was, as the reporter said: the left tower of the World Trade Center, our symbol of power, slowly sinking into the rubble of dust and debris. A few minutes later the other tower was attacked. Little by little the whole grizzly story was revealed.

The terrorists had managed to use our own passenger planes to accomplish the destruction! On the evening of that infamous day we heard our new president, George Bush, declare that he would fight the perpetrators with "all that it takes," and he would be doing that for a long time. In those days it was Osama Bin Laden and the Al Qaeda network that were suspected of being behind it all, so we escalated the operations in Afghanistan that had been started by then President Clinton in the early 1990s. I must say, so far such an attack has not been repeated, but we are sitting on the edge of our chairs fearing that one could happen any day.

At the beginning of September 2001, just before September 11 or 9/11, our grandson Jason joined the Air Force voluntarily. He had the same initiation into the service as our son Marty had in 1981, and the two airmen compared notes after Jason had completed boot camp in Lackland, Texas, and before he was sent to England to serve. Luckily so far Jason never had to serve in combat because he chose to go into the electronic field and is building bombs. But his decision to serve his country had another, less important effect: because of the imminent declaration of war against Iraq (highly debatable, but still a fact), he was not able to attend our big party in January of 2003, our Golden Wedding Anniversary.

Married for Fifty Years

Preparations: The celebration of our fiftieth wedding anniversary in January of 2003 was a very special event that had been planned for a whole year by the entire family. Everyone was contributing to make this a great party. We chose to reserve the big reception hall at Ironstone Winery in Murphys, in the foothills of the Sierra, to be close to our cabin but not quite as high up. Murphys is located on the Highway 49 at an elevation of about 1500 feet. Snow is rarely expected there, even in the middle of winter. Our wedding in 1953 had taken place on January 30, but that day would fall in the middle of the week in 2003. We chose Saturday, January 25 for our party and prayed for good weather.

Our daughter Barbara was in charge of the overall management and worked closely with the party coordinator at the winery. My job was to make the guest list and also put together posters with pictures from my numerous photo albums. Sharyn did the decorations, Doris the invitations, and Marty and Leo Hermann were willing to serve as photographers. The children helped too—Brandon ushering the guests, Donica receiving the guests and handling the guest book, Denali and Blair helping their fathers with picture taking, and Sequoia leading the play later in the evening. Patriarch Leo was willing to pay for everything.

The Party: It was a three-day affair. My sister Julie and her daughter Hedwig from Germany came a few days earlier and stayed with us in Castro Valley until the day before the party. Doris and Charlie had generously reserved the entire Dunbar House in Murphys, a five-star inn featuring five rooms with old-fashioned décor and fabulous service. Our closest relatives, Peter Deuel, whose wife Edith had passed away in 1999, my sister Julie, my niece Hedwig, Doris and Charlie, and Leo and I occupied the five rooms and had the inn for ourselves.

On Friday we drove up, settled in our royal abode—Leo and I occupying the bridal suite leading out into a little garden featuring a swing made for two people—and strolled around town. The weather was wonderful, the birds singing, and the daffodils sending up green shoots already. It was very much like our wedding day fifty years ago. That night Charlie had invited all the relatives and friends who were already there to a pizza parlor; an informal affair, just to get acquainted. All our children and grandchildren except the Michaels stayed at the cabin; all the other guests spent the weekend in hotels and bed-and-breakfast inns around the area. Quite a few guests had chosen to stay at the 150-year-old Murphys Hotel in the center of town. After dinner we had a nice evening at the fireside in our "private" inn.

The big day arrived, and Leo and I—used to getting up early—rose at six and hiked out to Ironstone Winery, just about half an hour away, where the big party would start at three o'clock in the afternoon. It was another beautiful day; the hills green from the recent rains, the little creek running through Murphys, was sparkling clear, and the air was warming up with the rising sun. When we came back to the Dunbar House, our guests were up and we were ready for our royal breakfast consisting of exotic delights, including edible flowers. We then had several hours to visit with friends, strolling through Murphys, sitting in the garden, and getting ready for the afternoon. After having done my face by my friend Shirley and my hair coiffed by Phyllis's daughter Johanna, I got into my precious golden dress (which I had purchased in New York just for the event) and I worked on my little speech. Leo looked wonderful in his rented tuxedo (with tails!), and golden bowtie and cummerbund. Julie and Hedwig appeared like queens in their festive gowns.

Marty and his children had picked up their maternal grandmother, Terry Grasso Munisteri from Houston—who graciously consented to coming and celebrating with us—at the airport in Sacramento. She had seen the children only as babies and was happy to be with them again.

The party was wonderful. Almost one hundred people came, and I'll never forget the thrill of seeing our guests walking slowly up the walk from the parking lot and being surprised by the festive spacious hall; they were looking forward to a great evening. When we came in early, not expecting any of our guests to be there already, we were dazzled by the sight of our family, lined up, and shouting their welcome. They had been there since one o'clock to make sure everything was running smoothly. We soon got into the swing of things. For two hours we greeted our guests, introduced them to each other, pointed out the family posters that were conveniently put on easels, munched delicious hors-d'oeuvres, had countless pictures taken, and enjoyed being king and queen for the day. Around five o'clock dinner was rolled in and the guests found their seats at the numerous round tables. We all lined up for the good food. Barbara and the Ironstone coordinator had done so well that everything went as planned. Doris had provided for lovely string music during the meal. Sharyn showed excellent taste in her choice of beautiful table decorations. The room was spacious enough, so that guests could visit with each other during and after the dinner.

After two hours the classical music stopped and was followed by the disc jockey, who told us that he was organizing the entertainment from there on. At first he announced the cake ceremony. A little table carrying the giant golden dessert was wheeled in and Leo and I had the honor of cutting the first slice of the cake. Waiters poured coffee for all the guests. Photographers circulated and took countless pictures, even of the kiss Leo and I gave each other, according to custom. That wedding celebration was so much more elaborate than our humble affair fifty years ago.

Next on the agenda were speeches—about a dozen of them. I had to go first and, since I was well prepared, I enjoyed sharing my feelings with the audience. We all were sorry that Jason could not be with us because of the pending war in Iraq. After greeting our guests and thanking them for coming so far in the middle of winter, I told then in a nutshell how Leo and I had met and how short our courtship had been—only four weeks. Other speakers were good friends and relatives; especially impressive was Shirley Kuller who became very emotional. A funny touch was a toast to our fifth "child," the Ford Falcon—both became part of our family in 1960—still carrying Leo to work every day. Leo's coworker, Phil Howard, gave that speech. The youngest speaker was Sequoia, who did very well. Doris was the mistress of ceremonies and did a wonderful job.

Now the audience was ready for the big event of the evening: the play. Sequoia and Doris had worked on the production for the last year, all by telephone and email since the younger Schmidts were then in New Zealand and the Michaels in New York. The Schmidts had planned coming to the party for over two years. All the young people of the family including Natalie and Rhoan Tussy were the actors. Denali, the artist in the family, had made all the props. For Lodi Lake a blue sheet was used and all four children donned bathrobes. Rhoan, adopted as an infant from Russia in 2001, portrayed young Marty, and when asked if he liked mountain climbing, the little guy clapped his hands enthusiastically. He was supposed to say "yes," but the little Russian-born preferred to use body language. At the end of the play—which included Mathilde coming from Germany, asking her sister whether or not to marry Leo, life in Lodi with four children, and buying the cabin—the big finale was staged with Opa and Omi being crowned with golden wreaths. The audience was very pleased with the play.

Before the dancing started, the owners of Ironstone, John and Gail Kautz, who had been invited also, had the huge electronic organ play for us, an unexpected entertainment. After that the music turned to dance tunes and soon the dance floor became crowded. Young and old moved around and not many guests stayed in their seats. If some elderly gentlemen decided they were too old for this, little Sequoia took care of them, and soon they were dragged from their table and hauled around on the floor. Two hours were allotted for the dancing, and that was just perfect timing. Around ten o'clock the DJ announced the last dance and started packing his gear together. The guests went home happily—most of them did not have to drive very far, which was fortunate since a heavy fog had developed during our party. As far as we know everybody made it home safely to their hotel or other commodity. Leo almost took the wrong turn when we drove out of the Ironstone estate, but luckily we made it and unwound happily in our wonderful Dunbar House, where we sat together for a happy hour with our guests. Leo and I had been represented by fifteen immediate family members at this reunion. I was reminded of our wedding in Lodi fifty years ago when it had been just Leo and I. I am quoting Golde from the *Fiddler on the Roof*:

> "For twenty-five years I've lived with him,
> Fought with him, and starved with him.
> Twenty-five years my bed is his.
> If that's not love, what is?"

How much more love if that is doubled!

Next morning we had another tasty breakfast, packed our belongings, said good-bye to our hosts, and drove the short distance to the Murphy's Hotel, where we had arranged for one more get-together with whoever wanted a bite to eat before heading to their respective homes.

We were surprised at how many of our guests decided to attend this last meal. We from the Dunbar House were not very hungry, of course, so we had time to circulate among our guests. It was especially gratifying to observe Grandma Terry enjoying her grandchildren whom she might not see again for a long time. Another happy event: Ann and Hans Deuel, children of Leo's sister Edith who had married the same year Edith had passed away in 1999, announced to us that they were expecting a new addition to the family in July. At noon the happy party broke up and everyone left.

After the Party: The next day Marty and the children had to leave for New Zealand because school started as soon as on January 29. Joanna, who was then still the legal guardian of the children, insisted on that and had a court order written stating that Marty bring them home on the day before at the latest. So January 27 was a busy day for us and our little house in Castro Valley was full to the rim. We had Julie and Hedwig still with us and around ten o'clock the Kreiders surprised us. Sequoia had just started to give manicures and pedicures with her brand-new set that Marty had bought her for Christmas. Alex, the Kreider's son, soon featured blue and green toenails and Phyllis's fingernails were filed down almost to the quick. Sequoia had convinced her that this was necessary because her cuticles had to be removed—a doubtful procedure leaving poor Phyllis with paper thin nails. Anyway, we all savored these last moments and were amazed at how skillfully Marty packed Leo's truck with never-ending sacks and containers. Finally the children were stuffed on top of all the baggage and off they went to the airport. Julie and Hedwig also left soon after and we were alone again in a peaceful house. Leo and I resumed our daily life.

Reminiscences

Looking back on my entire life, I see several patterns evolving. Though thrown into turbulent times by fate, I always emerged unscathed, protected by some guardian angel. I did not sit still and rest on my laurels; always new projects had to be developed and tackled. Nothing ever was a complete failure or success, but I always engaged in my favorite activities: reading, going to college (thirteen years altogether), gardening, hiking, and being with my family. From childhood on, I had had the desire to go to America.

Certain trends developed during my long life. Leo's family had come from Russia, had to move to Poland and from there fled to West Germany before they came west to the United States. My family had lived in Germany and my oldest sister moved west to Ohio. I followed her, but did not stay in the east of the United States. I went to California where I met my husband and stayed to raise my family. Now our youngest son has moved even farther west to New Zealand and is raising *his* dynasty down under. Amazing!

My life has been full of trials and tribulations, some caused by circumstances that I had no control over, some by my parents, but most of them by myself. However, I always managed to overcome obstacles and to return to my basically positive disposition.

My philosophy for a good life is as follows. It does not matter where you are or what your life style is; there is something good in any situation. If you have a dream and it comes true, consider yourself lucky. Do not want what you cannot have and be satisfied with what you have.

Above all, be happy! And if something should go wrong, take Scarlett O'Hara's advice:

"After all, tomorrow is another day."

Photos

Bremen

Marktplatz

Old quarter

Vier Stadtmusikanten

Old Farmhaus

The Goal of my Life

The Golden Gate Bridge

Beautiful Lake Chabot

Nature Galore

Yellowstone Falls

Yosemite Valley

Ancestors
1850

Ernst Friedrich
and
Otto Apelt

My Father's Family

Else, Cora, Otto, Thilde, Hermann
Apelt
1895

My Father

1876

1896

1909

1921

My Mother's Parents

Julie and Heinrich Nielsen
around 1870

My Mother's Family   1889

Luise, Emma, Julie, Paula, Carl, Lotte
after their mother's death

My Mother

1935

1907

1952

1976

The Older Children

Cornelie

Dorothee

Julie

Triadrich

Early Childhood

Our house at the Platz

1921

1925 with Klaus Rodewald

1928
1935

1931

Early Youth

Knitting

Swimming

skating

hiking

1935

Hermann and Markus

Wash day

and 1956
graduated from
Harvard

Wützchen 1936

Winter at
the Platz
1930

1929

Family Events

My parent's Silver
wedding Anniversary

back: Gustav Rassow, Mother,
Father, Tante Ilse,
housekeeper
front: Dorothee, Julie, me

1934

at
home
with
Tante
Thilde

My father
shows his port
to his grandson

↓

1956

1960
on his deathbed

The Bölkens

Annie

André

Pflichtjahr-
girl

Rose and me

Famous People connected with Bremen

Paul Ernst

Bürgermeister Spitta

Paula Modersohn-Becker

Rudolf Alexander Schröder

Getting to America at last!

Visitor From Bremen Entertained at A.B.A. Club

Miss Mathilde Apelt, of Bremen, was recently the guest of M. Pierre Grisar at a dinner given by him at the American Belgian Association of Antwerp. Miss Apelt is the daughter of Senator Dr. Apelt.

Guests of Pierre Grisar at A.B.A. Club are, l. to r., M. Baudouin (left, foreground), curator of Rubenshuis; M. Freddy de Man, Miss Mathilde Apelt, M. Grisar, M. Willem Eekelers, Alderman and Director of Education for the City of Antwerp; and Mme. Freddy de Man.

Phot. Climal

in the Grand Canyon

cotton-picking in Tennessee
↓

At the Houston Cotton port

Life in Dayton

Cornelie

Twins

Madeline
with
Sammie
and Model T

Walter
Ernst

Barb and Walt

Christmas 1952

Leo, Dec. 1952

Engaged, Jan. 6, 53

Wedding
Jan 30,
1953

Leo's Parents

Waldemar and Alice Schmidt

Leo Hermann
Oct. 24, 53

Doris
May 4, 55

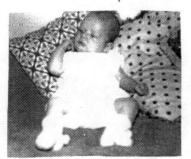

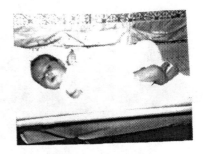

Barbara
Mar. 3, 57

Marty
June 10, 60

The Family is Growing

babies and baptisms

raising children and dolls

Moving in 1963

the old house in Lodi

the new house in Castro Valley

Activities

scouting 67

ready for church 63

trip to Lake Tahoe   1967

Scholastic Life

going to college
1966

teaching German to adults

1973

in my back yard
where I live most of the time

"Do you want Alice to be
your wedded wife?"
Play in honor of 50th anniversary
of Leo's parents in Lodi

1976

Our Cabin

Outdoor Life

Weddings

Sharyn and Leo H.
1978

Doris and Charlie
1980

Barbara and Randy
1979

The Graduate 1980

My class 1981

Squaredancing 1982

Doris and Ethel
1979

Marty and his father
in our study

On top of Denali

Kathy's Wedding, 1988

happy to be there

Kathy Barb John   Julie   Jim
Allen

Susie's Wedding 1988

all
fifteen
of us

four
children

five
grand
childre

Trips 1990

Me

Barb Allen
Sharyn, Barb
Cornelie

Kathy,
Doris, Phylli

Meeting of Apelt girls, Hearst Castle

Grandma comes back from Paris

Grandchildren

Denali and Sequoia

Jason and Brandon

1991

Barb's Birthday

like father, like son

Castro Valley

My Japanese friend, Machiko

our garden in Spring

Johanna's Wedding Brings
All of Us together

1993

The four sisters

Triplets

Christmas at the Michaels

Cabin in Winter
1993

out side

in side

big
one!

playing
chess
with
Opa

in Denali Park

Leo at Work

Leo
at Play

1995

The Four Sisters in Weimar,
Goethehaus

2000

Mathilde in her Garden

Jason,
Our Eagle Scout

Scouts: Jason, Randy, Barb, Brandon

2000

2001

Our Soldier

Denali,
on top of
the World ←

Uncle Peter,
the last of
our generation
with Sequoia, the
youngest of hers
↓

2004

Mother and Daughter in Tahiti

Camping at Lake Taupo
in New Zealand

Golden Wedding Anniversary
2003

Natalie, Sequoia, Mathilde, Leo
Brandon, Donica

Marty, Denali, Leo, Sharyn, Barb, Sequoia, Rand,
Donica, Mathilde, Leo, Blair, Charlie, Doris, Brandon

978-0-595-39748-8
0-595-39748-4

Printed in the United States
83274LV00005B/72/A